NEW FIELD, NEW CORN

NEW FIELD, NEW CORN

Essays in Alabama Legal History

edited by

Paul M. Pruitt, Jr.

FOREWORD BY BRYAN K. FAIR

QUID PRO BOOKS
New Orleans, Louisiana

Published in 2015 by Quid Pro Books, as part of the *Legal History & Biography* Series.

ISBN 978-1-61027-323-7 (hbk.)
ISBN 978-1-61027-308-4 (pbk.)
ISBN 978-1-61027-310-7 (ebk.)

QUID PRO BOOKS
Quid Pro, LLC
5860 Citrus Blvd., Suite D-101
New Orleans, Louisiana 70123
www.quidprobooks.com

qp

Publisher's Cataloging in Publication

Pruitt, Paul M. (Paul McWhorter), Jr., 1950–
New field, new corn : essays in Alabama legal history / edited by Paul M. Pruitt, Jr.
p. cm. — (Legal history & biography)
Includes bibliographical references and index
Includes photographs and map images
ISBN 978-1-61027-323-7 (hardcover)
1. Alabama—History—1819–1950. 2. Alabama—Politics and government. 3. Alabama—Biography. I. Title. II. Series.

F326.P46 2015

CONTENTS

FOREWORD

Critiquing Our Present, Interrogating Our Past: The Significant Contributions of Student Scholarship to Alabama Legal History

Bryan K. Fair

It has been my privilege to teach constitutional law courses at The University of Alabama School of Law for more than two decades. In addition to the basic first year introduction to Constitutional Law, I have taught Gender, Sexism and the Law, Race, Racism and the Law, the First Amendment, Free Speech, Freedom of Religion, and Equal Protection. Many of these advanced electives have been organized as seminars where students complete research papers or reflective essay exams. Such classes have allowed me to work with my students individually and to come to know many of them more personally than often occurs in larger first year courses. I can learn about their interests and about their goals. In addition, I can talk with them more extensively about the nature and scope of law, legal institutions, and law reform. Moreover, I can share my experiences, my research and writing, and my perceptions regarding various legal issues.

To say that this work has been a labor of love is a gross understatement. It has been truly exhilarating and enriching, especially the thousands of hours working with brilliant, curious, and thoughtful law students, examining myriad legal questions to clarify our understanding of legal subjects, as well as the function and force of legal principles. My students have been my teachers. Undoubtedly, I have learned far more from them than they have from me. This Foreword is written in tribute to our past, present, and future Alabama Law students, those who have, who are, and who will make Alabama Law's greatest contributions to our society.

Two principal thoughts frame this Foreword. First, I am reminded of Justice Holmes' oft-quoted phrase, "A page of history is worth a volume of logic." Second, I recall Faulkner's line, "The past is never dead; it's not even the past." As a student of the American Constitution and a teacher for the past 28 years, I have learned the value of excavating American history to understanding what has become of our grand nation on a hill. This is not an academic exercise. Personally and professionally, my thinking is a product of history. I have benefited from the guidance of exceptional teachers of History at Duke University and Law at UCLA, along with the kindness or mentoring of Dr. John Hope Franklin, Derrick Bell, Richard Delgado, and Jean Stefancic, as well as my exceptionally supportive colleagues at Alabama. Although I am not myself a classically trained legal historian, my writing is replete with references to law and history.

I see the legal world through historical lenses. They are not rose-colored; they are made clear by deconstructing the relevant past and by seeking to construct the past's influence on the present. I have come to know from colleagues like Dr. Tony Freyer and Dr. Paul Pruitt that much of the American past is not dead; it's not even the past. This is true in Ohio were I was raised, as well as in Alabama, where I reside. I have also learned these lessons through my own inquiry and through the ongoing, careful and rigorous research of my students. Legal education is collaborative, colleagues and students asking questions and seeking answers. I owe an important debt to colleagues and students.

The purpose of this Foreword is to illumine the substantial growth in the field of Alabama Legal History and the remarkable scholarly achievement of Alabama Law students in the emerging literature on Alabama's compelling and complicated story. First, I offer a word about history and then I explain the process and development of this important emerging work. Second, I describe the breadth of this new literature. Finally, I affirm its quality and value to me and to the general reader.

First, I offer a further word on history's relevance to the present and the future. My thesis is simply this: to understand any legal subject, no matter what it is, one gains a deeper understanding of its character and content by examining that subject in historical context. Indeed, without such context, I contend one has an incomplete picture. To understand current residential segregation, one has to look back to prior housing policy; to understand educational segregation, one has to look back to prior education policy; to understand voting discrimination, one must look back to prior voting policy; and so on.

Knowing historical context will not always produce one analysis or response. Reasonable observers might still reach different conclusions. However, a contextual analysis of legal issues affords us the chance to lay bare how previous generations wrestled with and resolved common legal dilemmas. We can reveal why choices were made, what those choices produced, and whether alternatives were considered? Asking such questions might also help us to examine current legal issues and to frame more effective solutions. I have no doubt that our past has important lessons to teach us, if we are willing to learn them.

Let me give two brief examples from my recent work on same-sex marriage and school segregation. I have been asked numerous times what I think about the constitutionality of government bans on same-sex marriage. In brief, I oppose such restrictions, believing they violate constitutional rights under due process and equal protection. For a fuller account of my views, please see my article in the *University of Miami Law Review*.[1] Here, I can only provide the following brief explanation, in light of important lessons from our history. First, over 50 years ago, the Supreme Court ruled that marriage is a fundamental right protected by the due process clause, and such right cannot be burdened by the government, absent a compelling justification. Second, at nearly the same time, the Court held that similar bans on interracial marriage were unconstitutional, notwithstanding then-existing popular opinions and state laws to the contrary. Third, the Court has said that government classifications that burden fundamental rights are presumptively invalid. Such government regulations are rarely sustained. Fourth, the Court has said that the federal constitution embraces a principle of freedom of association, including intimate associations. Perhaps the most intimate association we ever form is with a spouse or life partner. Finally, the Court has ruled that government regulations resting on group-based animus are illegitimate. When I reflect on such historical rulings from the Court, they provide a context for my current views on the constitutional protection of same-sex marriage. Although I never insist that my students share my opinions or conclusions, I do insist that they examine the relevant history and engage it in their analysis of contemporary legal questions.

A second example comes from my research on school districts seeking to avoid resegregation by voluntarily adjusting the racial makeup of schools to maintain broad enrollment diversity. The question arises whether such voluntary efforts violate the legal mandate of *Brown v. Board of Education*.[2] Looking back, I have asked what did the Court seek to achieve in *Brown*? Did the Court seek to proscribe policies advancing racial privilege? Did it seek to ensure equal educational opportunity for minority children? Did the Court seek to frame a broad constitutional remedy for a broad constitutional violation? Did the Court intend to prohibit policies advancing integration? My research suggests that the federal Constitution should not be read to proscribe educational policies that promote the benefits of diverse enrollments.[3] And these are exactly the types of interesting legal issues we may explore with our students.

Without a doubt, I have one of the best legal jobs in the world. I follow and critique the opinions of the nation's highest court, the Supreme Court of the United States (SCOTUS), and discuss with my students many of the most significant legal conflicts of our time: abortion, same-sex marriage, religious liberty, health care, affirmative action, and the scope of federal and state powers, among many others. I write about the Court's decisions, examining the Court's analysis and reasoning, and offering counter viewpoints and theories. I push my students to interrogate what they read, what

---

[1] Bryan K. Fair, *The Ultimate Association: Same-Sex Marriage and the Battle Against Jim Crow's Other Cousin*, 63 UNIVERSITY OF MIAMI LAW REVIEW 269 (2008).

[2] 347 U.S. 483 (1954).

[3] Fair, *Still Standing in the Schoolhouse Door: Deconstructing Brown's Bias and Reconstructing its Remedy*, 2 INDIANA JOURNAL OF LAW & SOCIAL EQUALITY 137 (2013).

they think, and what they hear, from others or from me. Moreover, I help train future lawyers, seeking to develop my students' practical skills, professional judgment, and ethics. With my colleagues, I take seriously the duties of preparing our students to render high quality legal services to the Bar and to their clients.

Unsurprisingly, history is relevant to the structure of legal education. For much of the past two hundred years, legal education has followed the traditional case method.[4] Students read and discuss cases from various courts, state and federal, examining how courts decide actual disputes, criminal and civil. Professors present students with probing questions about what they have read and with hypotheticals to test student understanding of legal issues and doctrine. Students learn to rely on and apply the reasoning from settled cases, as they consider the proper resolution of new ones, some hypothetical and some real. By reading thousands of cases, students gain the ability to model the analysis and reasoning provided by each judicial opinion. Generations of American lawyers have read law and discussed the implications of the cases with their professors.

In modern legal education, students have greater influence regarding their course of study, especially beyond the foundational first year. At Alabama Law and many other schools, students have few, if any, required courses beyond the first year. In this new environment, students can develop specific substantive expertise—for example, in criminal law, employment law, bankruptcy law, tax law, business law, or patent law, among many other areas—during their final two years of study, by taking a series of classes on one area of law. Some students also undertake clinical courses, working in live-client settings on real legal claims.

While I personally advise my students to think broadly about their legal education, I also recommend that they complete basic courses commonly tested on the Bar Exam in most states. As much as I want them broadly educated, I also want them well prepared for their ultimate examination. Notwithstanding new calls for continuing reforms in legal education, Alabama Law grads continue to enjoy great professional success. They acquire excellent skills that are transferable to many professional disciplines.

One of the best skills they develop is the ability to analyze and write about legal issues. At times, this is called thinking or writing like a lawyer. To be clear, I do not mean this in any pejorative sense. Instead, students acquire skills to dissect legal issues, to research law, to write and advise their clients. I regret widespread portrayals of lawyers as deceptive or dishonest; neither value is honored in legal education. To the contrary, my colleagues and I constantly remind our students of the importance of honesty, hard work, and fairness, notwithstanding their roles as zealous advocates.

---

[4] *See generally* Robert Stevens, LAW SCHOOL: LEGAL EDUCATION IN AMERICA FROM THE 1850S TO THE 1980S (1983).

Developing analysis and writing skills goes to the very heart of legal education. It is a central part of the first year core. At Alabama Law, we also require students to practice such skills in advanced courses, especially in seminars like Alabama Legal History. Professors Freyer, Pruitt, and other colleagues, including Wythe Holt and Albert Lopez, have expertly guided our students through these advance research and writing experiences.

In most of my elective classes for second and third year students, I offer the students the opportunity to conduct original research on a mutually agreeable topic. I assist the students in defining their topics, usually narrowing them in scope. I then work with each student, sometimes reviewing an outline, initial research results, an outline with references, a first draft, and then the final paper. Those seminar experiences have provided me with extraordinary teaching and learning opportunities, as well as important chances for my students to closely examine a narrow legal issue, deploying their recently acquired legal research and writing skills on a question of personal interest. They identify the essential sources, cases, statutes, literature—closely reading the record—and reach their own conclusions. In the process, they advance legal knowledge—their own, mine, and, if they publish their essays, the public's.

I recall so many exceptional papers. There was one on jury nullification in nonviolent criminal cases. Another one was on free speech and campaign finance regulations. One was on the legal foundation for Dr. Martin Luther King, Jr.'s Letter from Birmingham Jail. Another examined constitutional reform in Alabama. Students have written extensively about the establishment clause and school vouchers, public school prayers and religious displays in public space, criminal regulations of abortion, same-sex marriage, affirmative action, vote dilution schemes, the regulation of obscenity, sexual harassment, the right to privacy, the regulation of commercial speech or hate speech, and so on. The breadth of the topics and the depth of the research have been spectacular, and the quality has often exceeded expectations.

This rich tradition of excellent legal scholarship by Alabama Law students continues in the following pages. Prepare to be thrilled and surprised by the quality of the research and writing, and to learn about each subject in historical context. The diverse Alabama legal histories that appear below are well-researched and well-written. They are compelling, often unknown stories of tragedy, triumph, or both. Mike Dodson has examined the exciting history of one Alabama's leading law firms, Burr and Forman. Ellie Campbell has traced the extraordinary 1965 verdict in Anniston in *Strange v. State*. Courtney Cooper has carefully exhumed the early history of the Alabama Constitutions. Eddie Lowe has studied the leading forces of economic growth in Blount County at the turn of the twentieth century. Helen Eckinger has traced the dramatic events and forces that led to the establishment of a military focus at the University of Alabama in the 1850s. Warren Hoffman has excavated the fascinating history of the open range in the South and particularly in Alabama, and the forces behind the enclosure movement. Paul Rand has investigated the important history of property trusts in Alabama. And, Deirdra Drinkard has explored the significant impact of Hugo Black's military experiences on his Supreme Court opinions.

I have no doubt that you will think differently about each subject after consideration of the fresh analyses and perspectives offered by the authors. I salute each of them and their professors for their outstanding scholarly achievement!

BRYAN K. FAIR
Thomas E. Skinner Professor of Law
University of Alabama School of Law
June, 2015

ACKNOWLEDGMENTS

This book could not have been written and assembled without the generous assistance of many people. First, the editor thanks several deans who have taken an interest in legal history at the University of Alabama. These administrators—Kenneth C. Randall, William S. Brewbaker III, James B. Leonard, Jenelle Marsh, and Claude Arrington—facilitated the addition of new courses to the UA Law School curriculum and, in the case of James Leonard, encouraged the addition of rare books and valuable collections to the already substantial collections of the Bounds Law Library. Our faculty, including Wythe Holt, Bryan Fair, Tim Hoff, Tony Freyer, and Alfred Brophy, realized that Alabama legal history could be a distinct component of southern legal history and provided moral support and good advice to our dual (academic and publishing) enterprises. Tony Freyer, of course, taught the first Alabama Legal History seminar in 2011 and shared the instructional duties in the next two classes; certainly this book would not be in print without his involvement in the production of these excellent essays.

The editor also wants to thank several colleagues on the staff of the Bounds Law Library. These include Robert Marshal, Ruth Weeks, Julie Griffith, and Penny Gibson—in their varied expert roles of leadership and research support. Archivist David I. Durham, legal historian and archivist *par excellence*, has offered consistently good advice and has willingly stood by to help Alabama Legal History students with their research. The same goes for the attorneys and scholars who have served as resources for Alabama Legal History students and for the editor, including Guy Hubbs, Jim Lewis, Chris McIlwain, and Rob Riser.

Their editor particularly wishes to thank the young lawyers whose essays make up this book, whose fresh ideas and hard work never ceased to inspire him with respect for the coming generation. They provide him, consistently, with new insights into the functions of law—new examples, to put it another way, of what the fictional barrister Horace Rumpole has termed "a life-long subject of harmless fun."[*] A section of biographical summaries follows, to highlight their own achievements and successes, before and after their involvement in the extensive seminar research which they have shared in these pages.

[*] John Mortimer, THE FIRST RUMPOLE OMNIBUS 11 (1983) [from "Rumpole and the Younger Generation" (1983)].

Thanks, finally, to Alan Childress of Tulane University and Quid Pro Books, for his courageous approach to publishing and for his willingness to take on this project; and to Quid Pro's senior editor Lee D. Scheingold for her generous, detailed, and helpful suggestions.

PAUL M. PRUITT, JR.

Tuscaloosa, Alabama
July, 2015

About the Authors

Editor/Introducer **Paul M. Pruitt, Jr.** has served on the staff of the Bounds Law Library of the University of Alabama since 1986. He has been Special Collections Librarian for almost that long. He is co-editor and contributor to the *Occasional Publications of the Bounds Law Library*. He is the author of *Taming Alabama: Lawyers and Reformers, 1804–1929* (University of Alabama Press, 2010). At the Law School, he teaches two courses: From Domesday to the Black Death: English Legal History; and the Alabama Legal History Seminar. In addition to his undergraduate degree from Auburn University, he holds an M.L.S. from the University of Alabama and a Ph.D. in History from the College of William and Mary.

Foreword author **Bryan K. Fair** joined the faculty of the University of Alabama School of Law in 1991. Since 2000 he has been Thomas E. Skinner Professor of Law. Students have twice named him as the Law School's outstanding faculty member. He has also received the University's Outstanding Commitment to Teaching Award. He has served the University as an assistant vice president for Academic Affairs, and the Law School as the Director of Diversity and International Programs and as Associate Dean for Special Programs. He currently serves on the Board of Directors of the Southern Poverty Law Center. Professor Fair is the author of *Notes of a Racial Caste Baby: Colorblindness and the End of Affirmative Action* (NYU Press, 1997). His research remains focused on equality theory under the Fourteenth Amendment.

Contributors

Ellie Campbell is the Reference and Instruction Law Librarian at the Grisham Law Library at the University of Mississippi. She holds a J.D. and an M.L.I.S. from the University of Alabama, an M.A. in American Studies from King's College London, and an M.A. in Southern Studies from the University of Mississippi. She is from Anniston, Alabama.

Courtney Cooper graduated with honors both from the University of Alabama School of Law in 2014 and the University of Alabama in 2011, majoring in Broadcast News and Political Science. Courtney grew up in Eutaw, Alabama, a small town in the Black Belt, which inspired her passion for Alabama history. She hopes to continue her research and use her skills to serve the State of Alabama. She would also like to thank her parents, godparents, and Jake Gipson for their love and support.

Michael Dodson graduated *magna cum laude* from the University of Alabama School of Law in 2013 and *summa cum laude* in Business Administration from the University of Alabama in 2010. He served as an Articles Editor for the *Alabama Law Review*, and he was inducted into the Order of the Coif. After law school, Michael clerked for one year with the Honorable W. Harold Albritton, III of the Middle District of Alabama before beginning his career as an associate in the general commercial litigation section of Burr and Forman's Birmingham, Alabama office.

Deirdra Drinkard earned her undergraduate degree, *magna cum laude*, in journalism from the University of Alabama. She received her Juris Doctor from the University of Alabama School of Law in 2014. She has been a freelance writer for the *Mobile Press-Register* and works as Deputy District Attorney for the Tuscaloosa County District Attorney's office. She lives in Tuscaloosa with her husband, Michael, and their three pets.

Helen Eckinger received a B.A., with distinction, in English from Yale University and a J.D. *magna cum laude* from the University of Alabama School of Law, where she was a Hugo Black Scholar, a member of the Order of the Coif, and the Executive Editor of the *Alabama Law Review*. She is currently a law clerk for the Honorable Abdul Kallon of the Northern District of Alabama, and plans to pursue a career in healthcare litigation as an associate with Whatley Kallas, LLC.

Warren Hoffman received his bachelor's degree in finance from the University of Alabama in 2010. He received his Juris Doctor degree from the University of Alabama School of Law in 2013. He is an active member of the Alabama State Bar, and currently works in the Commercial Real Estate Department for BBVA Compass Bank in Birmingham, Alabama. His passion for land and property has lead him to where he is today, and he hopes to continue a successful career working on real estate matters in the future.

Eddie Lowe is a member of the University of Alabama School of Law class of 2013. In 2010 he received his undergraduate degree in political science from the University of Alabama, after transferring from UAB in 2008. He currently practices law in Oneonta, Alabama as an associate at the law office of Carl Dalton NeSmith, Jr.

Paul Rand is a 2013 graduate of the University of Alabama School of Law. He graduated with a B.A. in English Literature from the University of Alabama in 2005. Mr. Rand is an attorney with the Community Law Office of Jefferson County, Alabama, where he was awarded a Clark-Clemon Fellowship and currently serves as trial counsel to indigent criminal defendants.

NEW FIELD, NEW CORN

Alabama, 1854, published by New York mapmakers Ensign, Bridgeman & Fanning

Courtesy Barry Lawrence Ruderman Antique Maps, www.RareMaps.com, used by permission

INTRODUCTION: ALABAMA LEGAL HISTORY AS A FIELD OF STUDY

Paul M. Pruitt, Jr.

I. Introduction

Why has Alabama legal history not been written—until fairly recently? The answer is simple if we follow the reasoning of Frederic William Maitland, a great legal historian who, more than a century ago, asked an analogous question concerning English legal history. Both lawyers and historians were at fault, he thought, for the slow development of a shared, cross-disciplinary field of study. The problem lies partly in differences of training—historians, particularly, lack knowledge of the practical workings of law and legal practice—and partly with differing ways of thought. Feeling his way around the situation, Maitland advanced the theory that lawyers and historians are different beings, intellectually. What the latter want, he said, are *facts*, evidence, and the older and more deeply rooted in context, the better. What the former want is authority, in the form of rules or precedents laid down by some body with the power to do so, and the newer the better.[1] Broadly speaking, this division marks the difference between the lawyer's deductive mindset and the historian's inductive training. The differences are real, but as the careers of Maitland and numerous attorneys and scholars since his time have shown, the divide can readily be crossed.[2]

An examination of Alabama's historical literature reveals that the state's early historians (Pickett, Brewer, Owen, among others) were mostly lawyers.[3] As late as the mid-twentieth century, Birmingham attorney William H. Brantley was writing complex and well-researched Alabama histories on law-related topics, including a biography of Chief Justice George Washing-

[1] Frederic William Maitland, *Why the History of English Law Is Not Written,* in H.A.L. Fisher, ed., COLLECTED PAPERS OF FREDERIC WILLIAM MAITLAND, DOWNING PROFESSOR OF THE LAWS OF ENGLAND (1911), I: 480-97.

[2] *See* Paul M. Pruitt, Jr., *Root and Branch: Contexts of Legal History in Alabama and the South*, 17 JOURNAL OF SOUTHERN LEGAL HISTORY, 121-49 (2009), especially 121-22, for discussion of American legal historian James Willard Hurst.

[3] *See* Albert James Pickett, HISTORY OF ALABAMA AND INCIDENTALLY OF GEORGIA AND MISSISSIPPI: FROM THE EARLIEST PERIOD (1851); Willis Brewer, ALABAMA: HER HISTORY, RESOURCES, WAR RECORD, AND PUBLIC MEN (1872); and Thomas M. Owen, HISTORY OF ALABAMA AND DICTIONARY OF ALABAMA BIOGRAPHY (1921). For short biographies of these authors, see Owen, *op. cit.*, III: 213-14; IV: 1310-11; and IV: 1363. Pickett studied but did not practice law.

ton Stone and a two-volume survey of antebellum banking.[4] At roughly the same time a professional historian, Auburn University's Malcolm McMillan, published the indispensable CONSTITUTIONAL DEVELOPMENT IN ALABAMA, 1798–1901.[5] The decades that followed saw quite a number of academic professionals published well-regarded books touching on the history of law in Alabama. These works include (but are not limited to) Dan Carter's SCOTTSBORO: A TRAGEDY OF THE AMERICAN SOUTH (1969),[6] William Warren Rogers and Robert David Ward's AUGUST RECKONING: JACK TURNER AND RACISM IN POST-CIVIL WAR ALABAMA (1973),[7] Gene Howard's DEATH AT CROSS PLAINS (1984),[8] Robert J. Norrell's REAPING THE WHIRLWIND: THE CIVIL RIGHTS MOVEMENT IN TUSKEGEE (1985),[9] Roger Newman's HUGO BLACK: A BIOGRAPHY (1994),[10] Robert Saunders' JOHN ARCHIBALD CAMPBELL, SOUTHERN MODERATE, 1811–1889 (1997),[11] Glenn Feldman's POLITICS, SOCIETY, AND THE KLAN IN ALABAMA (1999),[12] Mary Ellen Curtin's BLACK PRISONERS AND THEIR WORLD: ALABAMA, 1865–1900 (2000),[13] Jonathan S. Bass' BLESSED ARE THE PEACEMAKERS: MARTIN LUTHER KING, JR., EIGHT WHITE RELIGIOUS LEADERS, AND THE "LETTER FROM BIRMINGHAM JAIL" (2001),[14] J. Mills Thornton III's DIVIDING LINES: MUNICIPAL POLITICS AND THE STRUGGLE FOR CIVIL RIGHTS IN MONTGOMERY, BIRMINGHAM, AND SELMA (2002),[15] David I. Durham's A SOUTHERN MODERATE IN RADICAL TIMES: HENRY WASHINGTON HILLIARD, 1808–1892 (2008),[16] Paul M. Pruitt, Jr.'s TAMING ALABAMA: LAWYERS AND REFORMERS, 1804–1929 (2010),[17] and

---

[4] *See* William H. Brantley, CHIEF JUSTICE STONE OF ALABAMA (1943); and Brantley's BANKING IN ALABAMA, 1816–1860, 2 volumes (1961–1967).

[5] Malcolm Cook McMillan, CONSTITUTIONAL DEVELOPMENT IN ALABAMA, 1798–1901: A STUDY IN POLITICS, THE NEGRO, AND SECTIONALISM (1955).

[6] Dan Carter, SCOTTSBORO: A TRAGEDY OF THE AMERICAN SOUTH (1969).

[7] William Warren Rogers and Robert David Ward, AUGUST RECKONING: JACK TURNER AND RACISM IN POST-CIVIL WAR ALABAMA (1973).

[8] Gene Howard, DEATH AT CROSS PLAINS: AN ALABAMA RECONSTRUCTION TRAGEDY (1984).

[9] Robert J. Norrell, REAPING THE WHIRLWIND: THE CIVIL RIGHTS MOVEMENT IN TUSKEGEE (1985).

[10] Roger K. Newman, HUGO BLACK: A BIOGRAPHY (1994). *See also* Steve Suitts, HUGO BLACK OF ALABAMA: HOW HIS ROOTS AND EARLY CAREER SHAPED A GREAT CHAMPION OF THE CONSTITUTION (2005).

[11] Robert Saunders, JOHN ARCHIBALD CAMPBELL, SOUTHERN MODERATE, 1811–1889 (1997).

[12] Glenn Feldman, POLITICS, SOCIETY, AND THE KLAN IN ALABAMA, 1915–1949 (1999).

[13] Mary Ellen Curtin, BLACK PRISONERS AND THEIR WORLD: ALABAMA, 1865–1900 (2000).

[14] Jonathan S. Bass, BLESSED ARE THE PEACEMAKERS: MARTIN LUTHER KING, JR., EIGHT WHITE RELIGIOUS LEADERS, AND THE "LETTER FROM BIRMINGHAM JAIL" (2001).

[15] J. Mills Thornton III, DIVIDING LINES: MUNICIPAL POLITICS AND THE STRUGGLE FOR CIVIL RIGHTS IN MONTGOMERY, BIRMINGHAM, AND SELMA (2002).

[16] David I. Durham, A SOUTHERN MODERATE IN RADICAL TIMES: HENRY WASHINGTON HILLIARD, 1808–1892 (2008).

[17] Paul M. Pruitt, Jr., TAMING ALABAMA: LAWYERS AND REFORMERS, 1804–1929 (2010).

Steven Preston Brown's JOHN MCKINLEY AND THE ANTEBELLUM SUPREME COURT: CIRCUIT-RIDING IN THE OLD SOUTHWEST (2012).[18]

Recently the lawyer-layman pendulum may have swung back the other way. Lawyer Pat Rumore has recently published two books that capture the outlines of legal practice across Alabama history and introduce readers to many of the attorneys whose influence permeates our history. These fine works are LAWYERS IN A NEW SOUTH CITY: THE LEGAL PROFESSION IN BIRMINGHAM (2000), and FROM POWER TO SERVICE: THE STORY OF LAWYERS IN ALABAMA (2010).[19] A Birmingham lawyer, Herbert James Lewis, has published a well-wrought, legally well-informed survey titled CLEARING THE THICKETS: A HISTORY OF ANTEBELLUM ALABAMA (2013).[20] A Tuscaloosa attorney, Christopher McIlwain, has a forthcoming book tentatively titled CIVIL WAR ALABAMA, which covers the myriad complexities of Alabama's secession, Civil War, and Reconstruction.[21] McIlwain is seeking to replace Walter L. Fleming's long-lived but opinionated CIVIL WAR AND RECONSTRUCTION IN ALABAMA and thereby to move the focus of state Civil War history away, somewhat, from the secessionists.[22] Covering the same period as Lewis and McIlwain but from a more technical point of view, attorney Daniel Reese Farnell, Jr. completed his Ph.D. at Auburn University in 2007 with a dissertation on a long-anticipated topic: "Alabama Courts and the Administration of Slavery, 1820–1860."[23]

As good as they are, none of the works cited in the paragraphs above are full-fledged histories of Alabama law. One reason? To this date, there is no proper narrative framework for an integrated approach to state law—nothing like Tony Freyer and Timothy Dixon's work on Alabama's federal courts.[24] For more on this point, see below. For the moment it is worth pointing out that over the last several decades there have been notable achievements in the broader, parallel field of southern legal history—itself a recent child of southern history and American legal history.[25]

---

[18] Stephen P. Brown, JOHN MCKINLEY AND THE ANTEBELLUM SUPREME COURT: CIRCUIT-RIDING IN THE OLD SOUTHWEST (2012).

[19] Pat Rumore, LAWYERS IN A NEW SOUTH CITY: A HISTORY OF THE LEGAL PROFESSION IN BIRMINGHAM (2000); and Pat Rumore, FROM POWER TO SERVICE: THE STORY OF LAWYERS IN ALABAMA (2010).

[20] Herbert James Lewis, CLEARING THE THICKETS: A HISTORY OF ANTEBELLUM ALABAMA (2013).

[21] Emails, Chris McIlwain to Paul Pruitt, July 11, August 13, 14, 2013.

[22] For a modern edition of Fleming's "Dunning school" classic, see Walter L. Fleming, CIVIL WAR AND RECONSTRUCTION IN ALABAMA, introd. by Sarah Woolfolk Wiggins (1978; orig. pub.1905).

[23] Daniel Reese Farnell, Jr., "Alabama Courts and the Administration of Slavery, 1820–1860" (Ph.D. dissertation, Auburn University, 2007).

[24] Tony A. Freyer and Timothy Dixon, DEMOCRACY AND JUDICIAL INDEPENDENCE: A HISTORY OF THE FEDERAL COURTS OF ALABAMA, 1820–1994 (1995).

[25] *See* Pruitt, *Root and Branch, supra* note 2, at 122.

II. The Development of Southern Legal History

By the mid-1980s several academic historians had realized, in the words of David J. Bodenhamer and James W. Ely, Jr., that "No part of southern history has received less attention from scholars than the region's laws and legal systems." This despite the fact that, as they added, "few things reveal social values more clearly than does law."[26] In 1984 Bodenhamer and Ely published AMBIVALENT LEGACY: A LEGAL HISTORY OF THE SOUTH, a collection of eleven essays whose authors examine aspects of the legal heritage of the south, with some attention to its distinctiveness, and suggest further avenues of study. Of course slavery and the racial regimes that followed its downfall have been among the most prominent, most studied feature of southern history. Yet contributors to AMBIVALENT LEGACY believed that legal historians could enhance our understanding of other pieces in the interlocked puzzle. Tony Freyer, for example, noted in his essay *Law and the Antebellum Southern Economy: An Interpretation,* that slavery "represented only one dimension of the southern legal and economic order."[27]

Other southern historical themes of interest to legal historians include the workings of class-relations among whites, the persistence of codes of honor alongside deep-rooted patterns of violence, and the predominance of economies based on a combination of staple crops and extractive industries.[28] Another groundbreaking study of 1984 considers a number of these issues, interwoven with that of race—historian Edward L. Ayers' VENGEANCE AND JUSTICE: CRIME AND PUNISHMENT IN THE 19TH-CENTURY SOUTH. Early on, Ayers observes that "southerners of both races wore shackles not entirely of their own making." At length, after examining examples of social and economic influences on the legal, police, and penal practices of several states, including the earnest efforts of reformers—Ayers concluded that "Crime and punishment, as much as anything, measure the continuity of the south with the past."[29]

After the seminal year of 1984,[30] studies of southern legal history began to appear with regularity, including Morris S. Arnold's UNEQUAL LAWS UNTO

[26] David J. Bodenhamer and James W. Ely, Jr., AMBIVALENT LEGACY: A LEGAL HISTORY OF THE SOUTH (1984), vii.

[27] Tony A. Freyer, *Law and the Antebellum Southern Economy: An Interpretation,* in Bodenhamer and Ely, AMBIVALENT LEGACY, 49-68, at 49. The essay explores Freyer's argument, "that southern courts and legislatures helped preserve social equilibrium through a proportionate distribution of goods and services from large properties classes to small or non-propertied classes." Freyer, *op. cit.*, 50.

[28] For two general treatments of these issues in the post-bellum era, see C. Vann Woodward, ORIGINS OF THE NEW SOUTH, 1877–1913 (1951); and Edward L. Ayers, THE PROMISE OF THE NEW SOUTH: LIFE AFTER RECONSTRUCTION (1992).

[29] Edward L. Ayers, VENGEANCE AND JUSTICE: CRIME AND PUNISHMENT IN THE NINETEENTH CENTURY SOUTH (1984), 4, 276.

[30] Though 1984 is a convenient starting date for serious study of southern legal history, it is true that many earlier works are of value and interest. These include books on topics as specific as Richard Maxwell Brown's THE SOUTH CAROLINA REGULATORS (1963); or as sweeping as

A SAVAGE RACE: EUROPEAN LEGAL TRADITIONS IN ARKANSAS, 1686–1836 (1985),[31] Gail Williams O'Brien's THE LEGAL FRATERNITY IN THE MAKING OF A NEW SOUTH COMMUNITY, 1848–1882 (1986)[32] and a collection of essays edited by Kermit L. Hall and James W. Ely, Jr., titled AN UNCERTAIN TRADITION: CONSTITUTIONALISM AND THE HISTORY OF THE SOUTH (1989).[33] In 1991, the Georgia Legal History Foundation launched the GEORGIA JOURNAL OF SOUTHERN LEGAL HISTORY, subsequently retitled the JOURNAL OF SOUTHERN LEGAL HISTORY.[34]

By the mid-1990s, the University of Georgia Press had announced a new series of books, Studies in the Legal History of the South. At least twenty-five titles have been published in this series,[35] including several of particular interest to students of Alabama history. Among the latter are Timothy S. Huebner's THE SOUTHERN JUDICIAL TRADITION: STATE JUDGES AND SECTIONAL DISTINCTIVENESS, 1790–1890 (1999), which contains a chapter on long-tenured Alabama supreme court justice George Washington Stone;[36] and Christopher Waldrep and Donald G. Nieman's edited volume LOCAL MATTERS, RACE, CRIME, AND JUSTICE IN THE NINETEENTH-CENTURY SOUTH (2001), with Michael W. Fitzgerald's article on Ku Klux Klan activities in the Alabama Black Belt.[37] A recent volume in the series is the compilation edited by Sally E. Hadden and Patricia Hagler Minter, SIGNPOSTS: NEW DIRECTIONS IN SOUTHERN LEGAL HISTORY (2013), containing seventeen essays on topics as diverse as grand jury presentments, married women's property rights, prohibition, and a reexamination of the constitutional theory of secession.[38]

Bertram Wyatt Brown's SOUTHERN HONOR: ETHICS AND BEHAVIOR IN THE OLD SOUTH (1982). For a pre-1984 study combining comparative history (of English and colonial legal practices) with long-term narrative, see A.G. Roeber, FAITHFUL MAGISTRATES AND REPUBLICAN LAWYERS: CREATORS OF VIRGINIA'S LEGAL CULTURE, 1680–1810 (1981).

31 Morris S. Arnold, UNEQUAL LAWS UNTO A SAVAGE RACE. EUROPEAN LEGAL TRADITIONS IN ARKANSAS, 1686–1836 (1985).

32 Gail Williams O'Brien, THE LEGAL FRATERNITY IN THE MAKING OF A NEW SOUTH COMMUNITY, 1848–1882 (Athens: University of Georgia Press, 1986).

33 Kermit L. Hall and James W. Ely, Jr., AN UNCERTAIN TRADITIONALISM: CONSTITUTIONALISM AND THE HISTORY OF THE SOUTH (Athens: University of Georgia Press, 1989).

34 The GEORGIA JOURNAL OF SOUTHERN LEGAL HISTORY (1991–1993); and the JOURNAL OF SOUTHERN LEGAL HISTORY (1993–present). This journal is an annual publication.

35 *See* http://www.ugapress.org/index.php/ugapress/results/85a1d6934d3255c3c37b01d2 3cb35855 (a list at the University of Georgia Press website, accessed July 10, 2013).

36 Timothy S. Heubner, THE SOUTHERN JUDICIAL TRADITION: STATE JUDGES AND SECTIONAL DISTINCTIVENESS, 1790–1890 (1999), 160-85 (*George W. Stone, Political Sectionalism, and Legal Nationalism*).

37 Michael W. Fitzgerald, *Extralegal Violence and the Planter Class: The Ku Klux Klan in the Alabama Black Belt During Reconstruction*, in Christopher Waldrep and Donald G. Nieman, eds., LOCAL MATTERS: RACE, CRIME, AND JUSTICE IN THE NINETEENTH-CENTURY SOUTH (2001), 155-71.

38 Sally E. Hadden and Patricia Hagler Minter, eds., SIGNPOSTS: NEW DIRECTIONS IN SOUTHERN LEGAL HISTORY (2013).

It would be wrong to give the impression that the University of Georgia Press has acted alone in working this new field. The last twenty years have seen the publication by several university presses of works that have significantly expanded our grasp of research possibilities. These include Peter W. Bardaglio's RECONSTRUCTING THE HOUSEHOLD: FAMILIES, SEX, AND THE LAW IN THE NINETEENTH-CENTURY SOUTH (1995),[39] Thomas D. Morris' SOUTHERN SLAVERY AND THE LAW, 1619–1860 (1996),[40] William G. Thomas' LAWYERING FOR THE RAILROAD (1999),[41] Ariela Julie Gross' DOUBLE CHARACTER: SLAVERY AND MASTERY IN THE ANTEBELLUM SOUTHERN COURTROOM (2000),[42] Sally E. Hadden's SLAVE PATROLS: LAW AND VIOLENCE IN VIRGINIA AND THE CAROLINAS (2001),[43] Dylan C. Penningroth's THE CLAIMS OF KINFOLK: AFRICAN AMERICAN PROPERTY AND COMMUNITY IN THE NINETEENTH-CENTURY SOUTH (2003),[44] Mark V. Tushnet's SLAVE LAW IN THE AMERICAN SOUTH: STATE V. MANN IN HISTORY AND LITERATURE (2003),[45] Lisa Lindquist Dorr's WHITE WOMEN, RAPE, AND THE POWER OF RACE IN VIRGINIA, 1900–1960 (2004),[46] and Laura F. Edwards' THE PEOPLE AND THEIR PEACE: LEGAL CULTURE AND THE TRANSFORMATION OF INEQUALITY IN THE POST-REVOLUTIONARY SOUTH (2009)[47] In addition, southern legal historians have had an impact upon more than one volume of the NEW ENCYCLOPEDIA OF SOUTHERN CULTURE, most notably its tenth volume, LAW AND POLITICS (2008).[48]

Southern legal historians have done wonderful things, but they have not yet reached the point at which the "whole" of the new field is greater than the sum of its parts. There is, as yet, no thesis or generally accepted interpretation of what makes southern law distinctive—whether in practice, concept, or experience. Hadden and Minter's SIGNPOSTS introduction sug-

---

[39] Peter W. Bardaglio, RECONSTRUCTING THE HOUSEHOLD: FAMILIES, SEX, AND THE LAW IN THE NINETEENTH-CENTURY SOUTH (1995) [University of North Carolina Press].

[40] Thomas D. Morris, SOUTHERN SLAVERY AND THE LAW, 1619–1860 (1996) [University of North Carolina Press].

[41] William G. Thomas, LAWYERING FOR THE RAILROAD: BUSINESS, LAW, AND POWER IN THE NEW SOUTH (1999) [Louisiana State University Press].

[42] Ariela Julie Gross, DOUBLE CHARACTER: SLAVERY AND MASTERY IN THE ANTEBELLUM SOUTHERN COURTROOM (2000) [Princeton University Press]; *see also* Gross, WHAT BLOOD WON'T TELL: A HISTORY OF RACE ON TRIAL IN AMERICA (2008) [Harvard University Press].

[43] Sally E. Hadden, SLAVE PATROLS: LAW AND VIOLENCE IN VIRGINIA AND THE CAROLINAS (2001).

[44] Dylan C. Penningroth, THE CLAIMS OF KINFOLK: AFRICAN AMERICAN PROPERTY AND COMMUNITY IN THE NINETEENTH-CENTURY SOUTH (2003) [University of North Carolina Press].

[45] Mark V. Tushnet, SLAVE LAW IN THE AMERICAN SOUTH: STATE V. MANN IN HISTORY AND LITERATURE (2003) [University Press of Kansas].

[46] Lisa Lindquist Dorr, WHITE WOMEN, RAPE, AND THE POWER OF RACE IN VIRGINIA, 1900–1960 (2004) [University of North Carolina Press].

[47] Laura F. Edwards, THE PEOPLE AND THEIR PEACE: LEGAL CULTURE AND THE TRANSFORMATION OF INEQUALITY IN THE POST-REVOLUTIONARY SOUTH (2009) [University of North Carolina Press].

[48] James W. Ely, Jr. and Bradley G. Bond, eds., LAW AND POLITICS, Volume 10 of the NEW ENCYCLOPEDIA OF SOUTHERN CULTURE (2008) [University of North Carolina Press].

gests that "the interaction of race and power" is one of several motifs that continue to fascinate southern legal historians; these editors also invoke the name and achievements of the late J. Willard Hurst (1910–1997), "whose research insisted that high court decisions were but one level of legal-historical action to be investigated."[49] Hadden's SLAVE PATROLS and Edwards' THE PEOPLE AND THEIR PEACE both show the particular benefits of grassroots legal history—revealing (to anyone who might have doubted it) that intense local research is a splendid way of following Hurst's advice. Hadden and Edwards outline parochial practices over a broad range of geography and time; each also places customary (*de facto*) laws and procedures in the larger context of common law. No doubt future historians can explore with profit the continuance of almost tribal features in numerous legal and quasi-legal aspects of southern life.

Speaking of local focus, the growth of southern legal history has been accompanied, in several of the states that neighbor Alabama, by the type of basic structural analysis so far lacking or unpublished here. Louisiana historian Judith Kelleher Schafer was a leader in this type of historical research, beginning with her SLAVERY, THE CIVIL LAW, AND THE SUPREME COURT OF LOUISIANA (1994),[50] followed by AN UNCOMMON EXPERIENCE: LAW AND JUDICIAL INSTITUTIONS IN LOUISIANA, 1803–2003 (1997), a substantial work that Schafer co-edited with Warren M. Billings.[51] Billings went on to edit, with Mark F. Fernandez, A LAW UNTO ITSELF?: ESSAYS IN THE NEW LOUISIANA LEGAL HISTORY (2001);[52] in the same year Fernandez published FROM CHAOS TO CONTINUITY: THE EVOLUTION OF LOUISIANA'S JUDICIAL SYSTEM, 1712–1862.[53]

Florida legal historians have not been far behind the Louisianans. The year 1997 saw the publication of two pioneering works of Florida legal history, James M. Denham's A ROGUE'S PARADISE: CRIME AND PUNISHMENT IN ANTEBELLUM FLORIDA, 1821–1861,[54] and Walter W. Manley II, *et al.*, THE

---

[49] Hadden and Minter, SIGNPOSTS: NEW DIRECTIONS IN SOUTHERN LEGAL HISTORY, 5, 8. *See also* Pruitt, *Root and Branch*, *supra* note 2, at 121-22.

[50] Judith Kelleher Schafer, SLAVERY, THE CIVIL LAW, AND THE SUPREME COURT OF LOUISIANA (1994).

[51] Judith Kelleher Schafer and Warren M. Billings, eds., AN UNCOMMON EXPERIENCE: LAW AND JUDICIAL INSTITUTIONS IN LOUISIANA, 1803–2003 (1997). Schafer also published BECOMING FREE, REMAINING FREE: MANUMISSION AND ENSLAVEMENT IN NEW ORLEANS, 1846–1862 (2003).

[52] Warren M. Billings and Mark F. Fernandez, eds., A LAW UNTO ITSELF?: ESSAYS IN THE NEW LOUISIANA LEGAL HISTORY (2001). *See also* Warren M. Billings and Edward F. Haas, eds., IN SEARCH OF FUNDAMENTAL LAW: LOUISIANA'S CONSTITUTIONS, 1812–1974 (1993). Billings has long been, also, a noteworthy historian of seventeenth-century Virginia; see, among others, his SIR WILLIAM BERKELEY AND THE FORGING OF COLONIAL VIRGINIA (2004).

[53] Mark F. Fernandez, FROM CHAOS TO CONTINUITY: THE EVOLUTION OF LOUISIANA'S JUDICIAL SYSTEM, 1712–1862 (2001).

[54] James M. Denham, A ROGUE'S PARADISE: CRIME AND PUNISHMENT IN ANTEBELLUM FLORIDA, 1821–1861 (1997).

SUPREME COURT OF FLORIDA AND ITS PREDECESSOR COURTS, 1821–1917.[55] Subsequently, Denham collaborated with William Warren Rogers, Sr., to publish FLORIDA SHERIFFS: A HISTORY, 1821–1945 (2001).[56] To the north of the Floridians, the late Erwin Surrency (1924–1912) published in 2001 his CREATION OF A JUDICIAL SYSTEM: THE HISTORY OF GEORGIA COURTS, 1733 TO PRESENT.[57] As for Alabama's western neighbor, there are many fine studies of Civil Rights struggles in Mississippi,[58] but the Magnolia State—like several of the former Confederate states—lacks the *recent* institutional studies[59] that have been completed in Louisiana, Florida, and Georgia.

III. Alabama Legal History: Motive, Opportunities

A southern man of letters, Willie Morris, once paraphrased a celebrated southern novelist, to this effect: "To understand the world, William Faulkner once said, you have to understand a place like Mississippi."[60] The same might be said with regard to the legal history of Alabama, a state that (like Mississippi[61]) kept its own bastardized version of common law pleading in place until—in Alabama's case—the law reforms of the early 1970s.[62] Pat Rumore's books make for a fine beginning in the quest for broad contextual narratives. Another start is a project undertaken by Paul Pruitt and Tony Freyer in the late 1990s—a project which produced a manuscript titled "Alabama's Supreme Court and Legal Institutions: A History" (1999). Still unpublished, this work is on file in the Bounds Law Library and the Ala-

[55] Walter W. Manley II, E. Canter Brown, Jr., and Eric W. Rise, THE SUPREME COURT OF FLORIDA AND ITS PREDECESSOR COURTS, 1821–1917 (1997); for a parallel work on federal courts, see Kermit L. Hall and Eric W. Rise, FROM LOCAL COURTS TO NATIONAL TRIBUNALS: THE FEDERAL DISTRICT COURTS OF FLORIDA, 1821–1990 (1991).

[56] William Warren Rogers, Sr. and James M. Denham, FLORIDA SHERIFFS: A HISTORY, 1821–1945 (2001).

[57] Erwin Surrency, CREATION OF A JUDICIAL SYSTEM: THE HISTORY OF GEORGIA COURTS, 1733 TO PRESENT (2001). Surrency was a historian of several broad topics of American law; see, for instance, his HISTORY OF THE FEDERAL COURTS, 2nd edition (2002).

[58] To pick one recent study, see Christopher Waldrep, JURY DISCRIMINATION: THE SUPREME COURT, PUBLIC OPINION, AND A GRASSROOTS FIGHT FOR RACIAL EQUALITY IN MISSISSIPPI (Athens: University of Georgia Press, 2010).

[59] The prolific archivist-historian-lawyer Dunbar Rowland (1864–1937) published COURTS, JUDGES, AND LAWYERS OF MISSISSIPPI, 1798–1935 (1935); the volume's spine identifies it as Volume I of what was evidently intended to be a longer work.

[60] Willie Morris, *Delta Blues*, NEW YORK TIMES, February 11, 1996. Evidently, Morris was either paraphrasing Faulkner or, perhaps, just making up a convenient remark. For discussion, see materials at http://liciabobesha.com/2013/02/quoteunquote/ (accessed July 16, 2013).

[61] L.G. Fant, Jr., *Procedural Law in Mississippi, Part I*, 34 MISSISSIPPI LAW JOURNAL 40-49 (1962–1963), especially 47-49.

[62] Tony A. Freyer and Paul M. Pruitt, Jr., *Reaction and Reform: Transforming the Judiciary Under Alabama's Constitution, 1901–1975*, 53 ALABAMA LAW REVIEW 77-133 (2001), especially 96-98, 120-33; and Tony A. Freyer, Paul M. Pruitt, Jr., and R. Volney Riser, *Clement Clay Torbert and Alabama Law Reform*, 63 ALABAMA LAW REVIEW, 867-94 (2012), especially 869-73, 876-77, 881-83.

bama State law Library.[63] Shortly thereafter (2001) Paul Pruitt and David I. Durham launched[64] a program of documentary publishing, the Occasional Publications of the Bounds Law Library. The Occasional Publications are designed to expand our concept of "legal documents" to include diaries, lectures, commonplace books, and speeches—anything generated by (or about) a legal professional in pursuit of his or her calling.[65] Such documents, typically, are illustrative of both structural and particular elements of legal practice.

Pending completion of these architectural works, students of Alabama legal history should employ the Hadden-Edwards grassroots approach to the study of the legal profession. We are in particular need of further research on the bar and its membership; on the peculiarities of local justice and its administration by justices of the peace, chancellors, circuit judges, and judges of city courts; on plaintiffs and defendants in civil cases; and on the statistics and demographics of criminal trials. Completion of such projects will require basic research in one or more of the state's archives, and in such county courthouses as preserve significant runs of old materials.[66] Why are these projects so important? A few observations on the legal profession will show what can be accomplished via studies, at whatever level of locality, of the bar and bench.

---

63 Tony A. Freyer, Paul M. Pruitt, Jr., Timothy W. Dixon, and Howard P. Walthall, "Alabama's Supreme Court and Legal Institutions: A History." This work, initiated by the Alabama State Law Library in 1997, is still an ongoing project; R. Volney Riser joined its authors in 2009. For a description of the work as a "Four-Headed Beast," see Pruitt, *Root and Branch*, *supra* note 2, at 126, 142 n. 54.

64 Many thanks for the encouragement and material support provided to the Bounds Occasional Publications by Dean Ken Randall, Dean Bill Brewbaker, and Vice Dean James Leonard.

65 To date, the titles of the Bounds Publications include: [No. 1] A GUIDE TO THE HOWELL THOMAS HEFLIN COLLECTION (2001); [No. 2] Wade Keyes' INTRODUCTORY LECTURE TO THE MONTGOMERY LAW SCHOOL: LEGAL EDUCATION IN MID-NINETEENTH CENTURY ALABAMA (2001); [No. 3] THE PRIVATE LIFE OF A NEW SOUTH LAWYER: STEPHEN CROOM'S 1875–1876 JOURNAL (2002); [No. 4] GILDED AGE LEGAL ETHICS: ESSAYS ON THOMAS GOODE JONES' 1887 CODE AND THE REGULATION OF THE PROFESSION (2003); [No. 5] COMMONPLACE BOOKS OF LAW: A SELECTION OF LAW-RELATED NOTEBOOKS FROM THE SEVENTEENTH CENTURY TO THE MID-TWENTIETH CENTURY (2005); [No. 6] A JOURNEY IN BRAZIL: HENRY WASHINGTON HILLIARD AND THE BRAZILIAN ANTI-SLAVERY SOCIETY (2008); [No. 7] A GOODLY HERITAGE: JUDGES AND HISTORICALLY SIGNIFICANT DECISIONS OF THE UNITED STATES DISTRICT COURT FOR THE MIDDLE DISTRICT OF ALABAMA, 1804–1955 (2010); and [No. 8] TRAVELING THE BEATEN TRAIL: CHARLES TAIT'S CHARGES TO FEDERAL GRAND JURIES, 1822–1825 (2013). Durham and Pruitt worked with Carol Rice Andrews on No. 4, with Tony Freyer and Timothy Dixon on No. 5, with R. Volney Riser on No. 7, and with Sally Hadden on No. 8.

66 The records of a few circuit and other courts are housed in archival facilities, for example: the Mobile County Courts at the Archives of the University of South Alabama; the Marengo County Circuit court at the Hoole Special Collections Library, University of Alabama; the Madison County Courts at the Archives of the Huntsville-Madison Public Library. Individual courthouses that contain significant collections of historic records include those of Green County and Tuscaloosa County. The judicial and other records of some counties have been preserved in microform thanks to recent projects of the Alabama Administrative Office of the Courts. See Pruitt, *Root and Branch*, 131-32, 146.

First consider frontier conditions in Alabama, which persisted in many parts of the state almost into the twentieth century. On the frontier, lawyers were perhaps the largest group of educated men available for a variety of important tasks. Certainly they were ubiquitous in the early intellectual life of the state, and remained so into the twentieth century. Many of the state's first men of letters were lawyers, including southwestern humorists Johnson Jones Hooper and Joseph Glover Baldwin; novelists Henry W. Hilliard, Jeremiah Clemens, and John H. Wallace, Jr.; poets Alexander B. Meek and William Russell Smith; newspaper editors John Forsyth of Mobile, George R. Cather of Ashville, and William Wallace Screws of Montgomery (among many); and law-trained educators, including Henry Tutwiler and Thomas Chalmers McCorvey.[67]

Lawyers were likewise deeply involved in the New South boom of industrial development following the Civil War. To take one instance: When businessmen met in 1873 to revive Birmingham's then-flagging iron industry, the result was the Eureka Mining and Transportation Company. Of the company's seven directors, two were lawyers: its president, Daniel S. Troy, and future state Supreme Court justice David Clopton. Within a year the Eureka Company was itself in need of rescue, and one of its prime rescuers was William S. Mudd, a Jefferson County lawyer and circuit judge.[68] Even when they weren't among the first movers of industry, lawyers served as public relations men, negotiators (for lands, right-of-way purchases, natural resources), and as legislative lobbyists.[69]

The mention of lobbying naturally calls to mind another of the legal profession's notable (if occasionally controversial) achievements: the large number of lawyers who are officeholders. This is verifiable in Alabama at the most fundamental level, that of delegates to constitutional conventions. Malcolm McMillan kept track of occupational groups among delegates. He counted 18 lawyers among the 44 men who wrote Alabama's 1819 constitution; thereafter the percentages of lawyer-delegates fluctuated until 1875, when a majority of delegates were lawyers. At the convention of 1901, lawyers numbered an astonishing 96 of 155 delegates.[70] We have less information concerning the personnel of the state legislature, though anyone familiar with the House and Senate *Journals* knows that attorneys have played a prominent role in legislative history—a truism exemplified by the fact that nearly all of Alabama's Speakers of the House have been lawyers.[71]

---

[67] *See* Benjamin Buford Williams, A LITERARY HISTORY OF ALABAMA: THE NINETEENTH CENTURY (1979), 27-28, 28-58, 69-94, 121, 157-61, 175-80, 181; and Owen, HISTORY OF ALABAMA AND DICTIONARY OF ALABAMA BIOGRAPHY, III: 80 (Baldwin), 308 (Cather), 348-49 Clemens), 598 (Forsyth), 814 (Hilliard), 839 (Hooper), and IV: 1100 (McCorvey), 1183-84 (Meek), 1515-16 (Screws), 1597-98 (Smith), 1694-95 (Tutwiler), 1721-22 (Wallace).

[68] Ethel Armes, THE STORY OF COAL AND IRON IN ALABAMA (1910), 255-59. See Owen, HISTORY OF ALABAMA AND DICTIONARY OF ALABAMA BIOGRAPHY, III: 352-55 and IV: 1256, 1685-86.

[69] Thomas, LAWYERING FOR THE RAILROAD, *supra* note 41, at 26-27, 89-90.

[70] McMillan, CONSTITUTIONAL DEVELOPMENT, *supra* note 5, at 31-32, 116, 190, 263-64.

[71] Speakers are listed at www.legislature.state.al.us/misc/history/past_house_ldrs.html. Of

Speaking in 1922, federal District Judge Henry D. Clayton said of lawmakers in the 1880s: "Calling the roll of the legislators in Alabama for a ten year period in those days would be like naming leading lawyers of the state."[72] Alabama governors have also benefited from legal training and the personal contacts that almost inevitably followed a legal career. From statehood through the present term of Governor Robert Bentley (in all, from 1819 to 2013), historians Samuel Webb and Margaret Armbrester have identified fifty-six Alabama governors; a hand count identified thirty-seven of them as lawyers.[73]

Having shown the importance of lawyers in state history, it goes almost without saying that we (students of history, however placed) need narratives of law and lawyers at work in the community. To put it another way, we need studies of how lawyers and lawmakers have figured in the evolution of the community known, in its various forms, as "Alabama." For the last three years at the University of Alabama, Tony Freyer and Paul Pruitt have taught Seminars in Alabama Legal History with the aim of building up just such a body of historical literature. The pieces that follow, with one exception,[74] are revisions of papers submitted in those classes. Individually, they cover a number of important areas of state legal history. Warren Hoffman and Paul Rand, respectively, explore the developing law of enclosures[75] and the nineteenth-century law of equity and trusts,[76] both "hard law" topics. Helen Eckinger provides a study of institutional governance at the Civil War-era University of Alabama.[77] Eddie Lowe and Michael Dodson

---

those serving from 1818 to 1927, a search in Owens' HISTORY OF ALABAMA AND DICTIONARY OF ALABAMA BIOGRAPHY revealed that every one was a lawyer except for Clement Clay Shorter (1888–1889). Shorter's biography is not available in any of the standard biographical directories, possibly because he died young. (For Shorter's obituary, see HUNTSVILLE WEEKLY DEMOCRAT, June 25, 1890, [p. 3, col. 4].)

72 Henry D. Clayton, *Some Past, Present, and Prospective Burdens of Lawyers*, 47 PROCEEDINGS OF THE ANNUAL MEETING OF THE STATE BAR ASSOCIATION 105-129 (1924), at 126.

73 Samuel L. Webb and Margaret E. Armbrester, eds., ALABAMA GOVERNORS: A POLITICAL HISTORY OF THE STATE (2001; 2nd ed., 2014). The hand count utilized the biographies in the 2001 edition of Webb and Armbrester. Webb and Armbrester count as governors General Wager Swain (1867), the Freedmen's Bureau official who had administrative charge of Alabama; and Jere Beasley (1972), who was acting governor during George Wallace's recovery from his gunshot wounds. The hand count did not count as lawyers John Murphy (1825–1829) or Hugh McVay (acting governor, 1837), both of whom were trained as lawyers but did not practice. Interestingly, most of the state's recent governors have not been lawyers, including Guy Hunt (1987–1993), James Folsom, Jr. (1993–1995), Forrest "Fob" James (1970–1983, 1995–1999), Bob Riley (2003–2011), and Robert Bentley (2011–present).

74 The exception is Deirdra Drinkard's *The Uniform Beneath the Robe*, which was submitted in Bryan Fair's 2012 Seminar in Alabama Constitutional Law.

75 Warren Hoffman, *Developments of the Enclosure Movement in Alabama: Disrupting the Free Roaming*.

76 Paul Rand, *Flush Times in the Chancery: A Brief Note on the History of Equity and Trusts in Alabama*.

77 Helen Eckinger, *The Militarization of the University of Alabama*. This paper was submitted and published by the ALABAMA REVIEW, and is reprinted here with that journal's generous

each present the history of significant legal developments in, respectively, a small town[78] and in the growing metropolis of Birmingham.[79] Courtney Cooper furnishes a treatment of Alabama's constitutional history, focusing on the always-controversial 1901 Constitution.[80] Deirdra Drinkard gives us a new insight into the mind of the School of Law's most celebrated alumnus, Justice Hugo L. Black.[81] Finally Ellie Campbell shows us a 1960s "hinge moment" in public attitudes toward members of terrorist groups such as the Ku Klux Klan.[82]

This book began with Bryan Fair's inspirational foreword, and ends with an encouraging tale from the mid-twentieth century. Taken all in all, these pieces represent a starting point in our search for knowledge. The students, though their work may be rooted in part upon the work of older scholars, have pointed the way for future students of Alabama legal history. Thus the collection's title: NEW FIELD, NEW CORN.[83]

permission. *See* 66 ALABAMA REVIEW 163-85 (July 2013).

[78] Eddie Lowe, *Economic Growth in Blount County/Oneonta: Attorneys, Companies, and Cases.*

[79] Michael Dodson, *Pioneers in Alabama Legal History: A Firm Understanding of the History of Alabama.*

[80] Courtney Cooper, *A Man in a Boy's Coat: The Evolution of Alabama's Constitutions.*

[81] *See supra* note 74.

[82] Ellie Campbell, *The "Breakthrough Verdict": Strange v. State.*

[83] The title plays upon Coke's remark that "assuredly out of the old fields must spring and grow the new corn." See John Henry Thomas and John Farquhar Fraser, eds., THE REPORTS OF SIR EDWARD COKE, KNT.: IN THIRTEEN PARTS (1826), I: xxx.

Developments of the Enclosure Movement in Alabama: Disrupting the Free Roaming

Warren Hoffman

I. Introduction

Often when people hear the phrase "enclosure movement" the first thought in their head is of the British Isles and the English enclosure that occurred there starting in the sixteenth century. This movement involved not only the closing off of the lands to roaming animals, but also closing off an entire public land system in which farming had been on the commons.[1] However, the extent of this enclosure was not as widespread as many believe. The movement failed to take hold in regions such as Scotland, Ireland, Wales, Cornwall, and the North and West Parts of England. The reason for this was that agriculture in these areas was undeveloped compared to other parts of the British isles, and the land was much more suitable for letting animals graze than for farming because of the hilly and forested terrain.[2]

While this was one of the principal enclosure movements in history, the United States has also undergone its own distinct enclosure movement. In the Postbellum South, there was a much less publicized closing of the range that significantly affected the individuals and society of the time. The South did not have a system of farming the commons such as England had developed earlier, and thus the focal point of the Postbellum South enclosure movement was the closing of the range, which would prevent herdsmen from allowing their animals to graze public and private lands not enclosed. The closing of the range in the South would prove to be no simple task, for the movement would have to uproot an open range system that was embraced by both the laws and the society of the time.[3]

The system of the open range that had developed in the South was very similar to that of the one that developed in the Celtic Fringe areas men-

---

[1] Donald N. McCloskey, *The Enclosure of Open Fields: Preface to a Study of its Impact on the Efficiency of English Agriculture in the Eighteenth Century*, 32 Journal of Economic History 15-35 (1972).

[2] Grady McWhiney and Forrest McDonald, *Celtic Origins of Southern Herding Practices*, 51 Journal of Southern History 165-182 (1985).

[3] Shawn Everett Kantor, Politics and Property Rights: The Closing of Open Range in the Postbellum South 17, 18 (1998) ("Instead of forcing livestock owners to control their animals, the fence law permitted citizens to let them roam the countryside.... It was impossible to prevent livestock from trampling and eating crops. The decision, therefore, was to pass laws requiring farmers to fence in their productive acreage and fence out animals.").

tioned above. One reason the South's system of grazing was similar to the Celtic method is that both were based on "allowing one's animals to run wild and root for themselves on just anybody's land," and this method was limited the extent to which natural food was available for the grazing animals to eat.[4] The Southern landscape featured abundant natural vegetation and oaks, which fit the herdsmen's lifestyle perfectly, requiring them to spend little labor or money in maintaining their animals.[5] Another affinity between the two regions was that in fact, many of the Southern herdsmen in the eighteenth and nineteenth centuries actually came from the Celtic portions of the British Isles, from 1715 all the way through 1837.[6]

While the system of the open range that had developed in the South was similar to that of the Celtic region, it was actually anything but similar to the system of land laws that had developed in the Northern part of the country. The system developed in the North is best summarized by one of Robert Frost's Yankee characters: "Good fences make good neighbors."[7] The English Puritans who settled New England brought their system of fences with them and continued to practice agriculture as they had in England, with a system that required that animals be restrained and fenced in.[8]

While the open range system had taken a solid hold in the South, and particularly in Alabama, it was eventually doomed by societal pressures. It was anything but a quick process, but in the end the range was closed. This chapter attempts to trace the development of the enclosure movement in that occurred in the Postbellum South and particularly in Alabama from its roots after the Civil War all the way through the movement's triumph in the mid to late twentieth century. The intent is to show that closing the range was not just a quick process, but filled with back and forth movement between the legislature, courts, and the public of the State of Alabama.

---

[4] Forrest McDonald and Grady McWhiney, *The Antebellum Southern Herdsman: A Reinterpretation*, 41 JOURNAL OF SOUTHERN HISTORY 158 (1975).

[5] *Id.* at 159.

[6] *Id.* at 156 ("Many of the American drovers of both the eighteenth and nineteenth centuries came from the Celtic Areas of the British Isles...if one tracks down where the Scotch-Irish went in their great migration that began soon after 1715...one has pinned down an important antebellum livestock country. They went to Philadelphia, thence to the uplands around that city, and thence to the uplands of the Pennsylvania valleys. From there they moved in two general directions: westward along the Ohio Valley, on both the Ohio and Kentucky sides of the river, and southwestward down the several valleys of Maryland and Virginia, back up to Virginia's Southside, down through the Piedmont of the Carolinas, and then into Tennessee and northern parts of Georgia, Alabama, and Mississippi, and ultimately into Arkansas, northern Louisiana, and Texas.).

[7] Quoted in J. Crawford King, Jr., *The Closing of the Southern Range: An Exploratory Study*, 48 JOURNAL OF SOUTHERN HISTORY 53 (1982).

[8] *See Celtic Origins of Southern Herding Practices*, *supra* note 2, at 170 ("'English puritans who came to settle in New England gave up as little of their former ways of doing things as possible. [They] . . . continued to practice the kind of agriculture with which they had been familiar in England.' In New England, just as in England, animals were yoked or otherwise restrained in ways totally foreign to open-range herding.").

First, this chapter will examine what made the open range so dominant (including statutes and case law supporting the open range); next it will examine the South after the War Between the States and the initial motivation behind the first push to close the range. The chapter then shifts focus to examine the case law, acts of the Alabama legislature, and code provisions that are the results of the push to close the range. Finally, the chapter examines last remnants of the open range system in Alabama that lasted well into the twentieth century, and then attempts to draw conclusions about the enclosure movement in Alabama as a whole.

II. The Times of the Open Range

From the Colonial times until after the Civil War, the general rule in the South was that farmers had to fence animals out in order to protect their crops from any trespassing animals.[9] In 1632 a law in the Virginia Colony provided that farmers were to fence in their crops, or plant at their "owne perill."[10] This same concept was the rule in Alabama: if a farmer did not have a proper fence around his crops and an animal caused damage to his crops, the loss was on the farmer.[11] This rule was in direct conflict with the common law. The common law required that a farmer keep his animals on his own property. Any animal that ventured onto another's property was considered a trespasser under common law, and the owner of the land could impound or kill the animal and then sue the owner of the animal for any damages to crops.[12]

Consequently, the Alabama Supreme Court confirmed this American system by explicitly rejecting any possibility that a common law rule (i.e., animals must be fenced in) was still operable.[13] In *Nashville & C.R. Co. v. Peacock* (1854), the Alabama Supreme Court discussed the process of repudiating the common law in the state. In this case, the facts showed that the Appellee's cow was found dead near the Appellant's railroad. The place the cow was killed however was not on the lands of the Appellee. The railroad tried to argue that because the cow was not on the Appellee's land, the company could not be liable for the loss.[14] In support of this argument, the railroad relied on the doctrine of the common law. In explaining that the common law was never adopted in this state, the court said:

> The laws of Mississippi Territory, which were adopted by the State of Alabama at the formation of our State constitution, contain provisions in direct repugnance to the common law on this subject, and to the extent of this repugnance repealed it.... Our present Code con-

---

[9] *See* King, *supra* note 7, at 56-57 and *passim* (53-70).

[10] *Id.*

[11] *See* Pruitt v. Ellington, 59 Ala. 454, 455 (1877).

[12] Kantor, POLITICS AND PROPERTY RIGHTS, *supra* note 3, at 17.

[13] Nashville & C.R. Co. v. Peacock, 25 Ala. 229 (1854).

[14] *Id.*

> tains similar provisions, which show conclusively that the unenclosed lands of this State are to be treated as common pasture for the cattle and stock of every citizen.[15]

Because the relevant common law never took hold in the state, the open range system was able to flourish throughout Alabama.

So what made the open range so appealing in Alabama? It was most likely an abundance of land in the state perfectly suited for grazing animals, which attracted herdsmen who moved here to take advantage of it. Frank Owsley describes the two types of herdsman that sought out the land in Alabama: the first ones were the "cutting edge" herdsman, who were primarily hunters and trappers and pursued livestock grazing as a secondary pursuit.[16] Members of this group were always on the move searching for better pastures and more game. Second was the genuine herdsman, whose primary occupation was livestock grazing.[17] This group of herdsman primarily remained in one location for long periods of time and maintained large herds of animals.[18] As for the land, in most areas of the state the vegetation was so lush and abundant that ranging animals could live off it all year round.[19] In the fall the oaks provided a great deal of mast for hogs to eat. Cattle in the fall were driven to the Tennessee River where they could live off the cornfields, canebreaks, and wild grasses until the spring.[20] Many historians have made the observation that the state contained a fine amount of food for grazing livestock.[21]

The open range thrived throughout early Alabama, and the case law of the state continuously supported the open range and its policies. A good example of the case law of the time is illustrated in *Woodward v. Purdy*, a case from the Supreme Court of Alabama in 1852. In this case, the Plaintiff's hogs broke into the Defendant's enclosed property and caused damage to his land.[22] The Defendant turned his dogs loose after the hogs, which the court describes as "worrying and tearing them with dogs." The hogs were injured by the Defendant's dogs, which led to the lawsuit in which the Plaintiff asked for $20 in damages.[23] The justice of the peace, with a jury, awarded the Plaintiff $142 plus costs for the damage to the hogs. The Defendant appealed to the circuit court, and offered evidence in recoup-

---

[15] *Id.*

[16] Frank Owsley, PLAIN FOLK OF THE OLD SOUTH 24 (1949).

[17] *Id.* at 25.

[18] *Id.*

[19] Grady McWhiney, *The Revolution in Nineteenth Century Alabama Agriculture*, in Sarah Woolfolk Wiggins, ed., FROM CIVIL WAR TO CIVIL RIGHTS: ALABAMA 1860–1960: AN ANTHOLOGY FROM THE ALABAMA REVIEW 115 (1987).

[20] *Id.*

[21] *Id.*

[22] Woodward v. Purdy, 20 Ala. 379 (1852).

[23] *Id.*

ment that he suffered damage to his crops from the hogs. The circuit court refused to hear evidence supporting this, and the Defendant appealed to the Supreme Court of the state.[24] The Supreme Court noted that at the time the hogs broke into the Defendant's land, the Defendant did not have a lawful fence around his crops (according to statute), and therefore had no action at law against the Plaintiff. With no action at law, the Defendant could not have a recoupment action either, and therefore the Supreme Court affirmed the rulings of the lower court.[25]

In addition to the courts, the code of Alabama also supported the open range system that fit the state so well. In the 1852 Alabama code the stray laws in §§1062-1063 can only be accounted for because of the open range.[26] Section 1062 specifically recognizes the prevalence of ranging animals, and allows the owner of a residence with stray animals on it to take up the strays if the owner is not known. Also, the 1852 code boasted stringent laws in relation to trespass on stock or cattle in §§1100-1101. In particular, §1100 of the 1852 code is the primary authority sanctioning the open range. This section states:

> If any trespass or damage is done by any animal breaking into lands not enclosed, as in the preceding section is provided, the owner is not liable therefor; and if any person injures or destroys any such animal, he is liable to the owner for five times the amount of the injury done, to be recovered before any court of competent jurisdiction.[27]

While this code section does not explicitly say that Alabama is declared an open range state, the fact that an owner of animals is not liable for his animals breaking into lands of another unless proper action is taken by the landowner reveals that Alabama is operating under an open range system. With the burden on the farmer to properly enclose his crops, the owner of animals could let them freely range without having to worry about being liable for damage they caused unless they managed to get into a properly enclosed field.

III. The Beginning of the End for the Open Range

The open range continued to be endorsed in Alabama per statutory authority through the late nineteenth century. However, there was increasing pressure from powerful sectors of society to close the range. During the post-Civil War era in the South, the once powerful slaveholders were trying to hold onto what power they had left. Immediately after the war, their biggest concern was losing their land and having it apportioned and given out to the freedmen.[28] While this would take away their source of income, it

---

[24] *Id.*

[25] *Id.*

[26] Code of Alabama 1852 Title 12, §§1062-1063.

[27] *Id.*, Title 13, §1100.

[28] *See* Steven Hahn, THE ROOTS OF SOUTHERN POPULISM: YEOMAN FARMERS AND THE TRANS-

would also cause them to lose what power they still had over the freedmen and society in general. Ultimately the elite retained control of the land;[29] however they now had to come up with more ways to ensure that they would not lose their power over the freedmen, landless whites, and holders of small farms (both white and black) in the future. Perhaps the biggest threat to the Elite's control was the open range system that was so deeply embedded in southern legal customs.

By the 1870's, sharecropping became a common way of life for the landless whites and freedmen. This was not necessarily by choice, but instead a necessity to put food on the table for their family. Sharecropping also allowed the elite landowners to retain control over the lower levels of society.[30] However, there was still one threat to the elites' control over the freedmen and landless whites, and holders of small farms: The open range laws that continued to dominate primarily throughout the South. The reason being that the open range allowed people who owned little or no land to still raise animals because the animals could roam and feed through the forests and fields of the South.[31] This didn't just allow them to raise animals for food, but they could also raise their own work animals to use in farming.[32] This system posed a big threat to the elites, because it allowed freedmen and landless whites to provide for their families somewhat more independently or even to provide for their families on their own. However, take away the open range, and the landless whites and freedmen would become entirely dependent on the elite landholders, thus ensuring continued control for the elites.

The elites were not the only ones pushing for closing the range. The developing railroad industry also saw a big advantage to a closed range—less liability when grazing animals were injured or killed by trains.[33] The railroads were one of the most frequent litigants in the courts during the times of the open range.[34] The laws of Alabama held railroad companies liable for injuries to stock on their tracks, and damages were usually pretty easy to

---

FORMATION OF THE GEORGIA UPCOUNTRY 1850–1890 153 (1983) ("Although the abolition of slavery struck the planting elite a telling blow, in a rural society control of land as much as control defined the boundaries of social relations. Had the federal government embarked upon a policy of confiscating large plantations and dividing them among the ex-slaves—a policy anticipated by the wartime military exigencies and supported by a handful of Radical Republicans—the postwar South would have been very different.").

[29] *Id.* ("The decision of President Andrew Johnson to restore confiscated property to its former owners and the commitment of most Republicans to the sanctity of private property and the revitalization of the cotton economy, however, combined to doom the federal initiative.").

[30] *Id.* at 163.

[31] *Id.* at 248.

[32] *Id.*

[33] *See* King, *supra* note 7, at 62.

[34] *Id.*

collect. There are even instances of stockowners deliberately "salting" the tracks in hopes that a train would hit their stock and they could collect.[35]

An example of a typical railroad case can be found in *Mobile & O.R. Co. v. Williams*. In this case, all the evidence presented showed that the Appellee had found one of his oxen dead near the railroad and it appeared to have been killed by a train.[36] There was also evidence that near the same place the owner also found one of his cows with two broken legs. The Appellant argued that this was not enough evidence to sustain the action.[37] The court discussed an 1852 act that "authorize[ed] the owner to recover, on mere proof of ownership, value and injury by the railroad company, its cars or locomotives."[38] The court next discussed an 1857 act that defined the duty of engineers in charge of a locomotive to give warning of an approaching train, and upon seeing an obstruction, to use all power and skill known to skillful engineers to stop the train.[39] In summarizing the two acts, the court said:

> The effect of the statutes is, that a railroad company is liable for injuries to stock when they result from the negligence of its servants or agents, whenever and wherever it may occur. If the injury occurs at or near any public road crossing, or any regular depot or stopping place, or within the corporate limits of any town or city, or because of an obstruction which could or ought to have been perceived, no degree of diligence will excuse the company from liability, unless all the requirements of the statute have been observed. In either case, the injury being shown, the burden of proof is on the railroad company to acquit itself of negligence, or to show a compliance with the statute.

The result in this case was that the previous proceedings were reversed and remanded because the court should have charged the jury that if the evidence showed the killing of the cattle by the railroad, then the Appellee was entitled to recover unless the Appellant could show the killing was not the result of negligence on its part.[40] While this might seem like a win for the railroad, how easy would it be to prove the killing was not the result of negligence for the railroad? Probably pretty hard if the jury was made up of common residents of Alabama at the time. In addition to the railroads, the timber companies in twentieth-century Alabama would also push to close the range. Owners of timberlands would gain interest in reforestation in the 1900s; however, the stock (mainly hogs) rooting for worms and insects posed problems for this effort.[41] The railroads and timber companies would provide the first push to close the range, as representatives of a soon to be

---

[35] *Id.*

[36] Mobile & O.R. Co. v. Williams, 53 Ala. 595, 598 (1875).

[37] *Id.*

[38] Acts of Alabama (1851–1852), 45.

[39] Acts of Alabama (1857–1858), 15.

[40] Mobile & O.R. Co. v. Williams, 53 Ala. 595, 598 (1875).

[41] *See* King, *supra* note 7, at 62.

industrializing and developing society. However, closing the range would prove to be much easier said than done.

The pressure starting to be generated in the public of Alabama for closing the range can be seen by examining the work of an increasingly active Alabama Legislature in the mid- to late-nineteenth century. The first legal restriction of Alabama's open range occurred in the form of a legislatively created district in 1866 known as the "Canebrake Agricultural District," which included parts of Greene, Dallas, Perry, and Marengo counties.[42] Within this district, stock running at large was strictly prohibited, and any domestic animal found running at large could be taken up immediately.[43] It is important to note that this district was centered in the cultivated parts of four primary Black Belt counties.[44] It is no coincidence that this district is in the heart of the Black Belt, and its creation was most likely the result of the power of the elites.

Otherwise, there were three primary means by which the range was slowly beginning to close in Alabama. The first method seen in Alabama was for the legislature to make it unlawful for stock to run free in a county or parts of a county. The earliest example of such an act occurred in 1866 in Dallas County.[45] In these areas, ranging animals could be taken up, and the owners of the animals were held liable for any damages or fees.[46] The second method used by the legislature became popular in the 1880s. Under this method, the legislature would delegate the power to decide whether or not to enact a stock law district to a county or local authority.[47] A good example of this is an 1881 Alabama act allowing the county commissioners or revenue courts in twelve counties (most of them located in or near the Black Belt) to establish or abolish districts where stock could not run at large.[48] To initiate the process, the act required a petition by ten landowners before the county commissioners could close the range. Once the proper petition and publication were made, it was up to the commissioners to make the decision. The third method (often used) was one by which the Alabama legislature authorized a local election to close the range. Under this system, the power of the legislature would be delegated to a county authority but voter participation ultimately decided the outcome. An example of this is an 1882

---

[42] King, *supra* note 7, at 58.

[43] Acts of Alabama (1865–1866), 334-37.

[44] King, *supra* note 7, at 58.

[45] Acts of Alabama (1866–1867), 46.

[46] Acts of Alabama (1866–1867), 46. *See also* Acts of Alabama (1870–1871), 94.

[47] King, *supra* note 7, at 58.

[48] Acts of Alabama (1880–1881), 163-65. The counties were Marengo, Sumter, Montgomery, Hale, Dallas, Autauga, Wilcox, Lowndes, Russell, Monroe, Lawrence, and Perry. They are wholly or partially located in the Black Belt, except for Russell County in the upper coastal plain (on the eastern edge of the Black Belt) and Lawrence County in the Tennessee Valley.

Alabama Act that required 50 freeholders to petition the probate judge before a fence-or-no-fence vote could be held.[49]

It is important to note that while all this activity in the legislature is going on, the Code of Alabama continued to have statutes in harmony with the open range. At the same time the code also lacked any provisions that would close the range. In the 1876 Alabama Code, §1587 was almost identical to §1100 from the 1852 code (discussed above).[50] Thus, the Code of Alabama remained in harmony with the open range concept up to and beyond 1876. Even after restrictions on the open range began to be enacted, such as legislatively created districts or options to create districts, the open range statutes themselves, such as §1587, continued to be a part the code.

After the legislature became active in creating ways to limit the open range, the courts of Alabama were soon filling with cases contesting every aspect of the laws. The Alabama courts in the late nineteenth century continued to uphold the general rule of the state that animals were allowed to run at large.[51] However, the courts did begin to note that the open range was limited when a law or statute was in place prohibiting it. It is also interesting that during this time in several cases the court still went so far as to state that the common law rule that an owner must restrain his animals to his own property was reversed or not applicable.[52]

A good illustration of the legislative acts discussed above can be seen in *Stanfill v. Dallas County Court of Revenue*. Leading up to this case, a petition was signed by Jere Johnson and 12 others and filed with the probate judge of Dallas County.[53] The petitioners prayed for an order of the court to establish the county's several precincts into a district in which stock could not run at large.[54] Counsel for counter-petitioners objected to consideration of the petition (original) on the grounds that the act of the general assembly approved February 28, 1881 giving the court of county revenue of Dallas County jurisdiction in such cases was unconstitutional and void. Despite this, the petition (original) was granted, and an order establishing the stock law district was made after the evidence was heard. Afterwards, John Stanfill, one of the counter petitioners, petitioned for the writ of

---

49 Acts of Alabama (1882–1883), 538-41; Acts of Alabama (1884–1885), 306-09.

50 Code of Alabama 1876, Title 13 § 1587; *see also supra* note 26.

51 Hurd v. Lacy, 93 Ala. 427, 9 So. 378 (1891).

52 Mobile & O.R. Co. v. Williams, 53 Ala. 595 (1875).

53 Stanfill v. Dallas County Court of Revenue, 80 Ala. 287 (1885).

54 Acts of Alabama (1880–1881), 163 ("The act of the legislature, under which the proceedings were had, provides that whenever any ten freeholders petition in writing the Court of County Revenue, stating that they desire an order to be made establishing a district, wherein stock shall not be allowed to run at large; that they are residents of the district, fully describing it; and such petition is filed with the judge of probate at least thirty days before the next term of the court, and notices of the application are posted at the court-house, and at three public places in the district, and once in a newspaper, if one is published in the county, the court must hear the petition, and any persons opposed to it, and make an order granting or dismissing such petition, in whole or in part.").

certiorari from the City Court, which was denied.[55] The case was carried to the Supreme Court; and in its opinion refusing certiorari, the court emphasized the importance of the county unit, and affirmed the constitutionality of acts delegating the closed range decision to county bodies:

> From the origin of the government counties have been organized and existed; and the entrusting to their local authorities *quasi* legislative powers and functions has never been considered as violative of the maxim that legislative power can not be delegated. Such conferred powers are the powers of the State, and are conferred for the purposes of local and political organization. The Court of County Revenue is the authority that acts for and exercises the powers of Dallas county; and conceding that the power conferred by the act is *quasi* legislative, it constitutes no valid objection to its constitutionality[56]

Another good example of a member of the public contesting the acts of the General Assembly can be seen in *Dunn v. Wilcox County*. In this case, the court was to determine the constitutionality of several acts of the legislature that authorized the court of county revenues of Wilcox County "to establish or abolish districts in which stock may be prevented from running at large."[57] In the case, the Plaintiff argued that the enactments were a violation of §50 of article 4 of the Alabama Constitution of 1875, which declared that "the general assembly shall not have power to authorize any municipal corporation to pass any laws inconsistent with the general laws of the state."[58] The court ultimately held that because counties are not "municipal corporations," the acts were not in violation of this section of the constitution. In reaching its decision, the court also noted that the stock laws in fact do not delegate any legislative power to the board of revenues by allowing them to "pass laws," because the laws are "complete within themselves," meaning absolutely none of the terms or provisions of the act are made by the county authorities, but are spelled out already by the acts. The county authorities only choose when to enact the acts.[59] While this case does not show any real confrontation between the public and the state, it is important because it shows how every angle of the stock laws was tested in the courts in an attempt to get them repealed.

Constitutionality was not the only standard by which the acts were contested. In *Flowers v. Grant,* the procedures and jurisdictional scope of the commissioners' court were under review. At issue was an act of December 1886 that authorized the commissioners' courts of Henry, Pickens, and Dale counties to establish or abolish districts within which stock could not run at

---

[55] Stanfill v. Dallas County Court of Revenue, 80 Ala. 287 (1885).

[56] *Id.*

[57] Acts of Alabama (1880–1881), 163; Acts (1884–1885), 531, 560; Acts (1886–1887), 851, 923.

[58] Dunn v. Wilcox County, 85 Ala. 144, 145-46, 4 So. 661 (1888). For the 1875 Constitution of Alabama, Art. IV, §50, see 1876 Code of Alabama, 135.

[59] *Id.*

large.[60] In order to establish a district, the act provided "[t]hat whenever any ten freeholders petition said court, in writing, stating that they desire an order to be made establishing a district wherein livestock shall not run at large, fully describing such district, and stating that petitioners reside in such district," etc., the court shall proceed in the manner directed afterwards in the act, to establish it or not, as to be determined through trial.[61] In this case, the Defendants objected to the petition of the twelve citizens by claiming that the petition was illegal and failed to state that the petitioners were freeholders and resided in the district sought to be established. On this subject, the Supreme Court noted: "The 10 'citizens' who it is averred owned lands in said district, might have resided in any other county of the state, or in any part of the county of Henry outside of the district described." Because the act had specified "freeholders," the Court held that the order establishing the district was void.[62]

In addition to late-nineteenth century case law focused on the Acts of the Alabama Legislature, the courts also had to address ranging animals in areas where there was no rule against the open range and stock was still permitted to run at large. *Hurd v. Lacy* (1891) is a good example of the case law of this type. In this case, the Appellee's mule was running at large (in a jurisdiction with no statute or law limiting the open range) and came into contact with and was injured by Appellant's barbed wire fence around a vacant lot.[63] Of the fence the court said, "The wire was supported by 5 posts, 30 or 40 feet apart, and was about 4 feet from the ground at the posts. It was stretched by hand only, and sagged between the posts from 8 to 12 inches. There was nothing but the posts and the single wire to warn stock or to prevent them from running against the wire."[64] After describing the condition of the fence, Justice Richard W. Walker reinforced the doctrine that the common law was not and never had been applicable in this state, and went into an in-depth discussion of the difference in the responsibilities of an owner of land in a closed range area compared to an open range area:

> Where ... the right to suffer such animals to run at large is recognized, it would seem as legitimately to follow that the owner of land, not properly inclosed, is without remedy for injury caused to his premises by stock running at large, and is also to be held to expose himself to liability for damages to such stock occasioned by erections or excavations so made on the land as to be obviously dangerous to animals straying thereon. Good reason for distinguishing the respective duties and liabilities of the land-owner [in an open range system vs. a closed

[60] Flowers v. Grant, 129 Ala. 275, 277-78, 30 So. 94 (1901); Acts of Alabama (1886–1887), 739.

[61] Acts of Alabama (1886–1887), 739. The date-approved note at the end of this act says that is was approved in December 1887; but that is a typographical error since the act is grouped with December 1886 acts (and the legislature was not in session in December 1887).

[62] Flowers v. Grant, 129 Ala. 275, 278, 30 So. 94 (1901).

[63] Hurd v. Lacy, 93 Ala. 427, 9 So. 378 (1891).

[64] *Id.*

> range system] ... is to be found in the consideration that the results of applying the maxim that "you must so use your property as not to injure the property of another" necessarily depend upon the state of the law as to the correlative rights of the land-owner, and of those who may be affected by his use of his property. [65]

Because the fence did not meet the requirements for a proper fence[66] in the code, the court affirmed the judgment of the lower court for the Plaintiff and its finding that the fence was negligently constructed.[67] Thus it is interesting that even with the push from legislative acts, the Court showed that overall the state was still strongly committed to an open range policy

In 1903, the Alabama Legislature became more involved in limiting the open range by requiring all cities and towns having five thousand or more people to adopt ordinances regulating livestock.[68] Additionally, in this same year the state legislature enacted a statewide law that set up standardized local option procedures.[69] This would provide the state with a standard formula for impeding the open range at the county level, without having to use a hodgepodge of local laws as done in the past. It is important to note however that the Alabama Courts continued to recognize prior local laws that established stock law districts as valid and not repealed as long as they did not conflict with the new 1903 General Law on creating stock law districts.[70] Soon after the legislature passed these two provisions, the Alabama Code followed suit and finally began to reflect these first provisions for limiting the open range.

Before exploring the new statutory development in the 1907 code that begins to limit the open range, it is important to recognize that statutes authorizing the open range continued to run strong through the 1907 Code of Alabama. In particular, §4245 was almost identical all the prior code sections supporting the open range, including the 1852 and 1876 sections mentioned previously.[71] If a fence was not proper and a neighbor's animal damaged crops, the loss still fell on the farmer according to §4245.[72]

The first of the new provisions restricting the open range in the 1907 Alabama Code made the penalties harsher for animal trespassing. These

---

[65] *Id.*

[66] 1887 Code of Alabama, §1364, provides that "all inclosures and fences must be made at least five feet high, and, if made of rails, not more than four inches apart," "or, if made of palings, nor more than three inches apart"; "but a rail fence five feet high, with rails not more than eighteen inches apart," "shall be a lawful fence, so far as cattle, horses, and mules are concerned."

[67] Hurd v. Lacy, 93 Ala. 427, 9 So. 378 (1891).

[68] Acts of Alabama (1903, General), 365.

[69] *Id.* at 431-38.

[70] *See* Mosely v. Hudson, 146 Ala. 682, 40 So. 217 (1906); Mayfield v. Court of County Com'rs of Tuscaloosa County, 148 Ala. 548, 550, 41 So. 932, 933 (1906).

[71] 1907 Code of Alabama §4245.

[72] *Id.*

sections do not conflict with the open range theory, but they show that the growing and developing society of Alabama was less tolerant to trespassing animals than it had been in the past. One of these sections, §4254 of the Alabama Code, read as follows:

> **4254.** Animal trespassing taken up.—Any horse, mare, mule, ox, bullock, cow, jack, jennet, sheep, goat, or hog, may be taken up and confined by any person into whose inclosure or ground such animal may have broken through a lawful fence, or which may be found on the part cultivated by anyone under a common inclosure, such person not having consented for the animal to run at large in the inclosure, and found running at large unlawfully in stock law districts.[73]

A close reading of this statute reveals that the burden is still on the landowner to fence his crops in. However, the owner of the land is provided a stronger legal remedy than he had before. Another addition to the 1907 code is §4255. This section provides that when a trespassing animal is taken up, confined, and/or cared for (by the owner of the land), the "owner [of the animal] shall pay to the person who has taken up and cared for it, twenty-five cents a day for the time it may be so kept."[74] Section 4256, also a new addition in 1907, adds to the authority of the farmer by requiring the owner of the animal, once notified, to promptly take away the animal away in two days.[75] Even though these sections still acknowledge and support the general open range theory of law, they begin to strip the open range of its once unlimited freedom and dominance.

Possibly the strongest evidence of the public's changing perception of open ranging animals was the addition of statutes in the 1907 code that gave Alabama citizens the option to create stock law districts in their respective counties.[76] These districts, if created, would generally prevent stock from running at large within their boundaries. The authority to create these districts came from the newly enacted §5881 in the 1907 code. This statute gave courts of county commissioners the power to supervise and hold elections to create or abolish a stock law district within their respective counties.[77] While the county commissioners had the power to hold the elections, the ultimate power to determine whether to hold a stock law district election was in the hands of the citizens. In particular, §5882 of the code allowed a majority of freeholders within a particular district of a county to file a petition saying they wished to hold an election in order to determine whether a majority of the qualified electors favor a law that would prohibit the running at large of stock in a district.[78] The Supreme

---

[73] *Id.*

[74] 1907 Code of Alabama §4255.

[75] 1907 Code of Alabama §4256.

[76] 1907 Code of Alabama §5881.

[77] *Id.*

[78] 1907 Code of Alabama §5882.

Court of Alabama described this new chapter of the code on stock law districts as "a practical codification of the general act of 1903," and held that it "operates as a repeal of all local laws in so far as they are in conflict with same, but leaves said local laws in full force in so far as they deal with any features not covered or provided for in said general law."[79]

While the previous stock laws discussed were optional, the 1907 code also created mandatory stock law districts in certain populated areas of the state. The newly enacted §§5898-5899 of the code required municipalities with five thousand or more people inside its limits to adopt ordinances and laws as necessary to prevent stock from running at large within the city limits.[80] This is the first instance of mandatory code provisions in Alabama that start closing the range.

The case law that developed after the 1903 General Assembly Acts and the 1907 code was similar to the case law that developed after the earlier legislative acts, in that the stock law option generated many contests in the courtroom. One problem in particular with the provisions was the question of how to handle a situation in which an animal, owned by a person residing outside a stock law district, wanders into a stock law district and causes damage. A 1908 case that discusses this concept and how it relates to the 1903 act is *Jones v. Hines*. In this case, the plaintiff alleged that the defendant had unlawfully permitted his hogs to run at large and destroy the plaintiff's corn in Gadsden.[81] The corporate authorities for Gadsden had passed an ordinance making the city of Gadsden a stock law district. The plaintiff lived in the county outside the city limits of Gadsden, but his hogs had made their way into plaintiff's garden within the city limits and destroyed part of it. In evaluating the case, the court reasoned that the Gadsden census showed a population of much less than 5,000, and believed that this had not changed. The court also noted that the ordinance itself did not even state the population, which was required by the 1903 act to be 5,000 or greater. In the opinion, Justice R.T. Simpson further said:

> It cannot be said that the act itself fixes any liability on the Defendant, for the act is directed at the city authorities, and evidently means that it shall be unlawful for them to permit the stock to run at large, and places upon said authorities, not the duty of punishing personally those whose hogs run at large, but merely the duty of making laws for impounding the stock. In other words, both the act and the ordinance are directed against the animal, and not against the owner except as he may be affected by the taking and selling of his animal.[82]

---

[79] Almon v. Court of County Revenues of Lawrence County, 179 Ala. 662, 663 (1913) (citing Blount County v. Johnson, 145 Ala. 553 (1906); *Phillips v. Bynum*, 145 Ala. 549 (1906)).

[80] *See* 1907 Alabama Code §§5898-5899.

[81] Jones v. Hines, 157 Ala. 624, 628-29 (1908).

[82] *Id.*

So at worst, the owner would not be able to recover his animal; however he could not be subject to civil liability for any damage caused by his stock. In reversing the lower court and holding that the owner could not be liable, the court noted that "[t]he passage of the ordinance certainly could not have the effect of making every citizen in the country keep up his hogs, lest they might wander into the city. No limit could be fixed to the distance from which a hungry hog might wander. All that can be said is that the citizen in the country who allows his stock to run at large takes the chances of their being impounded if they wander into town."[83] The Supreme Court showed in this case that just because stock laws were becoming common, they still did not control in all areas of the state and were not favored over the open range.

In 1918, the Supreme Court faced a decision with a similar set of circumstances, but analyzed it under the §4251 of the 1907 code instead of the 1903 acts. In *Ex parte Fowler*, the Plaintiff alleged that Defendant's "yellow and white spotted milk cow" caused $20 worth of damages to the Plaintiff's garden that was located in the town of Brighton (a stock law district in Jefferson County).[84] The Court of Appeals found that the Plaintiff must prove the damage had occurred inside a properly enclosed fence or that the animal was turned loose in a stock law district. In reversing this decision, the Supreme Court of Alabama found that the owner of the cow was liable for the damage committed by cow to the garden in a stock-law district, regardless of whether he was a resident of such district or was negligent in permitting cow to wander therein.[85]

In addition to cases about stock wandering from the open range into stock law districts, there was also an abundance of cases contesting just about every aspect of stock law elections. In *De Kalb County v. Price*, the Appellee was contesting a stock law election for precinct number 10 in DeKalb County.[86] The result of the election was against a stock law by the slimmest of margins—a vote of 39 votes in favor of a stock law and 38 votes against a stock law. This result is interesting because the election managers claimed they could not ascertain the intention of the 39th vote (that evidently favored a stock law), so they ultimately decided it to be against the stock law and, and therefore found no majority obtained in support of the stock law.[87] In the probate court, a number of the ballots were thrown out, so the final vote turned out to be 32 votes in favor of the stock law and 31 against. In reviewing the record, the Supreme Court noted that several of the "yes" votes were actually cast by voters not residing within the county, and thus invalid. Therefore the court reversed the lower court's decision in

---

[83] *Id.* at 629.

[84] *Ex parte Fowler*, 203 Ala. 98, 99, 82 So.112, 113 (1919).

[85] *Id.*

[86] De Kalb County v. Price, 188 Ala. 419, 420, 66 So. 12, 13 (1914).

[87] *Id.*

favor of the stock law and rendered the judgment against the stock law.[88] This case shows just how divided the community was over the stock law issue. It also shows how meticulous the courts had to be in examining the results of elections to ensure a fair result.

IV. Continuing the Trend

Again in the 1923 code of Alabama, new provisions were introduced that continued to slowly lock down the range. However, the code continued to also have provisions consistent with the open range. The open range policy in §7975 of the 1923 code still held valid the proposition that an animal was not trespassing on a farmer's land unless the farmer had a lawful enclosure around his land.[89] Again, this provision remains substantially similar to its predecessors discussed above. Even though the open range still had a presence in the code, more new closed range provisions were introduced and they continued to chip away at the power of the open range statutes. First, the newly enacted §7991 limited the reach of article 3 regarding trespass by stock.

> **7991. Limitations to article.**—The provisions of this article as to lawful fences and the trespassing of animals shall not apply or be held to control as to stock law districts in which it is made unlawful for animals mentioned in the article to run at large; but shall apply to districts and territories in which it is lawful for such animals to run at large.[90]

While this may not seem to be a significant development, it is an acknowledgment by the state legislature that stock law district statutes override any open range provisions of the code such as § 4245. This was a reinforcement to the prior case law discussed, and a sure sign that stock law districts were there to stay, and that more changes were likely on the horizon.

Another new provision in the Alabama code was added to stiffen the penalty for the owner of stock running at large in a stock law district. While the 1907 code had also provided a penalty for this act, the 1923 criminal code introduced § 3224, which increased the penalty to "double the damages sustained by the injured party or parties... and [persons convicted] may also be imprisoned in the county jail, or sentenced to hard labor for the county for a term not exceeding six months, at the discretion of the court or jury trying the case."[91] These penalties were very harsh for the time, and proof that a significant portion of the public was less and less pleased with the free roaming of the open range in Alabama.

---

[88] *Id.*

[89] *See* 1907 Code of Alabama §7975.

[90] *See* 1923 Code of Alabama §7991.

[91] *See* 1923 Code of Alabama §3224.

The case law following the 1923 code appeared to have a different focus from much of the prior litigation. The stock law districts and county option appeared to be permanent fixtures, so there were not quite as many cases challenging the validity of the acts themselves. The focus of much of the case law seemed to have shifted from the constitutionality of the process to now contesting the results of the elections through the statutes.[92] In some instances, the owners of animals would actually use the technicalities of the stock laws to get themselves out of trouble. For example, in *Prestwood v. Bagley*, thirteen cattle were found running at large in a stock law district by Tom Bagley.[93] He took them up and claimed they caused damages to his crops. The owner of the animals challenged Bagley's right to detain the cattle because he failed to give the required notice under §10216 of the Alabama Code.[94] The court found for the Defendant (the animal owner), and afterwards the Plaintiff still refused to give up the cattle. On appeal, the Supreme Court again affirmed the lower court decision and found for the Defendant.[95]

Another interesting development in the case law during this time is that cases involving motor vehicles become more prevalent—perhaps a sign of the advancing society pushing for a closed range. In *Pelham v. Spears*, the Plaintiff was seeking $60 for damages done to his vehicle when a cow ran in front of it while his agent was driving down a public road in Geneva, Alabama.[96] The court still recognized that open range laws are the rule of the state unless prohibited by statute. It was not specifically averred in the complaint that the accident was in a stock law district, but the court held that even assuming it was, §10215 of the 1923 Alabama Code made it unlawful for stock to go onto the premises of another,[97] but not the highway.

---

[92] *See* Yates v. Walker County Bd. of Revenue, 232 Ala. 537, 168 So. 549 (1936); White v. Clarke County, 219 Ala. 233, 121 So. 913 (1929); Campbell v. Jefferson County, 216 Ala. 251, 113 So. 230 (1927); and Board of Revenue v. McDanal, 213 Ala. 349, 105 So. 191 (1925).

[93] Prestwood v. Bagley, 227 Ala. 316, 149 So. 817 (1933).

[94] 1923 Code of Alabama, §10216, provides: "Any person who is the owner of or in the lawful possession of any land, or his agent, shall have the right to take possession of any animal or stock found at large and uncontrolled on his premises, or premises of which he has chare, and when so taken up, he shall notify personally the owner of such animal or stock, when known, or by leaving a written notice at the usual place of residence of such owner within twenty-four hours after so taking up such stock or animal."

[95] Prestwood v. Bagley, 227 Ala. 316, 149 So. 817 (1933).

[96] Pelham v. Spears, 222 Ala. 365, 367, 132 So. 886, 887 (1931).

[97] §10215 of the 1923 Alabama Code provides: "when an election is held in any precinct, and the majority of the qualified electors therein cast their votes in favor of prohibiting stock from running at large in such precinct, it shall be unlawful for the owner of any stock or animal to knowingly, voluntarily, negligently, or willfully permit any such stock or animal to go at large on the premises of another, in such precinct, and the owner of such stock or animal so permitted to run at large shall be liable to any person injured thereby for all damages done to crops, shade or fruit trees, ornamental shrubs of another, to be recovered before any court of competent jurisdiction."

The Supreme Court of Alabama summarized the prior case law in the area by saying:

> There seems to be considerable difference of opinion as to the liability of owners of animals who injure others on the highway, and liability is most generally found where the animal was there in violation of a statute or ordinance, but the best adjudicated cases hold that, if the animal is not unlawfully on the highway, the owner is not liable for injuries therefrom unless it was of such disposition and possessed such propensities, known to the owner, as would likely or probably suggest the infliction of damage to third persons or their property.[98]

The Supreme Court affirmed the circuit court's finding for the Plaintiff based on the fact that according to the prior case law and the statute the owner was not liable.

In another case, *Crittenden v. Speake*, a mule was running at large in a stock law district at night and was hit by a car.[99] The Plaintiff was suing for damages to the automobile as a result of the collision. In finding for the Defendant, the Supreme Court noted that this did not come within the type of damages proscribed by §10215 of the 1923 Alabama Code.[100] In reversing the Court of Appeals and finding for the Defendant, the Supreme Court held that there was no evidence that the Defendant had knowingly, negligently, willfully, or voluntarily allowed the mule to go at large in the stock law district.

V. The End of the Open Range

In 1939, the Alabama legislature enacted a comprehensive stock law. The act was titled "The Local Option Stock Law for the State of Alabama with the County as the Unit."[101] Section 2 stated "[t]hat it shall be unlawful for the owner of any livestock or animal, as herein defined, to knowingly, voluntarily, negligently, or willfully permit any such livestock or animal to go at large in the State of Alabama either upon the premises of another or upon the public lands, highways, roads, or streets in the state of Alabama."[102] It is under these provisions that Alabama should be declared a closed range state. There were, however, provisions whereby a county could elect to become open range. Sections 90, 91, 92, and 93 of the act provided that upon petition of twenty-five percent of the qualified electors of a county an election might be held to determine if a county should be open range or closed range.[103] One additional interesting development in this act was that the automobile was now a part of the fence laws of the state. The 1939 act

---

[98] Pelham v. Spears, 222 Ala. 365, 367, 132 So. 886, 887 (1931).

[99] Crittenden v. Speake, 240 Ala. 133, 198 So. 137 (1940).

[100] *See* 1923 Code of Alabama §10215, quoted *supra* note 97.

[101] Acts of Alabama (1939), Act No. 368, at 487.

[102] *Id.*

[103] *Id.*

required that no driver be liable for any injury to livestock on a public highway regardless of whether or not there is an open range.[104]

The 1940 code did not provide much as far as new substance to the enclosure movement. The code predominantly featured refined sections concerning the local option to enact stock laws to make it illegal for animals to roam at large. Apparently the closed range was still not automatic; but making stock laws easier to enact locally would continue to deplete the open range. One interesting addition within the local option laws was §78. This provision provided that through the optional election procedures it could be made unlawful for stock to run at large on public property within a jurisdiction.[105] Another interesting provision new to the local option was §93. This section provided that it could be chosen through local option that stock law districts not be abolished by county elections.[106]

In 1951, the legislature finally declared it unlawful for livestock to run at large in any county. The legislature also abolished all open range counties and repealed any code section that allowed for the creation of an open range county, as well as all other laws that were in conflict with the act.[107] After this law was passed, the local election was no longer an option, and all livestock was prohibited from running at large. What finally pushed the legislature over the edge? More than likely it was the society that was significantly different from the times of the open range. There were now cities with big populations, paved roads, and automobiles, all of which put roaming stock out of place.

Even after Alabama was finally declared no longer an open range state, there were still times when animals would wind up on the lands of a neighbor for extended periods of time. However, the landowner now had the lawful remedy on his side. In *Glover v. Pugh*, Appellant Pugh notified Appellee Glover several times that his (Glover's) cattle were on Pugh's land.[108] Over several months, Glover failed to get his cattle, and Pugh eventually penned two of them up. Pugh notified Glover of this action too, and at the same time fed and watered the two penned cattle. Glover (the owner of the cows) then sued Pugh in a detinue action to recover the cattle. Pugh then filed a plea in recoupment to recover the costs for taking care of the cattle and the damage they had caused. The Court of Appeals ultimately found that the Appellant was not entitled to sue in detinue because he failed to pursue the remedies provided in §88, Title 3, of the 1940 Code of Alabama.[109]

---

[104] *Id.*

[105] *See* 1940 Alabama Code, §79 [Title 3].

[106] *See* 1940 Alabama Code, §93 [Ch. 5, Art. I].

[107] Acts of Alabama (1951), No. 53, at 266.

[108] Glover v. Pugh, 40 Ala. App. 258, 262, 122 So.2d 142, 146 (1959).

[109] Section 88, Title 3, 1940 Alabama Code sets out the method by which the owner of seized cattle may regain possession of same where no judgment has been entered for such damages. He must first pay the damages agreed upon, and should the parties be unable to agree, either

In another case, *Randle v. Payne*, the Plaintiff was driving on U.S. Highway 11 in Jefferson County when he collided with a bull owned by the Defendant on the highway.[110] Initially, a jury returned a verdict of $800 for the Plaintiff. However, after further review, the Court of Appeals held that after the 1939 act, liability for breach of the act was limited to those cases where an owner knowingly or willfully placed stock on a highway. The court then said it found "no evidence in this record that this Defendant placed his bull upon Highway 11 knowingly, or willfully. The value of the bull ($1500.00) in and of itself would tend to negative completely the elements of knowingly and willfully placing him on a highway highly travelled." So even after the state had moved completely to a closed range, the courts were still reluctant to subject animal owners to unlimited liability.

While the 1951 act would seem to be the end of the open range, the code continued to have provisions that at first glance support the open range. In particular, the relevant 1975 code provision said:

> **§3-4-6. Liability of owner of animal breaking into lands not enclosed by lawful fence for trespass or destroying such.**
>
> (a) If any trespass or damage is done by any animal breaking into lands not enclosed by a lawful fence as defined in this chapter, the owner shall not be liable therefor.
>
> (b) If any person injures or destroys any such animal, he shall be liable to the owner for five times the amount of injury done....[111]

Even though the 1951 acts clearly declared provisions such as the one above invalid, §3-4-6 continues to be a part of the code. Not only was the provision invalid, but it was also clearly contradictory to the closed ranged statutes enacted in the 1975 code. The primary closed range code provision enacted in the 1975 code is still in effect today. This statute provides:

> **§3-5-2. Permitting livestock or animals to run at large upon premises of another without permission or upon public lands, highways, etc., generally.**
>
> (a) It shall be unlawful for the owner of any livestock or animal, as defined in 3-5-1, to knowingly, voluntarily, negligently or willfully permit any such livestock or animal to go at large in the state of Alabama either upon the premises of another or upon the public lands, highways, roads or streets in the state of Alabama...
>
> (c) There shall be no "open range" counties in this state. This section shall apply to all counties within the state.[112]

---

party has the right to go before a justice of the peace within the precinct where the cattle is seized and have the issue tried after giving the opposite party one day's notice.

[110] Randle v. Payne, 39 Ala. App. 652, 656, 107 So.2d 907, 910 (1958).

[111] 1975 Code of Alabama §3-4-6.

[112] 1975 Code of Alabama §3-5-2.

Provisions such as §3-4-6 were expressly prohibited from having any effect anymore in Alabama by both the 1950 act and §3-5-2(c), yet open range issues still cropped up in the courts from time to time. In *Monfee v. Seymore*, a 1981 case in the Court of Civil Appeals of Alabama, the court was still discussing whether the concept of the open range was applicable in Alabama.[113] In this case, the Plaintiff filed an action against Defendant to recover possession of six head of cattle. Defendant counterclaimed, alleging that on two separate occasions the Plaintiff's cattle came onto his land and damaged his crops. The jury found in favor of Defendant on the counterclaim and assessed damages at $1,300. The circuit court denied Plaintiff's motion for a new trial, and the Plaintiff appealed. Additionally, the Defendant wanted the trial court to instruct the jury that the code precludes liability where the landowner has not erected a lawful fence to protect his crops. In addressing this issue, the Supreme Court specifically looked at §3-4-6 of the 1975 Alabama Code, and found that it was in fact in harmony with the open range concept, and therefore in conflict with present law.[114] In its decision, the court ultimately cited the 1951 act as authority for repealing §3-4-6 of the 1975 code. However, the fact that the Alabama courts were still discussing an open range provision late in the twentieth century shows just how hard it was to change the law of the state—even though attempts had been made well over half a century before this case.

VI. Conclusion

It didn't happen overnight, but eventually the open range was completely removed from the lands of Alabama. What makes the movement so interesting is that there wasn't really a single driving force behind it; instead it was a collaboration of forces that eventually forced the range out. The movement started out with a push by the elites after the Civil War to limit the open range and therefore keep the lower classes dependent upon them. Soon, railroads and developing towns were having many problems with stock on the open range. Eventually automobiles, paved roads, and an emphasis on an overall "cleaner" society were what finished off the open range regime.

What is even more interesting about the movement is that the sources of law were almost never on the same page. The Alabama Legislature would always be the first to introduce a new rule limiting the open range. This would soon be followed with action in the courts—a sign that the general public was contesting the new restrictions. Eventually the lagging code would catch up and everybody would all be on the same page, until the next round of restrictions were introduced.

---

[113] Monfee v. Seymore, 392 So.2d 1198 (Ala. 1981).

[114] *Id.*

FLUSH TIMES IN THE CHANCERY: A BRIEF NOTE ON THE HISTORY OF EQUITY AND TRUSTS IN ALABAMA

Paul Rand

I. Definitions and Deep Background

In frontier Alabama, property—and the essentiality of alienability—was the essence of civilization and commerce.[1] The laws governing these forces were inherited from English law, which had originally treated the trust relationship as one created by courts of equity. Trusts arose as an equitable remedy, attaching *in personam* and acting on (activated by) the conscience of the individual. This was due to the nature of the Courts of Equity—they stepped in where the common law failed, in order to restore justice or to give it effect where the local common law courts had lacked discretion.

The historical distinction between law and equity is essential to an understanding of the Alabama courts' approach to cases in which fraud and parol issues were to be considered. In theory, the Chancellor's courts were empowered with the King's residuary jurisdiction to do justice where the regular courts failed.[2] The Chancellor was a minister of the crown, and although they were not established with this jurisdictional separation in mind,[3] the Courts of Chancery came to be responsible for ordering equitable remedies according to divine, natural law. The rules developed at common law were destined to be imperfect, since no general principle could be fairly applied in every situation: no matter how identical the facts might have appeared when described in the abstract, firsthand experience of the circumstances, testimony, or personalities could reveal differences that might tip the balance of justice differently.

The Chancellor was not thought to have a law of his own. Rather, "he was to extend the benefits of the law to those for whom the regular courts hold no hope of success."[4] Milsom points out that "the channels of justice themselves were not part of the immutable order,"[5] but rather were the mechanisms by which human reason worked to do justice. Equity took up the slack not accounted for in this system, which was overall an imperfect

[1] Stephen Davis II and Alfred Brophy, *"The Most Solemn Act of My Life": Family, Property, Will, and Trust in the Antebellum South*, 62 ALABAMA LAW REVIEW 757 (2011).

[2] John Hamilton Baker, AN INTRODUCTION TO ENGLISH LEGAL HISTORY 38 (2002).

[3] *See* S. F. C. Milsom, HISTORICAL FOUNDATIONS OF THE COMMON LAW (1969). Milsom tracks the concurrent history of the common law court and Chancery, and indicates that they overlapped frequently. The distinction was one of hindsight, rather than design.

[4] Baker, AN INTRODUCTION TO ENGLISH LEGAL HISTORY 40-41.

[5] Milsom, HISTORICAL FOUNDATIONS OF THE COMMON LAW 76.

replacement for the wisdom and judgment supposedly embodied in the Church.[6]

While the common law came to be conceptualized as a body of rules applicable to given sets of facts, the Chancellor concerned himself with individual cases—expressing divine justice by determining the result demanded by Conscience. As put in *The Earl of Oxford's Case*, 1615, "The office of the Chancellor is to correct men's consciences for frauds, breaches of trust, wrongs and oppressions of what nature so ever they be, and to soften and mollify the extremity of the law."[7] This meant that equity looked to the conscience of the individual, acting *in personam*, as opposed to the law, which sought to uphold its rules as expressions of principles that recognized no anomalies.

The problem that emerged was that without precedent or fixed rules, any given Chancellor's individual sense of what conscience "demanded" might vary from his predecessor's.[8] Chancery came to be reviled and ridiculed for its inefficiencies,[9] and in the colonies, its association with executive power was a source of Revolutionary-era resentment.[10]

The phrase "trust law" refers to a body of law that has evolved in America and Britain which includes a wide range of legal practices and mechanisms.[11] A trust, or the relationship between trustee and beneficiary, was originally conceived of as an "obligation depending upon personal confidence," and proved so useful and flexible that the term "trust" now implies a wide interest in property.[12]

The trust devolved from its equitable roots to represent a more pedestrian and inert interest, which also made it more flexible and broadly applicable–essentially, the trust became a transferable, proprietary right. Coke treated the trust's beneficiary as a chose (what we would now call a "cause") in action, which meant that it could not be assigned. This limited its effectiveness, and was the result of its origin in equity.[13] Coke defined a "use" or "trust" in land as "a confidence reposed in some other, not issuing out of the land, but as a thing collateral thereto, annexed in privity to the estate . . . for which the *cestui que trust* has no remedy but by subpoena in the Chancery."

---

[6] Baker, AN INTRODUCTION TO ENGLISH LEGAL HISTORY 41. Human reason, that is, as distinguished from "spiritual proof."

[7] *Id.* at 42.

[8] *Id.* at 43. Baker notes Selden's quip: If the measure of equity was the Chancellor's conscience, one might as well make the measure of one foot the Chancellor's foot.

[9] *See* Charles Dickens, BLEAK HOUSE 2 (1853): "This is the Court of Chancery . . . which so exhausts finances, patience, courage, hope, so overthrows the brain and breaks the heart; that there is not an honourable man among its practitioners who would not give—who does not often give—the warning, 'Suffer any wrong that can be done you rather than come here!'"

[10] Lawrence M. Friedman, A HISTORY OF AMERICAN LAW 55 (1985).

[11] George Williams Keeton, THE LAW OF TRUSTS 2 (9th ed. 1968).

[12] *Id.*

[13] *Id.* at 3 (citing 6 Lit. 272b).

Before the formulation of this restrictive view, the beneficiary's interest was regarded as more proprietary, and not a cause of action depending on a private confidence between two humans. For such a confidence to be effective at law, it depended on the awareness of all parties (no bona fide purchaser would be bound, for example, because he was innocent of any special terms), and on the continued existence of the estate itself.[14] Maitland objected that the existence of a trust should not depend on reliance—the unborn, for example, cannot "rely" as such, but may nonetheless benefit from a trust.[15] Ultimately, the emphasis on a trust's obligation binding the conscience of the feoffee or trustee—so important in the law of uses—declined. Thus, the king and chartered corporations became capable of being trustees. As Joseph Story would put it more broadly than Coke: "A trust may be defined to be an equitable right, title, or interest in property, real or personal, distinct from the legal ownership thereof."[16]

A major influence on the developing nature of property law would be the conflict between private and public intent—that is, much of the litigation that concerned wills and trusts arose because there was a conflict between what individuals wanted to do with their property and what the sovereign would allow them to do.[17] For example, the Married Women's Property Acts liberalized women's rights of ownership. Before their passage, "property left to a woman might pass out of the testator's bloodline, might even fall prey to creditors of the woman's husband."[18] But trusts could be used to provide usage and even ownership rights on the testator's husband. These arrangements allowed a couple to avoid some of the societal bias against women's rights, but they also preserved the husband's supremacy, since the protections and rights provided by these trusts would often terminate upon the widow's remarriage.

Hostility to dynastic wealth emerged as another factor in trust law. The common law Rule Against Perpetuities developed near the close of the seventeenth century, and in response many landowners began to use trusts to ensure that no current member could sell his interest in the estate, or that no one (including the trustee) could treat land or improvements as market commodities. This practice was evident in the plantation South, even as wealth came to mean things other than land, such as "factories, banking houses, ships, and stocks and bonds,"[19] not to mention slaves.

---

[14] Keeton, THE LAW OF TRUSTS 3.

[15] *Id.*

[16] *Id.*

[17] I will use these phrases—"private intent" and "public intent"—as shorthand for the tensions described above. These tensions seem to be at the heart of most legislative acts, case opinions, and private actions concerning property, at least in the sense that developments in the law are mostly reactive to developments in circumstances, priorities, and behavior.

[18] Friedman, A HISTORY OF AMERICAN LAW 251.

[19] *Id.* at 252. For the formal beginnings of the Rule Against Perpetuities, see 22 Eng. Rep. 931 (1682).

Trusts, then, can be seen as a mechanism for giving effect to the intentions of the *cestui que trust* in spite of public policy, and as public policy evolves for better or worse, the trust is frequently employed to insulate the owner from its coercion.

II. Property and Trust Trends in Alabama's *Flush Times*

During the 1800s, Alabama was settled, experiencing from the beginning an influx of planters with "cotton fever." The world these planters made was thrown into upheaval by their eventual rebellion against the U.S. government; but while it lasted it was complex and imposing.[20] By the time of the Civil War, there were 115 planters in Greene County (a leading "Black Belt" county) who owned 50 people or more.[21] Most of these planters must have had family, business partners, and other acquaintances in what would become Union territory, and the exploding economy ran headlong into the Civil War. In the midst of this chaos, trust and estate law was (as it remains) an important "legal technology" for the preservation and manipulation of wealth. The importance of the family as a societal unit focused many institutions around it.[22] The laws of intestacy, for example, prioritized family descendants over others as the default path for property, as they do to this day.[23]

As people traveled farther and farther from home to seek their fortunes, personal property and property rights made it possible for them to bestow the benefits of their wealth on family who were not with them on the frontier. Examples of this include the ability to transfer stocks, options, and profits from real property: although it might not make sense to leave a cotton plantation in Alabama to a nephew in Pennsylvania, the rights to a portion of the profits from that plantation *could* be easily assigned to someone far away, and these mechanisms became important enablers in the relatively young "Southwestern" agricultural economy.

Along with marriage and estate law, another important institutional factor in the flow and accumulation of wealth was, of course, slavery. Human property was flexible, in that a slave could be transported (often to the disruption of the slave's own personal or family life), could be put to various uses which would increase the profitability of his owner's business or household, and slaves were often bred so that they would multiply. Slaves would be left to a widow to help her around the home, or they might be left to a son for use in his fields, or the profits of specified slaves and their "increase" might be reserved to pay debts, after which they would be put to

---

[20] William Warren Rogers, *et al.*, ALABAMA: THE HISTORY OF A DEEP SOUTH STATE 54-222 (1994).

[21] Davis and Brophy, *supra* note 1, 62 ALA. L. REV. at 757.

[22] *Id.* For contemporary information on the law of slavery, see Thomas R.R. Cobb, AN INQUIRY INO THE LAW OF NEGRO SLAVERY 235-39 (1858); *see generally* Thomas D. Morris, SOUTHERN SLAVERY AND THE LAW, 1619–1860 61-131 (1996).

[23] Davis and Brophy, *supra* note 1, 62 ALA. L. REV. at 757.

other purposes.[24] Trust law affected slave property in that slaves could be the "subject" of a trust. A slave could also, however, be the beneficiary of a trust, and wills often attempted to provide for the emancipation of a slave—an act prohibited by law before the Civil War in most slave states, and an example of the direct conflict between a testator's intent and public policy.[25]

During the Civil War, the Union passed Confiscation Acts, which used *in rem* court proceedings to confiscate Confederate property. In retaliation, the Confederate legislature passed its Sequestration Acts,[26] which provided for the confiscation of enemy property.[27] The Confederate version went farther than the Union's, giving the rebel government title to property held by alien enemies. This meant that debts owed to Union creditors would now be payable to the Confederate Treasury, and that devises of property to Union citizens would be invalidated, and the property they concerned would transfer to the Confederate treasury. Confederate receivers—part of a sprawling bureaucracy for which the Confederacy is not popularly known—would implement the law. Although exact figures are not available, William Robinson, Jr. describes the Sequestration Acts' effectiveness and points to thousands of cases yielding millions of dollars[28]—an impressive figure, although somewhat short of the tens of millions the acts' proponents had predicted.[29]

Many cases from the Alabama Reports concern the fate of testators' property. Frequently we see the court system having to balance conflicting interests, where a property owner's intentions for his property run up against the cultural or governmental priorities. Some slave owners would wish for their slaves to be freed after the owner's death, for example by placing them in trust to be freed or transported to Liberia.[30] Trusts and

---

[24] *Id.*

[25] Cobb, AN INQUIRY INO THE LAW OF NEGRO SLAVERY 296-311; and Morris, SOUTHERN SLAVERY AND THE LAW 371-423, especially 400-23.

[26] For the Confiscation Acts, see 12 Stat. 319 (1861) and 12 Stat. 589 (1862). For the Sequestration Act, see ACTS AND RESOLUTIONS OF THE THIRD SESSION OF THE PROVISIONAL CONGRESS OF THE CONFEDERATE STATES 57-67 (1861).

[27] Daniel W. Hamilton, THE LIMITS OF SOVEREIGNTY: PROPERTY CONFISCATION IN THE UNION AND CONFEDERACY DURING THE CIVIL WAR 20-40, 82-110 (2007).

[28] William M. Robinson, JUSTICE IN GREY: A HISTORY OF THE JUDICIAL SYSTEM OF THE CONFEDERATE STATES OF AMERICA 626 (1941).

[29] Paul M. Pruitt, Jr., Review of Hamilton, THE LIMITS OF SOVEREIGNTY, at 75 JOURNAL OF SOUTHERN HISTORY 449-52 (2009).

[30] The public policy of the antebellum Slave States usually prohibited this. For example, some trusts allowed for the slave to choose whether or not he wished to be freed, which choice the courts would refuse to recognize as possible, and upon which the devise would be invalidated. To get around these difficulties, testators were forced to express their intent that the slave be treated well. For cases cited by Davis and Brophy as prohibiting the emancipation of slaves by will in Alabama, see *Trotter v. Blocker*, 6 Porter 269 (Ala. 1838); *Alston v. Coleman*, 7 Ala. 795 (1845); *Harrison v. Harrison*, 9 Ala. 470 (1846); *Carroll v. Brumby*, 13 Ala. 102 (1848); *Welch's Heirs v. Welch's Adm'r*, 14 Ala. 76 (1848); *Pool v. Harrison*, 18 Ala. 514 (1850); *Roberson's Heirs v. Roberson's Ex'rs*, 21 Ala. 273 (1852); *Evans v. Kittrell*, 33 Ala. 449 (1859).

decedents' estates have always offered opportunity to avoid debts, and this was the subject of shifting judicial and legislative rules throughout the nineteenth century.

III. *Kennedy's Heirs v. Kennedy's Heirs*: Imported Principles

The 1841 case of *Kennedy's Heirs and Executors v. Kennedy's Heirs*[31] introduced into Alabama's judicial precedence many of the property, equity, and trust problems that the state would face in its boom times before the Civil War.[32] The Court had an uncommonly rich record to draw upon; the trial lasted ten days and unfolded the story of two brothers, William and Joshua Kennedy, pioneering the land around Mobile, before and after it ceased (1813) to be a Spanish colony.

Joseph S. Kennedy, son of William E. Kennedy (together with other children of William E. Kennedy), brought suit in Chancery in 1839.[33] Their claim concerned property that was deeded from William to his brother Joshua in 1824. According to William's heirs, the conveyance to Joshua was made so that William, who had lost his wife in 1821 and become "intemperate," could preserve some of his wealth in order to pass it on.

More precisely, William was a drunkard and had been making irresponsible transfers of land: easily influenced, he would sell parcels for next to nothing, or perhaps give them away. William and Joshua had shared many business dealings; Joshua "acted as [William]'s business agent, consulted and advised him as to the management and disposition of his property."[34] Accordingly, and after repeated solicitations, William transferred much of his property in and around Mobile to Joseph via deed on December 13, 1824.

Cases cited by Davis and Brophy as permitting limited rights granted to slaves via trust, such as the right to decide whether to remain enslaved or to be taken to another state for emancipation: *Atwood's Heirs v. Beck*, 21 Ala. 590 (1852); *Abercrombie v. Abercrombie*, 27 Ala. 489 (1855); *Hooper v. Hooper*, 32 Ala. 669 (1858).

The opinion in *Trotter v. Blocker* provides some wonderful insight into the problem posed and the early history of solutions considered. In 1821, the law imposed a condition that the slave be removed from the State. After 1822, the law required that the owner give a bond to the State to cover the costs of the emancipated slave becoming a "public charge." *See* Clement Clay, A DIGEST OF THE LAWS OF THE STATE OF ALABAMA 545 (secs. 37-40) (Tuscaloosa, 1843). An act passed in 1834 provided for the emancipation of slaves by upon petition of their owner, for "long, faithful and meritorious services performed, or for other good and sufficient cause shown." *Trotter v. Blocker*, 6 Porter 269 (Ala. 1838), acknowledged that statute, but held it to be consistent with the proposition that slaves in servitude could not be the beneficiaries of a property bequest–i.e., that of their own freedom–regardless of their owner's intent or reasons.

[31] 2 Ala. 571 (1841).

[32] For the hard times that had preceded this case (in the aftermath of the Panic of 1837), see Rogers, *et al*, ALABAMA: THE HISTORY OF A DEEP SOUTH STATE 138-45; for the boom times of the 1850s, see *id.* at 172-81.

[33] Kennedy's Heirs and Executors v. Kennedy's Heirs, 2 Ala. 571, 574 (1841).

[34] *Id.*

William's children's complaint asserted that the deed was intended to create a trust for the benefit of William's children. They claimed that no part of the stated consideration (of more than ten thousand dollars) was ever paid, and that their uncle Joshua himself repeatedly admitted and referred to the deed's trust purpose and his role as a trustee. They, the plaintiffs at trial, alleged that Joshua's business ventures had been suffering in the few years prior to 1824 and that by no "manner or means" could he have paid the stated consideration.[35]

Joshua's heirs, for their part, asserted a number of claims that were ultimately distilled by Chief Justice Henry W. Collier into two arguments. First was an assertion under the statute of frauds. There could be no action on an agreement concerning land unless the agreement was in writing,[36] they argued, and therefore Joshua's alleged undertaking to maintain the properties conveyed by the 1824 deed for the benefit of William's heirs was void. The second point was that because the deed expressed a "specified monied consideration, and nothing else," no proof of any other inducement for the conveyance was permissible.[37]

These arguments, in turn, would bring in much discussion of the nature of trusts, their government under the law of equity, and the possibility of creating and enforcing a secret trust into Alabama's jurisprudence for the first time. The facts of the case were considered in detail by the Court in fashioning its decision. It is notable that in this case, real property was the only asset at issue. In later cases under the precedents set in *Kennedy v. Kennedy*, the Court would consider not just other types of assets, but also broader policy concerns as the state and national legal systems grew more complex.

William died in 1825, and his children claimed that although William left only $100.18 in cash, his brother Joshua (as executor) obtained control over a great deal of real estate, beyond that conveyed to him by the 1824 deed.[38] They said that he sold most of the land obtained by that deed, for which he was paid handsomely, and that what land he held onto was earning rent. Joshua died in 1838, and left as his only heirs his widow and their children—in no way did he provide for William's children. The plaintiffs asked for the deed to be set aside, for Joshua's executors to be restrained from selling any of the property concerned, and that his heirs and any purchasers of the land in question be compelled to convey title to William's children.[39]

Most importantly from an equitable standpoint, Joshua's executors asserted that there was no fraudulent inducement, and that the 1824 deed was

---

35 *Id.* at 575.

36 *Id.* at 599.

37 *Id.* at 600.

38 *Id.* at 576.

39 *Id.*

made on the terms described above—for adequate consideration paid at the time of the conveyance, which was absolute and without conditions. They supported their defense by attempting to prove that the deed had no terms other than the consideration expressed on its face. They retorted that Joshua had taken William in, along with his infant children, and paid many of their expenses from his own estate—and that if he had kept an account (which he did not), that it would be William who owed Joshua, not the other way around.

The defendants claimed that the $10,800 consideration recited in the deed was paid "in money, or its equivalent." They asserted that land in Mobile was not worth much in 1824, and that this figure was a full consideration, especially considering that the title was imperfect and its "confirmation was exceedingly uncertain." This latter point had some substance to it: Joshua's heirs pointed out that the land was obtained by the Kennedy brothers during Spanish reign over that region, and that the subsequent confirmation of title was expensive, and they claimed that this process succeeded "primarily due to Joshua's efforts."[40]

The facts, however, were complicated, and the Court sifted a great deal of testimony in order to evaluate the circumstantial claims being offered by the parties. One allegation made by Joshua's heirs was that much of the land in question was gotten by Joshua and was rightfully his, and that the conveyance had been made in William's name simply because the property was acquired during the time of Spanish reign in that region, and William, having married a Spanish subject, was the only brother eligible to hold title to Spanish land.[41]

The lots at issue were located between "the Iberville and Perdido," and were mostly located within two large tracts that were, at the time William acquired them, "subject to the dominion of the King of Spain."[42] Between 1815 and 1820, William granted many lots from within these tracts to Joshua, either for money or for a recited "valuable consideration."[43] For example, in November 1818, William granted Joshua 80 arpents (roughly 80 acres), the recited consideration for which was $500 paid by Joshua at the time of purchase. Between 1817 and 1825, William made 100 deeds to various people for widely differing considerations. There were also some transfers from these tracts made by the brothers jointly, and some made just by Joshua.

---

[40] *Id.* at 578.

[41] Mobile was ceded to the British by the Treaty of Paris in 1763, as a part of French Louisiana east of the Mississippi River, but was captured by the Spanish in 1780. During the War of 1812, Mobile was seized by the United States. A "tide of immigration" drastically changed the makeup and character of Mobile after that war. The City Charter was granted by the Mississippi territorial legislature in January, 1814, and by the Alabama state legislature in December, 1819. ENCYCLOPEDIA BRITANNICA (11th ed. 1911), 15: 635-36. *See also* Harriet E. Amos, COTTON CITY: URBAN DEVELOPMENT IN ANTEBELLUM MOBILE 1-17 (1986).

[42] Kennedy's Heirs and Executors v. Kennedy's Heirs, 2 Ala. 571, 575 (1841).

[43] *Id.* at 579.

The convolution of these deals highlights not just the collaborative nature of the brothers' relationship on either side of the Mobile Bay, but also the speculative and pioneering nature of landholding in the region at the time. Mobile had been settled for some time, but its surrounding areas had been subject to three sovereign rulers in as many decades.[44] Once these lands came under the flag of the United States the titles would stabilize, but the maneuvers that had served to simplify transactions in the brothers' younger years would complicate the descent of their property later on—for example, in the litigation at hand.

Indeed, the Court rejected the "agency" argument, finding that Joshua's sophistication in the land business would have led him to put the lands in his own name promptly upon the Mississippi territory's assumption of Mobile in 1813—if, that is, the lands were really his.[45] Instead, Joshua would later pay William for bits and pieces of the tracts—a fact the Court found to speak in favor of William's outright ownership of the property he acquired from the Spanish.[46]

Another circumstance put forth by the defendants as evidence of the deed's purity was that shortly after William and Joshua executed the 1824 deed, Joshua made a trip to Cuba.[47] They claimed that he was in poor health at the time, and that the trip was made in hopes that the climate in Cuba would improve his breathing, and that given Joshua's precarious situation, no one would have made him trustee of anything. To the contrary, some witnesses testified that this trip was actually for the purpose of selling timber: apparently, Joshua brought with him 80,000 feet of lumber.[48] Other witnesses asserted that Joshua's trip was to inspect Spanish records regarding titles to lands he either owned or was interested in buying.[49] In any case, the Court agreed that Joshua's health was in decline at the time of his trip to Havana; but since he went with such a load of lumber and without anyone to assist him, the Court concluded that his health cannot have been so bad as to foreclose the possibility that William would subsequently trust Joshua to dispose of his affairs.

---

44 Amos, COTTON CITY 1-17; Rogers, *et al.*, ALABAMA: THE HISTORY OF A DEEP SOUTH STATE 26-37.

45 *See* 2 Ala. at 615.

46 *Id.* There were other grounds for rejecting this assertion. A map of the brothers' holdings was produced at trial, on which the brothers had initialed their respective holdings. The map was evidence of a partition they had done in 1818 or 1819, and the Court found this to speak against the notion that Joshua owned everything outright.

47 *Id.* at 584.

48 *Id.* (testimony of William Kitchens). This trade has not gone out of style. According to an article in *The Economist* quoting Ron Sparks, then-Commissioner of the Alabama Department of Agriculture, Alabama is responsible for one half of the chickens exported from America to Cuba, and almost all of its utility poles. *See* "Chickens for Cuba," *The Economist,* January 25, 2007 (http://www.economist.com/node/8599033, last accessed May 27, 2014).

49 2 Ala. at 585.

Overall, the facts reported in the opinion serve to illustrate not just the legal problems facing pioneers in the antebellum South; they also allow a look at what facts the Court found salient in establishing its own precedence on the establishment of trusts and the disposition of property according to an owner's intent. The Court's opinion by Chief Justice Collier cites many English cases for various rules surrounding the law of trusts and estates, particularly those relating to equity's jurisdiction over cases involving fraud, secret trusts, and parol proof. For example, Collier noted that "neither the common law . . . nor the statutes of frauds and perjuries, inhibit the admission of parol evidence to vary, or totally defeat, a written contract tainted with fraud."[50] And he pointed to the case of *Boyce's Executor v. Gundy*[51] to show that although reducing a contract to writing would provide an "argument against fraud," an agreement entered into on the basis of "false suggestions" was not *varied* by parol evidence proving a fraud, but rather that the agreement itself was "vitiated by fraud, which vitiates every thing."[52] So the Court began by following the equitable tradition of asserting its authority not over the agreement (or will) itself, but rather as an instrument of justice which would intervene to protect against or remedy fraud.

In cases where the statute was in danger of being permitted to serve as a cover for fraud (i.e., taking advantage of the parties' failure to reduce an agreement to writing by then pleading the statute of frauds to prevent its enforcement), the Court would intervene. And although, as Collier paraphrased an English source, "within the intention [of the parties], it cannot be said a trust is declared under these circumstances, it is clear a trust would be created upon the principle, on which this Court acts as to fraud."[53]

As far as the statute of frauds itself was concerned, Collier (after elaborate discussion of case law) cited to Aikin's Digest. The latter shows the statute to have been enacted by the territorial legislature in 1803. It was amended in 1823 to exclude bona fide conveyances, and again in 1828 to void deeds of trust as against creditors who had no notice, unless such a deed was recorded with the county clerk within thirty days of its creation.[54]

---

[50] *Id.* at 589 (citing 2 Story's Eq. 55).

[51] *Id.* (citing 3 Peters' Rep. 219).

[52] *Id.* at 590.

[53] *See id.* at 590-91, citing the wonderfully named Chancery case *Muckleston v. Brown*, 6 Ves. [jun.] Rep. 51-69, at 69 (1801), as well as multiple English cases and treatises.

[54] *See* 2 Ala. 588-99, especially 598-99 citing J. G. Aikin, DIGEST OF THE LAWS OF THE STATE OF ALABAMA 206-07 (1833). Aikin's cameo in the *Kennedy* opinion went beyond citation to his Digest. Another Kennedy brother, Maxfield, had turned up at trial and announced that William had been tried for the murder of a Colonel Maxwell in South Carolina in 1797. Maxfield claimed to have paid $10,000 for his brother's defense, and that Joshua had assumed payment but only paid back $1,600 of the debt: Maxfield had appeared to hold Joshua's estate liable. Waddy Thompson, a respected lawyer "known to the Court" and in South Carolina at the time, testified that William's defense resulted in acquittal and could not have cost more than $500. Furthermore, Thompson said, Maxfield Kennedy "could not have paid the one hundredth part of ten thousand dollars, either in money or in credit." John G. Aikin supported Thompson's assertion, testifying that "he knew Maxfield Kennedy in Tuscaloosa County—he

Collier cited equity's expansive role in the enforcement of trusts that would not be recognized at common law. In order to be remediable at common law, a fraud would have to relate to the execution of an instrument, in that the written agreement would have to have been misread by the promisor, or the entire arrangement would have to have been fraudulently obtained. Equity, on the other hand, could "interfere and grant redress" in cases of injury or loss "by mistake, accident and frauds, as well as undue advantages and impositions, betrayals of confidence and unconscionable bargains."[55] This would cover cases where, for example, the consideration was inadequate or otherwise the result of mistake, or the written agreement was obtained on the basis of a further promise—for example, where a will had been written to devise property to A on the basis of A's oral promise that he would provide for B and C.[56] In equitable proceedings, pleadings could describe these agreements as such without having to go further in order for parol proof to be admissible.[57]

Ultimately, the Court found it "incredible" that Joshua would have paid the cited consideration in the deed, and found instead that the consideration for the 1824 conveyance was Joshua's promise to keep the property for the benefit of William's heirs. The Court found a fraud established either in obtaining the deed, or in "perverting it to a purpose in opposition to the agreement between the grantor and grantee, and that it should consequently be set aside."[58] The doctrine of trusts, "or rather the manner in which they shall be declared," required no examination, since the resolution of the dispute was to find a trust *implied* rather than *entered into*—the Court imposed an equitable remedy in response to a constructive fraud, as opposed to a legal remedy for an actual fraud. The Court affirmed the decision of the Court of Chancery, and took pains to note Joshua's many good qualities ("he was industrious, temperate, energetic, persevering and affectionate to his relatives") in spite of his "temptations."[59]

IV. *R. Bishop's Heirs v. The Administrator and Heirs of S. Bishop*

Bishop v. Bishop[60] provides an illustration of the purposes a trust could serve, and the circumstances of the people who used them, as much as the law that had developed around their use. Reuben and Stephen Bishop were

---

was very poor." And, Aikin said, he had been told by Joshua of the $1,600 advance to Maxfield, but that the money was given as a gratuity, and decidedly not as payment on any debt. According to the opinion, some 60 or 70 witnesses ultimately testified in the *Kennedy* case. *See* 2 Ala. at 584 and 620.

55 2 Ala. at 592.

56 *Id.*

57 *Id.* at 597.

58 *Id.* at 622.

59 *Id.* at 623.

60 13 Ala. 475 (1848).

brothers. According to the facts of the case, Reuben lived in Greene County, Georgia.[61] He owned property, including slaves, but was in debt. He was also suspicious of his wife and her father, thinking that they might try to get control of his assets after he died. To protect some slave bequests he wanted to make to his children, he wished to send seven of his slaves to his brother Stephen, who lived in Alabama. Reuben deeded the slaves to a nephew, James Fannin, to whom Stephen had given power of attorney for the purchase. The deed recited $6,700 consideration, but Reuben's children would later claim that no money actually changed hands.

After Fannin brought the slaves to Alabama, Stephen sold two of them in order to pay his own debts.[62] After his death, Stephen's children, who were the defendants in the case, claimed that Reuben had been in crisis with creditors and sold the slaves to pay the debts: Stephen, they asserted, had paid $500 in cash and assumed some of Reuben's debts.

The Court was adamant about the admissibility of parol evidence to show the nature of a promise relating to a conveyance. That is, even though "a deed, or bill of sale be absolute on its face, parol proof may be received to show that it was intended as a mortgage, or that it was executed and delivered upon certain trusts, not reduced to writing, but existing in parol, and which the grantee, or donee promised to perform."[63]

For precedent the Court pointed to *Sledge v. Clopton*.[64] In that case, an absolute deed for slaves was intended first as security for a debt owed by their seller. Once the debt was paid they were to be given in trust so that the profits from their labor could provide for the seller's wife. The complexity of such arrangements goes beyond the contents of a land deed, and in order for a churning economy to be able to make use of such possibilities, the law would have to stay more flexible than the typical rules of conveyances would permit. Reuben Bishop's scheme was exactly the kind of promise that would allow the Court to look into the circumstances surrounding a sale that appeared untouchable by virtue of a properly executed sale. For analogy, the Court affirmed the principle that if A makes a promise to B in order to get B to change the terms of his will or some other conveyance, A's promise will be enforced by the Court.[65]

---

[61] In the present day, Interstate 20 goes through Greene County, which is east of Atlanta and south of Athens.

[62] Those two are identified as Peter and Dinah. No other details are given about them, and the human drama of being moved around, separated and reunited with family members is intimated but never made explicit in this or other court opinions. But it seems likely that the two may have been more valuable as a couple, since with title to a slave often came title to that slave's offspring.

[63] Bishop v. Bishop, 13 Ala. 475, 483 (1848).

[64] 6 Ala. 589 (1844).

[65] *Id.* at 600-01 (citing *Kennedy's Heirs v. Kennedy's Heirs, supra* note 31).

V. *Barrell v. Hanrick*: A New Wrinkle in the Use of Parol Trusts

During the Civil War, the Sequestration Acts provided yet another potential conflict between a testator with family and acquaintances who were citizens of the Union and the Confederacy's confiscation of any property left to such alien enemies. The most prominent Alabama case on point, *Barrell v. Hanrick*,[66] was decided in 1868. There were two brothers: George, who lived in New Jersey, and Charles, who had settled in Alabama. Charles wanted to create a will that would leave his property to his brother George, but as a citizen of the Union, George was considered an alien enemy, and any property devised to him would be unreachable—since to claim it would invite the scrutiny of Confederate receivers, who would confiscate it. Edward Hanrick was Charles Barrell's lawyer, and appears to have come up with a plan whereby Charles would deed all the property intended for George to Hanrick, who would hold onto it until the war was over, at which point he would convey it safely and legally to George.[67] Charles and his lawyer executed a deed that was absolute on its face, and Hanrick, somewhat improbably, died intestate shortly thereafter. Hanrick's son, also named Edward Hanrick, became the administrator of Barrell's estate, and failed to transfer the property to George Barrell, who in turn sued.

Barrell's lawyers pointed to the Alabama Statute of Frauds, enacted in the Code under §1320, which states that "no trust concerning lands, except such as results by implication or construction of law, or which may be transferred or extinguished by operation of law, can be created, unless by instrument in writing, signed by the party creating or declaring the same, or his agent or attorney authorized thereto in writing."[68] This tension between the requirements of the Statute of Frauds to put agreements in writing in order to avoid fraud, and the possibility that there may truthfully be more to

---

66 42 Ala. 60 (1868).

67 The suggestion that this scheme was Hanrick's idea comes from the Court at page 71, where Justice Thomas J. Judge infers as much "from their long acquaintance, and the strong friendship that existed between them, the character and business capacity of each, and the great confidence of the testator in Hanrick, and the peculiar control and influence of the latter over the former as to all business transactions." What to make of the darkness appearing toward the end of that description? Maybe the Court was not interested in any possibility of sinister intentions on Hanrick's part, since as a suggestion it is oblique at best, or maybe it should be considered a factor in the Court's willingness to endorse Barrell's intentions.

68 The quotation is from the 1852 Code of Alabama, §1320. The exception for trusts resulting by implication or construction of law remains pivotal in disputes of this kind: when the Court wants to enforce what might otherwise be disallowed as a parol trust concerning lands, it will have to characterize the trust as one arising by "implication or construction of law." The logical effect of this is that the trust—here, that Hanrick will get the property to Barrell's brother—is not considered as an agreement between the parties, but instead as an equitable remedy generated by the Court to prevent fraud. This is the sort of theoretical distinction that invites ridicule, but nevertheless allows the Court to avoid the destruction of a perfectly good rule (one that seeks to avoid fraud by ignoring anything that is not in writing) while leaving space for exceptions.

the agreement than that which was put in writing, is the subject of much tortured reasoning, some of which will be discussed below.

In *Barrell v. Hanrick*, Barrell's lawyers locked on to the circumstances under which one *induces* or *discourages* a conveyance by making a promise that the promisor has no intention of keeping. Citing a contemporary treatise, they pointed out that the Court should not "permit the Statute to become an engine of fraud."[69] This reasoning is directly descended from the structure of the Courts of Equity and the precedent set in cases such as *Kennedy v. Kennedy*. An oft-cited example of such a circumstance is one in which the youngest son convinced his father to leave the family estate to him, under the promise that he, the youngest, would give £10,000 to the eldest. That promise would be enforced, notwithstanding the Statute.[70]

Hanrick's lawyers argued that the exceptions did not apply in this case, since Charles Barrell and Hanrick, Sr. had both been perfectly clear as to their intent—which was to create an illegal parol trust. Hanrick had not induced Barrell to change his plans in bad faith; rather they had both done exactly what the Statute disallows, and in the absence of a fraudulent inducement, they argued, the exception did not apply.

Writing for the Court, Justice Thomas J. Judge disagreed, pointing to Alabama precedents in which the rule was developed that even though a deed may have been executed in good faith, if the deed were later put to fraudulent use ("or to one wholly different from the one intended by both parties at the time of its execution"[71]) a constructive trust could be created by the court to correct the injustice. The Court declared that "there [was] no reason to believe that Hanrick practiced any fraud or deceit in procuring the bequest to him in the will of Charles Barrell." But Hanrick, Sr. died before complying with the agreement, and the failure of his son, "for whatever cause, is a constructive fraud, against which relief should be decreed."[72]

The Court then dealt with the defendants' argument that the Barrells were coming into court with unclean hands—an argument they based on the plaintiffs' reliance on a trust that was made for the express purpose of avoiding the sequestration acts.[73] In their pleadings, the Hanrick lawyers encouraged the Supreme Court to consider how the situation would be handled if the War had been won:

> Suppose the Confederate States had achieved their independence, and this cause was now pending with all the facts and circumstances

---

[69] LEWIN ON TRUSTS 38 (cited in *Barrell*, 42 Ala. at 64).

[70] *See* Kennedy's Heirs v. Kennedy's Heirs, 2 Ala. 571, 594 (1841), discussed *supra* note 31 (cited by Hanrick's counsel as a case collating the precedents on the rule of exceptions for implied or constructive trusts).

[71] 42 Ala. at 73.

[72] *Id.*

[73] The "clean hands" doctrine is "a rule of equity that a plaintiff must . . . be free from reproach in his conduct." *See* BLACK'S LAW DICTIONARY 337 (3d ed. 1933).

> connected with it, what would the chancellor be compelled to say? Plainly, he would declare, that the testator not only has attempted to evade the statute against parol trust upon the statute book, . . . but has attempted to defraud the government. . . . Suppose the complainant to have filed his bill saying, "I was and am an alien. When this will was made I was an alien enemy, and any property I had in Alabama was subject-matter for confiscation. My brother made his will so as to avoid that law, in fraud of it, vesting the property in a friend of mine absolutely, but with the *secret* understanding that he would turn it over to me, and thus enable me successfully to cheat your law of confiscation." What would the court have said to such a bill? The answer would clearly have been: "Who comes into this court, must come with clean hands." . . . Is the law of legal morality relaxed? Are the precincts of the court less sacred? Are its maxims less pure? In God's name, if we have lost our liberty, let us preserve our morality.[74]

The Court looked to a decision in North Carolina, *Blossom v. Van Amringe*,[75] in which the Supreme Court of that state had ruled that it was a coordinate branch of a rightful state government forming a part of the United States, and that it could not entertain an objection under the "clean hands" doctrine, where the objection was based on violation of a Confederate law which had not been adopted by the Union after the Civil War.[76] Justice Judge pointed to decisions upholding the validity of "executory contracts based on the treasury notes of the late Confederate states, *after they had become the currency of the* country," and held that "it was unnecessary to elaborate this proposition."[77]

It is notable that in an 1874 decision, *Morriss & Blair v. Poillon,*[78] the Court expressed no concern whatsoever for the effect of the Sequestration Acts. One New York-based partnership had turned over a promissory note to another for the payment of a debt. The note was made by a citizen of Alabama, and during the War it had fallen into the hands of sequestration agents. Although the defendant tried to invalidate the transfer on the grounds that it was technically the property of the Confederate government when the transfer was made, the Court declared the acts of the sequestration agents in taking the note to be "wholly void." "In law," the Court hold, "they were nothing." This remarkable statement is a reflection of how much

---

[74] 42 Ala. at 69-70.

[75] 62 N.C. 133 (1867).

[76] The language of the North Carolina Supreme Court in that case is striking. In dismissing the notion that his evasion of Confederate law rendered a plaintiff incompetent to seek the aid of the Court, they commented that: "In our view, the complainant did but 'fight fire with fire;' that is, he resorted to artifice and deceit, *ex necessitate*, to avoid loss by reason of the acts of a public enemy of the nation. He is justified, or rather is not to be blamed, on the ground that artifice, deceit and stratagem may, during war, be resorted to deceive the enemy." 62 N.C. at 138-39.

[77] 42 Ala. at 73-74 (italics in original).

[78] 50 Ala. 403 (1874).

the Confederacy had fallen into oblivion, notwithstanding efforts to describe its legal mechanisms as the rules of either a partially successful insurrection, or a belligerent government, or both.[79]

VI. *Patton*'s New Rule, and the Repudiation of *Barrell*

Judging from *Barrell* and other post-War cases, by 1868 the Alabama Supreme Court was unhindered by the lingering legalities of the Confederacy. George Barrell was awarded title to his brother's property, and his court costs were reimbursed. But what would happen to the rules on parol trusts? The Court was able to get around the inconvenience of the Sequestration Acts and their invalidation by Union victory, and at the same time avoided making an embarrassing exception to well-established rules. But there was still a rapidly developing national economy, and the American and Alabamian legal systems' approaches to the Statute of Frauds, and parol problems in property agreements, were far from settled. At one time the Court could fashion solutions on a case-by-case basis, as demonstrated by the *Bishop* court's casual application of an exception to the rule against parol trusts. The *Barrell* ruling, that two parties could enter willingly into a conveyance of land and simultaneously agree that a parol trust should be formed, was distinct from most exceptions to the rule against parol trusts. The problem that would emerge is that most authorities would seek to narrow the "fraud" exception under the rule against parol trusts. While the Barrell/Hanrick trust was entered into willingly by both parties—they knew full well what they were doing, and did it to avoid the Sequestration Acts—this would later be understood as an unfortunate exception. It would be better, the Court would later hold, to construe the Statute narrowly, so that only frauds which arose at the *formation* of the agreement (and not by some later breach of the promise) would permit the Court, in equity, to imply a trust that could then be enforced.

In his 1878 decision in *Patton v. Beecher*,[80] Chief Justice Robert Coman Brickell would establish a new doctrine, contrary to the rule announced in *Barrel v. Hanrick*. The plaintiff was Mrs. Elizabeth Patton, who had inherited a lot in Montgomery in 1869. Her husband, J. O. Patton, "had failed in business" and became concerned that the lot might be vulnerable to his creditors.[81] To protect it, Mrs. Patton deeded that property to Edwin Beecher, "an intimate friend and member of the family," who was living with the Pattons at the time. The deed recited consideration of $4,000, and the parties agreed that he would hold it in trust for her, and would not record the deed, but would "reconvey to oratrix whenever requested." Beecher,

---

[79] *See generally* JUSTICE IN GREY, *supra* note 28, for a discussion of the treatment of the Confederate legal structure by post-war courts. It is also possible, of course, that Morriss & Blair's success where Hanrick failed says more about the relative power of corporate interests over individuals than it does about the Confederacy's legacy in court.

[80] 62 Ala. 579 (1878).

[81] *Id.* at 580.

perhaps predictably, likewise failed in business, without having reconveyed the property to Mrs. Patton. He made an assignment of the deed to one W. L. Chambers, who was named by the Pattons as a co-defendant.[82]

As Chief Justice Brickell saw it, the Statute of Frauds (and analogous Alabama statute law) was clear on its requirement that parol trusts be reduced to writing; the only question at hand was what circumstances would bring an agreement into the Statute's exception, under which an implied trust would be created by the Court. Brickell cited a common illustration where A purchases land with B's money, taking the title for himself; under these circumstances the law would imply a trust of the title for B. But such trusts, Brickell noted, arise from facts proved, and not from the agreement of the parties.[83]

Brickell focused in on the contours of the exception: "The fraud which will withdraw a case from the operation of the statute is not simply that fraud which may be imputed to every deliberate breach of a contract or promise."[84] Rather, there must have been an original "intention to circumvent . . . by the confidence reposed."[85] Brickell characterized *Barrell* as establishing that "though no fraud, no imposition, no violation of confidence was practiced or intended at the execution of the deed, its conversion to other uses than such as were expressed by the parol agreement, is a fraud against which courts of equity will relieve."[86] Brickell cited *Barrell v. Hanrick*, as well as *Bishop v. Bishop* and *Kennedy v. Kennedy*. The latter two cases are distinguished from *Barrell*, as described above, in that the agreements were ruled to have arisen from the suggestion of the donee, and any fraud was therefore perpetrated at the time of the agreement.[87] Brickell distinguished *Barrell* on the grounds that it was Hanrick, Jr. who failed to meet the terms of the agreements, and held that the rule against creation of a parol trust could not be avoided on such a violation.

VII. The Fate of the *Barrell* and *Patton* Decisions in Later Parol Trust Cases

The Brocks lived in Anniston. Mr. Brock sold their land to Mrs. Brock, after they separated on account of his "intemperate habits, and his unkind

---

[82] *Id.*

[83] 62 Ala. 585-87.

[84] *Id.* at 590.

[85] *Id.* (quoting from BROWN STAT. FRAUDS §94).

[86] *Id.* (citing *Barrell v. Hanrick*, 42 Ala. 60; *Bishop v. Bishop*, 13 Ala. 475; and *Kennedy v. Kennedy*, 2 Ala. 571).

[87] In all cases the parties were brothers; the *Bishop* agreement was allegedly made out of Reuben's mistrust for his wife and her father; the *Kennedy* agreement was entered into because of the granting brother's "intemperance." Because the *Barrell* grant was intended to get the property to Barrell's brother, one cannot ignore the popularity of familial transfers as a feature of wealth preservation.

treatment of her."[88] The fee simple deed was free on its face from any words of condition or of trust. The land, according to the opinion, was worth about $2,000 when the deed was made, but sold seven years later for $56,000—a fact which may explain the lawsuit. Mr. Brock tried to establish an express trust on the basis of letters exchanged between him and his estranged wife after the transfer had been completed; failing that, he sought to have a trust implied against her as a trustee *ex maleficio*, under the Statute's exception. His version of the sale was that it was made on the condition that if he returned home "a sober man, free from his habits of dissipation, his said wife would return to him, and live with him as his wife, and the deed in such event was to become null and void."[89] Mrs. Brock, for her part, denied having made any such promises in the first place.

The opinion, written by Justice Henderson Somerville, points approvingly to *Patton v. Beecher*, quoted Brickell's language for the rule that "it is *fraud then*, and not *subsequent fraud*, if any exist, which justifies a court of equity in intervening for the relief of the party injured by it."[90] To put a fine point on the topic, Somerville made his own contribution:

> The main point which we wish to emphasize is that the mere breach of an oral agreement, standing alone, though often a moral wrong, is not sufficient to establish that fraud in procuring the title which is requisite to render the grantee or devisee a trustee *ex maleficio*; although the fact of such breach may, of course, be looked into, in connection with the other circumstances of the case, as sometimes constituting one of several links in a chain of facts going to prove fraud.[91]

The idea of the conveyance under these circumstances started with Mr. Brock, unsolicited by his wife ("it matters not whether in a motive to rescue the property, then worth only about two thousand dollars, from the hazard of financial wreck nearly always incident to drunken habits. . .").[92] It was not the first time Mr. Brock had left home under disreputable circumstances: the Court found that on more than one prior occasion, Mrs. Brock had stayed with her father during one of her husband's drunken rages.[93] The Court allowed that the promises were made, but found no fraud on the part of Mrs. Brock, in whose favor it ruled.

The *Barrell* rule emerged at a time when the Statute of Frauds had only been codified as such in Alabama for fifteen years. One theme that emerges from the lines of cases dealing with its implications is that the jurisprudence

---

[88] Brock v. Brock, 90 Ala. 86, 90 (1890).

[89] *Id.* at 89.

[90] Brock v. Brock, 90 Ala. 86, 91 (1890) (quoting *Patton v. Beecher*, 62 Ala. 579) (italics in original).

[91] 90 Ala. at 93.

[92] *Id.* at 95.

[93] *Id.*

around the Statute would harden into a centralized set of interpretations. At the time of the *Bishop* decision in 1848, four years before the 1852 Code was adopted, the legal authorities were far-flung. There were some local precedents, but the Court also looked to other States' decisions and, of course, to English common law. But even the English heritage was complicated: there were traditions of only looking to English common law as it existed *prior* to the emigration of the colonists; recent developments, therefore, would sometimes be excluded or ignored.[94]

Another observable trend through these cases is the order of operations for judicial reasoning. If the underlying facts were such that the Court was suspicious of the promisor, or felt that the promisee would suffer unjustly unless the parol trust were characterized as such and enforced in spite of its failure to meet the requirements of the Statute, it could simply find as it needed in order to apply the exception to the rule.

An intriguing if frustrating aspect of such cases—beyond the larger developments of frontier, and later wartime, jurisprudence—are the glimpses that judicial records give us into the lives of the parties to these suits. Why did the Brock property in Montgomery appreciate from $2,000 to $56,000 in just seven years? What happened to the slaves, Peter and Dinah, and their "increase" after the Court ruled that they should be reunited with the other five and returned to Reuben Bishop? Such questions have nothing to do with doctrine; but they are firmly within the purview of legal history. Indeed the court reports cited above—like the whole body of Alabama case law—can serve as points of departure for the legal historian.

---

[94] For a discussion of the history of the "reception" of English common law in post-Revolutionary America, see Friedman, A HISTORY OF AMERICAN LAW 109-15.

"Rotunda and the Quad at The University of Alabama in 1859"

A view of the Quad, the Rotunda, designed by
William Nichols [1780–1853], and the campus in 1859.

Courtesy University Libraries Division of Special Collections, The University of Alabama, used by permission

THE MILITARIZATION OF THE UNIVERSITY OF ALABAMA

Helen Eckinger

On June 4, 1858, the University of Alabama experienced an unwelcome first: its first student-on-student homicide.[1] According to an account of the incident released by the university to *The Independent Monitor*, a Tuscaloosa newspaper, the victim, Edward Nabors, was one of several students eating breakfast at a Tuscaloosa boarding house that morning.[2] During the meal, the residents of the boarding house taunted a fellow boarder, a student and Mississippi native named David Herring, about Mississippi's recent debt default, as they had done during the previous days. Afterward, a third resident, Walter Gilkey, confronted Herring outside the house and struck him on the head with a stick.[3] Herring pulled a pistol from his pocket, and seeing this, Nabors attempted to intervene, striking Herrring at least twice.[4] Herring shot Nabors dead.[5] He was promptly arrested, and the next day was tried for murder before two justices of the peace.[6] While student sentiment was strongly in Nabors' favor,[7] the witnesses overwhelmingly agreed that Herring was not the aggressor and was acting only to protect himself.[8] Moreover, two of his professors, Andre DeLoffre,[9] who taught modern languages, and Dr. J. W. Mallett, who taught chemistry, testified to his "mild, orderly and gentlemanly" character.[10] The justices of the peace

---

[1] James B. Sellers, HISTORY OF THE UNIVERSITY OF ALABAMA, VOLUME 1: 1818–1902 253 (1953)

[2] *To the Patrons of the University of Alabama*, THE INDEPENDENT MONITOR, June 10, 1858.

[3] *Id.*

[4] *Id.*

[5] *Id.*

[6] *Id.*

[7] Landon Cabell Garland, ANNUAL REPORT TO THE TRUSTEES OF THE UNIVERSITY OF ALABAMA (July 1858) (on file with the W. S. Hoole Special Collections Library) [hereinafter ANNUAL REPORT, 1858].

[8] *To the Patrons of the University of Alabama*, THE INDEPENDENT MONITOR, June 10, 1858.

[9] Professor DeLoffre would later earn the respect of bibliophiles and researchers by unsuccessfully pleading with Union officers to spare the University's library during the 1865 burning of Tuscaloosa. Sellers, *supra* note 1, at 285.

[10] *To the Patrons of the University of Alabama*, THE INDEPENDENT MONITOR, June 10, 1858.

found that Herring acted in self-defense. Having been exonerated, he promptly left town.[11]

The most remarkable thing about Nabors' homicide is that it was the first time in the university's twenty-seven-year existence that one student killed another. Violence was commonplace during the early years of the University of Alabama. Following its establishment in 1831,[12] its early years were blighted by poor attendance and even poorer behavior on the part of its students.[13] After numerous futile attempts to curtail the excesses of its student body,[14] the school successfully lobbied the state legislature for permission to establish a Military Department at the university.[15] Although mounting political tension with the North motivated the legislators' votes,[16] university officials believed that the military system had the potential to transform their pupils from spoiled young men who were "ruined in moral character"[17] into productive citizens.[18] This article will explore the shift in the university's paradigm from a classics-based model to what essentially amounted to a military institute, and by extension, the revitalization of an institution of higher learning that heretofore had been a failure.

Superficially, the university's faculty and trustees had some success at cultivating an image of an academically prestigious institution. The university's students were drawn from the state's wealthiest families.[19] Its admission requirements included knowledge of Greek, Latin, mathematics, and geography,[20] and in 1850, the university was permitted to establish a chapter of the prestigious Phi Beta Kappa honor society, which, the faculty noted, placed it in company with institutions such as Yale College.[21] These marks of respectability, however, were a façade that hid the university's instability. Soon after its creation, it was forced to unofficially relax its admissions requirements to ensure an adequate flow of incoming students, and tension quickly settled across campus as unprepared pupils failed to meet their professors' lofty expectations.[22] Few students actually obtained

---

[11] *Id.*

[12] *Id.* at 1.

[13] ANNUAL REPORT, 1858.

[14] *Id.*

[15] L. C. Garland & J. J. Ormond, UNIVERSITY OF ALABAMA MILITARY DEPARTMENT 1 (1861).

[16] *Id.*

[17] Letter from Landon Cabell Garland, president, University of Alabama, to John Gill Shorter, governor, Alabama (Nov. 24, 1862) (on file with the W. S. Hoole Special Collections Library).

[18] Garland & Ormond, *supra* note 15, at 1.

[19] Royal C. Dumas, *My Son and My Money Go to the University of Alabama?: The Students at the University of Alabama in 1845 and the Families that Sent Them*, 1 ALA. C.R. & C.L. L. REV. 67, 77 (2011) (noting that the average slaveholdings of the students' families in 1845 placed them "within the top 12% of Southern society at the time").

[20] *Communicated for the Intelligencer*, ALABAMA STATE INTELLIGENCER, April 20, 1831.

[21] SELLERS, *supra* note 1, at 183, 185.

[22] Suzanne Rau Wolfe, THE UNIVERSITY OF ALABAMA: A PICTORIAL HISTORY 16 (1983).

degrees during the university's early years.[23] Even the establishment of the school's Phi Beta Kappa chapter was punctuated by an element of insubordination that underscored the lack of discipline on campus.[24] When the faculty received the organization's response to its application, it was shocked to learn that the university *already* had a chapter of Phi Beta Kappa; perturbed by his colleagues' reluctance to join the organization because of their general suspicion of secret societies, Professor F. A. P. Barnard had secretly submitted a successful application during the previous year.[25]

Any public perception of the university as an academic bastion was undercut by its students' propensity to resort to violence, which was a problem on campus from the school's beginning.[26] Many students arrived on campus armed with pistols, knives, and swords—and they often used them.[27] In an 1834 letter, Lawrence Sellers, who would go on to become a United States and Confederate Senator, wrote to his father that a group of students had chased the university's president, Alva Woods, across campus one night the previous week, firing pistols and hurling projectiles at him.[28] Woods escaped the mob by jumping into a dormitory through an open window, and hid until the crowd dispersed.[29] The tone of Sellers' letter does not suggest that the melee was an unusual occurrence; on the contrary, he marvels that the president's commitment to education was such that he was willing to regularly endure this kind of abuse.[30] Before long, the public at large was aware of the dangerous climate on campus. In an article entitled "Teaching the Young Idea How To Shoot," a New Orleans newspaper described an 1837 incident on campus:

---

[23] *Id.*

[24] Sellers, *supra* note 1, at 183.

[25] *Id.* Barnard, who would later go on to found Barnard College at Columbia University, was viewed as "free spirited" by his colleagues, and was a perpetual thorn in the side of the highly moralistic Basil Manly, who was the University's president from 1837–55. Wolfe, *supra* note 22, at 22.

[26] Dumas criticizes Sellers' portrayal of the student body, which he argues inaccurately characterizes it as being composed of "uneducated frontiersmen." Dumas, *supra* note 19, at 87. Even if Dumas is correct when he argues that Sellers uses anecdotal evidence to project the poor behavior of a few students onto the student body as a whole, *id.* at 87, factors other than their backgrounds may have fueled the university's students' tendency toward violence. Students "acted out adolescent rebellion by testing the rules, rioting, shooting into buildings, and striking professors" at colleges and universities in both the North and the South during this period. Jennifer R. Green, MILITARY EDUCATION AND THE EMERGING MIDDLE CLASS IN THE OLD SOUTH 62 (2008). Moreover, many students at the University of Alabama were likely adherents to the principals of "southern honor," namely to never give or, more importantly for these purposes, suffer an insult. *Id.* at 76 (noting that duels were not uncommon during the antebellum period).

[27] Sellers, *supra* note 1, at 227.

[28] Wolfe, *supra* note 22, at 20.

[29] *Id.*

[30] *Id.*

> Some of the Professors of the Alabama University at Tuscaloosa, lately fired several pistols at some refractory students. The students returned the fire, and the Alma Mater of our sister state was suddenly converted into a scene of commotion and smoke. We have heard of above a dozen rows at this college, and should suppose, from their frequency, that 'Plato's philosophic care' is not much regarded at this seat of learning.[31]

During the university's early decades, knife and pistol fights were considered a matter of course,[32] and such was the students' tendency to make use of what was at hand that the university's ineffective ban on deadly weapons included "large spades and shovels."[33] The faculty also struggled to curtail student pranks, such as an elaborate 1848 incident in which a two-year-old calf was tied to the lightning rod of the university building's rotunda,[34] and were constantly at odds with the general rebellious nature of youth; President Woods resigned in 1837 after a prolonged student insurrection following his decision to suspend one-third of the student body for illicitly attending a circus.[35]

Drunkenness also caused behavioral problems, with one historian suggesting that incidents connected to alcohol caused nine-tenths of the ill-will between Tuscaloosa residents and the university.[36] Such was the degree of the problem that, in 1847, the legislature passed a law punishing merchants who sold liquor to the university's students with fines of up to $500.[37] There are records of several Tuscaloosa vendors actually being subject to stiff penalties for violating the law, but the university never found a way to sufficiently curtail its students' alcohol consumption during its early years.[38]

This atmosphere of constant low-level violent squabbles punctuated by occasional more serious incidents was rendered untenable by Nabors' killing, which attracted national attention.[39] Locals seem to have seethed silently through the fall; no further mention of Nabors' death appeared in *The Independent Monitor* during the remainder of 1858. Then, on January 8, 1859, the *Monitor* printed an editorial that railed against the university.[40] It criticized the poor morals and violent behavior of the students and noted that the size of the student body had diminished precipitously in recent

---

[31] *Teaching the Young Idea How To Shoot*, THE PICAYUNE, April 23, 1837.

[32] Sellers, *supra* note 1, at 231.

[33] *Id.* at 228.

[34] *Id.* at 240.

[35] Wolfe, *supra* note 22, at 21.

[36] Sellers, *supra* note 1, at 245.

[37] *Id.*

[38] *Id.*

[39] *A Chapter of Tragedies: Murder by a University Student*, THE NEW YORK TIMES, June 23, 1858.

[40] *The University*, THE INDEPENDENT MONITOR, January 8, 1859.

years.[41] More such articles followed in the *Monitor*, and other newspapers around the state reprinted the *Monitor*'s articles and began publishing their own critiques of the university.[42] Although the criticisms levied a variety of charges against the university, they were united in their demand that something needed to be done.[43]

Officially, the university's president, Landon Cabell Garland, was indignant. In a series of nine editorials published in the *Mobile Register*, reprinted in newspapers throughout the state, and circulated independently by the university, Garland vigorously defended the university against its critics.[44] He devoted most of the editorials to explaining the drastic decrease in the size of the university's student body;[45] in 1859, just 70 students attended the school, compared with an all-time high of 145 enrolled students earlier in the decade.[46] He primarily blamed Nabors' killing for the decline, claiming that thirty students had left the university in the aftermath of Herring's acquittal in protest of the verdict, and estimated that another twenty failed to matriculate in the fall of 1858 because of the poor publicity the killing generated for the university.[47] This decrease, Garland wrote, was just a temporary setback.[48]

But even Garland admitted there was something more to the dwindling size of the student body than backlash from negative publicity. After discussing the effect the murder had on attendance, he noted that when its student body was at its largest, in the mid-1850s, the university had more non-professional students per capita than the University of Virginia, which was considered to be the gold standard of higher education in the South at the time.[49] It was unfair, he reasoned, to criticize the size of the university's student body based on comparisons to institutions in more populous states.[50] He also offered several additional explanations for the university's small size, only one of which—its inaccessible location—was its own fault.[51] He noted that many of Alabama's residents were born outside of the state, and suggested that they had lingering affinities to institutions of higher

---

[41] *Id.*

[42] Sellers, *supra* note 1, at 256.

[43] *Id.*

[44] Landon Cabell Garland, ANNUAL REPORT TO THE TRUSTEES OF THE UNIVERSITY OF ALABAMA (July 1859) (on file with the W. S. Hoole Special Collections Library) [hereinafter ANNUAL REPORT, 1859]. The articles are unavailable on microfilm. However, Garland pasted an original copy of the version circulated by the University into the Annual Report, accompanied by a note concerning the particulars of its publication.

[45] *Id.*

[46] *Id.*

[47] *Id.*

[48] *Id.*

[49] *Id.*

[50] *Id.*

[51] *Id.*

learning located where they grew up, which they themselves perhaps attended.[52] Moreover, the majority of the states' residents who had attained prestige and power had done so by accumulating wealth earned by farming, without the aid of a collegiate education. Because a university diploma was not seen as a building block to achieving financial success, Garland argued, it did not hold the same cache in Alabama as it did elsewhere.[53]

At times, Garland went on the offensive. Most seriously, he alleged that many of the university's woes were due to its small budget, which in turn, he claimed, was the result of the legislature's serious fiscal mismanagement of the trust used to fund the university.[54] Throughout, he strongly implied that were his critics charged with running a university, they might see things differently.[55]

In communications to the university's trustees, however, Garland admitted that factors particular to the university were driving current and potential students away. In an 1858 report, he noted a 33 % decrease in matriculation the previous fall, a decrease that preceded the student exodus and poor publicity following Nabors' murder and Herring's acquittal. He pointed to three factors that he believed were responsible for the recent decrease in the size of the student body.[56] The first two were the school's strict admission standards and the rigor of its studies. These, Garland refused to alter, noting that "[t]o lower our standards is to introduce indolence."[57] The third was, as Garland termed it, "the moral condition of the University."[58] In particular, Garland deplored the students' fondness for drink and their insistent refusal to leave their lodgings unless heavily armed.[59] The later tendency had worsened after a student claimed to have been twice attacked by a knife-wielding assailant while returning to his lodgings late at night during the 1857–58 school year, although Garland's retelling of the incidents reflects skepticism about the victim's truthfulness.[60] In spite of his admissions about the student body's shortcomings, which appear even more significant when compared with his defense of the school in the following year's letters to the *Mobile Register*, Garland's suggestions for improvement in the 1858 report were insubstantial and lackluster; he merely expressed confidence that with some minor changes, the situation would be improved.[61]

---

[52] *Id.*

[53] *Id.*

[54] *Id.*

[55] *Id.*

[56] ANNUAL REPORT, 1858.

[57] *Id.*

[58] *Id.*

[59] *Id.*

[60] *Id.*

[61] *Id.*

In fact, Garland did have a dramatic plan to transform the university and its students. By his own account, as soon as he assumed the presidency of the university, he began lobbying the legislature to allow him to create a military department.[62] Bills were introduced to that effect, but they failed to garner sufficient support, largely because of concerns about the associated costs.[63] However, by 1860, fears generated by John Brown's raid on Harper's Ferry and looming uncertainty about the stability of the Union made fiscal concerns secondary,[64] and on February 23, 1860, the Senate passed the bill into law.[65]

The legislature's approval of Garland's plan was clearly motivated by current events.[66] But for Garland, any benefit the state's military interests might derive from the university's new department were purely secondary to his primary goal: to introduce a new system of education at the university.[67] In an 1862 letter, he explained his motivations:

> [T]he military system was adopted in this University before the apprehension of war—before the need of military education became so universal—and with but a secondary reference to the military qualifications it might impart. The old collegiate system had proved a failure. The Institution was doing more harm than good. For one good scholar it sent out perhaps two, who were ruined in moral character. . . . It was to correct these evils that for six years I labored to effect the introduction of the Military System.[68]

Prior to the commencement of the fall term of 1860, Garland and university trustee J. J. Ormond published a pamphlet explaining the purpose of the new military department and what changes students could expect when they arrived on campus. It began by emphasizing that the university was not transforming itself into a military institution along the lines of, for example, the Virginia Military Institute.[69] Rather, it compared the military department to the university's law and medical schools.[70] It was an imperfect comparison, as the military department would govern the entire student body, but the practical implication seems to have been that by claiming

---

62 Letter from Landon Cabell Garland, president, University of Alabama, to John Gill Shorter, governor, Alabama (Nov. 24, 1862) (on file with the W. S. Hoole Special Collections Library).

63 Garland & Ormond, *supra* note 15, at 1.

64 *Id.*

65 JOURNAL OF THE SENATE OF THE STATE OF ALA., Feb. 23, 1860.

66 Garland & Ormond, *supra* note 15, at 1.

67 Letter from Landon Cabell Garland, president, University of Alabama, to John Gill Shorter, governor, Alabama (Nov. 24, 1862) (on file with the W. S. Hoole Special Collections Library).

68 *Id.*

69 Garland & Ormond, *supra* note 15, at 3.

70 Garland is referring to the short-lived Montgomery Law School, which operated from 1860–1861. *See generally* David Durham, *Introduction to Wade Keyes and the Montgomery Law School*, in WADE KEYES' INTRODUCTORY LECTURE TO THE MONTGOMERY LAW SCHOOL (2001).

the military element of the school was vested in a single department, the university would be able to continue offering instruction in areas like literature, which had no direct bearing on a purely military education.[71] Although they would be required to take courses in military tactics, the students would be otherwise free to choose their own course of study.[72]

The primary purpose of the military department, according to the pamphlet, would be to effectuate a new system of education that would replace the former model that Garland deemed a failure.[73] Its authors opined that "[t]he Legislature must have supposed that military discipline was better calculated to secure the ends of education than that prevailing in American Colleges."[74] Physical education, in the form of "vigorous exercise,"[75] would play an integral role in the new system; the authors noted that the old order produced "good mathematicians and incurable dyspeptics . . . it is not unfrequently [sic] the case that those who graduate with the highest distinctions and carry off the prizes of the institution, have bodies too much enfeebled by neglect, to be the useful depositories of highly cultivated and active minds."[76] Similarly, students would be required to keep their physical appearance, dress, and living quarters in adherence with strict guidelines.[77] "It is frequently revolting to see the slovenly and careless manner in which some students live," the authors noted.[78] In an attempt to curtail "extravagance," the university also planned to pay for all of its students' needs directly, using their tuition payments, although this goal might be circumvented by imprudent parental gifts of pocket money, the authors admitted.[79]

Most importantly, the new system would be devoted to the "preservation of morals."[80] "We are persuaded that the military throws around the student a better protection against the numerous temptations which assail him than any other can," the authors wrote.[81] Two elements of the system would work together to insulate students from debauchery.[82] The first was constant supervision.[83] Students would be subject to a dozen daily roll calls and nightly room checks, and sentries would patrol the campus.[84] The

[71] Garland & Ormond, *supra* note 15, at 2.

[72] *Id.* at 13.

[73] *Id.* at 4.

[74] *Id.*

[75] *Id.* at 5.

[76] *Id.*

[77] *Id.* at 6.

[78] *Id.*

[79] *Id.* at 7.

[80] *Id.* at 8.

[81] *Id.*

[82] *Id.* at 8-10.

[83] *Id.* at 8.

[84] *Id.*

second was the enforcement mechanism of this supervision: it would be undertaken by the students themselves.[85] The authors did not address the obvious potential flaw in this plan—that students who were used to behaving as they pleased might not be inclined to enforce a system aimed at sharply abridging their freedoms—but expressed great confidence in its expected success: "It is perhaps the only remedy for the defects in [the students'] early training—the only surviving hope of making [them] useful and honored member[s] of society."[86]

This was not the first attempt in recent years to overhaul the structure of the university. In 1852, the university's trustees commissioned then-President Basil Manly, Sr. to visit the country's preeminent colleges and universities.[87] During his trip, he observed the differences between the two leading educational models being employed by institutions of higher learning: the traditional, classics-based model, which allowed students little opportunity to deviate from the established curriculum, and a more flexible model, introduced by Thomas Jefferson at the University of Virginia, which allowed students more leeway when choosing their course of study.[88] Following Manly's trip, in 1854 the university's trustees adopted a resolution to align the university's curriculum more closely with that employed by the University of Virginia.[89] The trustees were concerned that university's rigid requirements for graduation were deterring students from attending, and hoped that the new measures would increase enrollment.[90] But in practice the university's curriculum changed little,[91] and within a few years, the

---

85 *Id.* at 9-10.

86 *Id.* at 13.

87 Sellers, *supra* note 1, at 151.

88 *Id.*

89 F. A. P. Barnard, *Report on a Proposition to Modify the Plan of Instruction in the University of Alabama* 3, in PROF. BARNARD ON COLLEGIATE EDUCATION AND COLLEGE GOVERNMENT (1855).

Professor Barnard (discussed *supra* note 25) and several of his colleagues were charged with preparing a report for the trustees detailing the proposed changes. *Id.* Instead, Barnard prepared an impassioned defense of the status quo. In particular, he believed the proposed changes would lower the university's standards and provide its students with a superficial education, which was anathematic to its true purpose: to create scholars, even if fairly few students were capable of achieving that status. *Id* at 25-50. Barnard proposed an alternative model that retained a four-year core curriculum, but allowed students whose professors determine they showed sufficient intellectual acumen to pursue electives in their third and fourth years. *Id.* at 95-96.

Perhaps skeptical about the reception his report would receive, Barnard begin writing anonymous letters to Tuscaloosa newspapers in which he opposed the adoption of the Virginia plan. James A. Fuller, CHAPLAIN TO THE CONFEDERACY: BASIL MANLY AND BAPTIST LIFE IN THE OLD SOUTH 173. When then-Governor Collier, a supporter of the Virginia plan, learned that Barnard was the author of the letters, he demanded that the board of trustees find some way to remove Barnard. *Id.* But Barnard resigned, *id.* at 174, and accepted a position at the University of Mississippi. Sellers, *supra* note 1, at 152. Upon hearing of his nemesis' resignation, Manly remarked, "[O]ne great incubus thrown off—Barnard is gone." Fuller, *supra*, at 174.

90 Barnard, *supra* note 89, at 7.

91 Sellers, *supra* note 1, at 153.

Virginia model was deemed a failure. Instead, students were allowed to receive a "diploma of graduation" for completing substantially less work than that required to obtain a "bachelor of arts and sciences" degree.[92]

Nor was Garland's idea of a military university novel in the South during the antebellum period. The region's first military school, the Virginia Military Institute, was founded in 1839.[93] By the outbreak of the Civil War twenty-two years later, it had been joined by eleven additional state-sponsored military academies in the South and over 70 private academies.[94] Unlike the sons of planters who attended the University of Alabama and similarly situated schools,[95] most of the students who attended these academies were the sons of professionals or tradesmen, rather than of men whose fortunes were tied to the land.[96] Scholar Jennifer Green has identified three key ways in which these students benefited from receiving a military academy education: funding, curriculum, and discipline.[97] Many of the schools were state-funded and offered students forms of financial assistance.[98] The curriculum had a more scientific and practical focus than the classics-based curriculum at more traditional universities, which helped prepare the students for professional careers.[99] As well, the schools' rigors encouraged a degree of self-discipline that curtailed the violent outbursts that often accompanied traditional notions of southern male honor.[100] Although Garland's pamphlet shows little interest in increasing the availability of student funding and explicitly rejects significantly modifying the university's curriculum, Green's research indicates his (as it turned out, well-founded) belief that implementing a military system would instill the student body with a sense of self-discipline.

When students, now known as cadets, arrived on campus in the fall of 1860, they were escorted to their new living quarters—not the dormitories (now known as barracks), but to a nearby field.[101] For the next six weeks, they and their professors, including President Garland, lived in tents and spent their days practicing military drills.[102] According to John Massey, who attended the university at the time, many of his fellow cadets, especially returning students, were "disgusted" by their newfound circumstances.[103] "It

[92] Wolfe, *supra* note 22, at 33.

[93] Green, *supra* note 26, at 1.

[94] *Id.*

[95] Dumas, *supra* note 19, at 77.

[96] Green, *supra* note 26, at 25.

[97] *Id.* at 8.

[98] *Id.* at 37.

[99] *Id.* at 130-31.

[100] *Id.* at 76-77.

[101] John Massey, REMINISCENCES 138 (1916).

[102] *Id.* at 138-39.

[103] *Id.* at 139.

struck some of the old students as a most incongruous thing in a University which stood for humanities and high culture," he wrote in his memoirs.[104] But soon, the ritual of the exercises, glamour of their uniforms, and attention of the townspeople—especially the "admiring lady spectators"—who often came to watch the drills engendered a change in the cadets' attitudes.[105] Garland, not one to overlook an opportunity to encourage his cadets' zeal, once remarked to Massey that "Venus always showed a penchant for Mars."[106] The increasing likelihood of war also increased the cadets' enthusiasm for all things military.[107] Massey recalled that "[t]he novelty of the military feature made it very attractive during the first few months, and later on the rising war spirit added to its interest."[108]

In mid-October, the cadets moved into the barracks. There, they were subject to the rigorous schedule that Garland and Ormond had envisioned.[109] They awoke at 6:00 a.m. to the sound of a three-minute reveille, during which the cadets dressed, rushed outside, and lined up for roll call.[110] They then had a half-hour to bathe and clean their living quarters, followed by a short study period, prayers, and breakfast.[111] They spent the day studying and making recitations, punctuated by dinner.[112] In the late afternoon, they drilled, followed by a brief recreation period and supper.[113] They then had another short recreation period, followed by more studying, before retiring at 10:00 p.m.[114] In Massey, at least, the routine produced the effect Garland had hoped for: "I found also that the regular habits of sleep and exercise enforced by the military system were a good thing for me. . . . Through this experience I learned that unexpected good comes to us by the patient endurance of unavoidable inconveniences and hardships," he remembered.[115]

The legislature's concerns about the financial drain of a Military Department proved to be well-founded, and by the end of 1860, the university was badly in need of funds.[116] In response, Garland conceived a plan that would amount to either a brilliant public relations move or an enormous blunder: to accompany his request for a budget increase, he proposed

---

104 *Id.*

105 *Id.*

106 *Id.*

107 *Id.*

108 *Id.*

109 *Id.* at 141.

110 *Id.*

111 *Id.*

112 *Id.*

113 *Id.*

114 *Id.*

115 *Id.*

116 *Id.* at 133.

sending the entire cadet corps on a steamship down the Tombigbee River to Mobile, then up the Alabama River to Montgomery, where they would drill before the state legislature.[117] Although the general consensus was that the military system had greatly improved the students' behavior, in late 1860, the faculty did not yet share Garland's confidence in his cadets.[118] "Fears were entertained that the discipline of the corps could not stand the strain of passing through Mobile and of going through the entertainments that would be proffered in Montgomery. Drunkenness and demoralization were dreaded," Massey recalled.[119] Even several of the cadets' parents advised Garland against the trip.[120]

Garland's gamble paid off.[121] The cadets behaved laudably during the January 1861 trip.[122] "On the steamboats, their behavior was all that could be desired, and in Montgomery everybody was proud of their appearance and deportment. . . . Camp discipline was maintained and perfect order prevailed," recalled Colonel Caleb Huse, who oversaw the trip on Garland's behalf.[123] In particular, Huse remembered proudly that although there were bar rooms on the steamships that ferried the cadets to Mobile and Montgomery, not one cadet imbibed.[124] In addition to impressing their commanding officer, the cadets made a favorable impression on the legislature, which suspended its procedural rules to rush into effect an appropriations bill benefiting the University of Alabama.[125]

As the war progressed, enrollment swelled. In the fall of 1862, 256 cadets matriculated.[126] In the fall of 1863, 345 cadets matriculated.[127] In Garland's view, the addition of the Military Department had been an enormous success.[128] In a letter to Governor Shorter, he recalled the "drunkenness," "gluttony," and "vice" prevalent among the students before the introduction

---

117 Sellers, *supra* note 1, at 258. Presumably the trip by water, although four times as long as passage overland, was the more practical of the two options.

118 Massey, *supra* note 101, at 133.

119 *Id.*

120 Caleb Huse, SUPPLIES FOR THE CONFEDERATE ARMY, HOW THEY WERE OBTAINED IN EUROPE AND HOW PAID FOR (1914), *available at* http://www.archive.org/stream/thesuppliesforth24469gut/24469-8.txt.

121 Sellers, *supra* note 1, at 258-59.

122 Huse, *supra* note 120.

123 *Id.*

124 *Id.*

125 *Id.*

126 Landon Cabell Garland, ANNUAL REPORT TO THE TRUSTEES OF THE UNIVERSITY OF ALABAMA (July 1863) (on file with the W. S. Hoole Special Collections Library) [hereinafter ANNUAL REPORT, 1863].

127 Landon Cabell Garland, ANNUAL REPORT TO THE TRUSTEES OF THE UNIVERSITY OF ALABAMA (July 1864) (on file with the W. S. Hoole Special Collections Library) [hereinafter ANNUAL REPORT, 1864].

128 Letter from Landon Cabell Garland, president, University of Alabama, to John Gill Shorter, governor, Alabama (Nov. 24, 1862) (on file with the W. S. Hoole Special Collections Library).

of the military system.[129] "It has corrected these evils to an extent surpassing the most sanguine expectations of its friends, no one who has enjoyed an opportunity of marking the contrast will deny," he wrote.[130] He anticipated the program to continue to thrive after the war.[131]

Garland believed that the university's Military Department would serve three purposes during the war. First, it would train young men to be officers in the Confederate Army.[132] "[T]he Institution has been one of the most useful feeders of the Army—supplying it with well drilled and competent officers," he wrote to a recruiting officer in 1864.[133] As a corollary to this purpose, he routinely sent cadets around the state to train and drill volunteer troops who were about to travel to the front.[134] John Massey recalled traveling to Montgomery and to north Alabama in late 1861 and early 1862 for such a purpose,[135] and in March 1862, Governor Shorter assigned the cadets the duty of drilling 12,000 volunteer troops at a dozen encampments around the state, where their performances received complimentary reviews.[136]

Second, Garland planned for the cadets to serve as a militia akin to the present-day National Guard if they were suddenly needed to protect the state.[137] During the early years of the war, the cadets were periodically sent out to defend the state against raiding bands of Union soldiers, but no actual combat resulted.[138] He also expressed confidence that they could defend the Tuscaloosa area from an invading Union Army.[139]

Garland feared the dangers posed by potential slave revolts almost if not more so than he feared attack by the Union, and he repeatedly suggested that the cadets could be used to suppress such a revolt if one took place.[140]

---

129 *Id.*

130 *Id.*

131 Letter from Landon Cabell Garland, president, University of Alabama, to John Gill Shorter, governor, Alabama (Oct. 16, 1862) (on file with the W. S. Hoole Special Collections Library).

132 Letter from Landon Cabell Garland, president, University of Alabama to Jno. W. Slaughter, captain and enrolling officer at Tuskaloosa [sic] (May 24, 1864) (on file with the W. S. Hoole Special Collections Library).

133 *Id.*

134 Letter from Landon Cabell Garland, president, University of Alabama, to Gideon J. Pillow, general, Confederate Army (Dec. 18, 1863) (on file with the W. S. Hoole Special Collections Library).

135 Massey, REMINISCENCES, *supra* note 101, at 154-55.

136 Letter from Landon Cabell Garland, president, University of Alabama, to Gideon J. Pillow, general, Confederate Army (Dec. 18, 1863) (on file with the W. S. Hoole Special Collections Library).

137 ANNUAL REPORT, 1863.

138 *Id.*

139 *Id.*

140 *E.g.*, *id.*; Letter from Landon Cabell Garland, president, University of Alabama, to John Gill Shorter, governor, Alabama (Oct. 30, 1862) (on file with the W. S. Hoole Special Collections Library).

He was particularly wary of the dense slave population in the middle part of Alabama, and believed that the cadets' presence in Tuscaloosa and their public displays of skill served as a deterrent to unrest.[141] His fear of a slave revolt was such that in October 1862, he confidentially suggested to Governor Shorter that provisions be made for "the removal of all the [male slaves] between 15 and 60, into cantonments far into the interior, where they may be guarded by a comparatively few soldiers, and if necessary marched out of the reach of Lincoln's troops"—a duty, he suggested, which could be performed by the cadets.[142]

By envisioning the cadets playing a role in protecting the white population from black slaves, and thereby preserving the power balance of slavery, Garland was continuing the university's tradition of promoting the institution. During the antebellum years, the university hosted many pro-slavery speakers, and published several of their speeches.[143] For some of these speakers, the university served as a platform from which they could share their ideas with the public.[144] Others, in particular Joseph Wright Taylor, who delivered a speech in 1847 entitled "A Plea for the University," pointed to the direct role the university could play in upholding the institution of slavery. "[T]he champions of the South," he argued, "must be her sons, their weapons the pulpit and the press, their schools of discipline our own Colleges and Universities."[145] In other words, Taylor was calling upon universities, like the University of Alabama, to better train its students to counter the ever-increasing abolitionist arguments from their Northern opponents.

Third, Garland hoped to use the university to ensure that the state had a supply of educated young men when the war ended.[146] "Educated talent will be extremely scarce by the time we get through this war; and young men are serving the country more effectually by abiding here and improving their opportunities of mental culture than they would do by going into the army," he wrote in an 1864 letter to the father of one cadet.[147] At times, Garland

---

141 ANNUAL REPORT, 1863.

142 Letter from Landon Cabell Garland, president, University of Alabama, to John Gill Shorter, governor, Alabama (Oct. 30, 1862) (on file with the W. S. Hoole Special Collections Library).

143 Alfred L. Brophy, *The Law of the Descent of Thought: Law, History, and Civilization in Antebellum Literary Addresses,* 20 LAW & LIT. 343 (2008) (analyzing almost forty addresses given at the University of Alabama between 1832 and 1860, many of them concerning the topic of slavery).

144 *Id.* For example, in 1843, Albert Forney delivered a speech in which he argued that slavery contributed to the development of the intellectual elite, because "to high intellectual culture, a class of individuals, upon whom devolves the sowing the seed and ingathering of the harvest is indispensible." *Id.* at 364. Similarly, in 1861, William Russel Smith delivered a speech in which he argued that slaves were "greatly benefitted" from being removed from Africa and "march[ed] onward from savage to civilized life." *Id.* at 389.

145 *Id.* at 369.

146 Letter from Landon Cabell Garland, president, University of Alabama, to Dr. A. G. Mabry, Selma (May 26, 1864) (on file with the W. S. Hoole Special Collections Library).

147 *Id.*

couched similar statements in terms of preparing the cadets for positions as officers in the Army: by remaining longer at the university, he reasoned, cadets would be more capable officers in the field.[148] But at others, he clearly envisioned training a group of young men who would rebuild the state when peace returned.[149]

This third purpose touches on two of the most significant challenges Garland faced during the war: the struggle to justify his efforts to keep cadets ineligible from conscription into the Army, and the similar struggle he undertook to keep cadets from deserting their posts and entering the Army on their own volition.[150] "Anxiety again begins to spring up in the minds of some parents relative to the conscription of their sons in the Corps—and a corresponding desire upon the part of their sons to resign and volunteer rather than be conscribed," Garland wrote to Governor Shorter in 1863.[151] In spite of opposition from military officials[152] and the general public,[153] the university's cadets remained ineligible for conscription during the War.[154] Various justifications were given for the exemption, including that, as members of the University Corps, the cadets were already members of a military organization,[155] and Garland's oft-repeated assertion that the cadets would be better officers if they remained longer at the university.[156]

---

148 Letter from Landon Cabell Garland, president, University of Alabama, to Thomas Hill Watts, governor, Alabama (March 29, 1864) (on file with the W. S. Hoole Special Collections Library).

149 Letter from Landon Cabell Garland, president, University of Alabama, to Dr. A. G. Mabry, Selma (May 26, 1864) (on file with the W. S. Hoole Special Collections Library).

150 Conscription was a contentious matter in the Confederacy during the Civil War. In April 1862, the Confederate Congress passed an act obligating all white males between eighteen and thirty-five to three-year terms of service in the Confederate Army; the age limit was raised to forty-five in September. Emory M. Thomas, THE CONFEDERATE NATION, 1861–1865 152-53 (1979). "Classes" of men, including national and state officers, railroad employees, druggists, professors, schoolteachers, miners, ministers, pilots, nurses, and iron-furnace and foundry laborers. *Id.* at 153. Men who would otherwise be subject to the draft did not have to serve if they could secure someone who would have otherwise been ineligible for the draft as a substitute. *Id.* The rampant abuse of the substitute and exemption system point to the draft's unpopularity. *Id.* at 154. Moreover, it amplified already tense class tensions: in October 1862, the Confederate Congress added owners and overseers of twenty slaves or more to the "classes" of exempt men. *Id.* This move was not well received by Southern yeoman, who saw it as "a symbol of the 'rich man's war' as 'poor man's fight.'" *Id.*

151 Letter from Landon Cabell Garland, president, University of Alabama, to John Gill Shorter, governor, Alabama (Feb. 3, 1863) (on file with the W. S. Hoole Special Collections Library).

152 Letter from Landon Cabell Garland, president, University of Alabama to Jno. W. Slaughter, captain and enrolling officer at Tuskaloosa [sic] (May 24, 1864) (on file with the W. S. Hoole Special Collections Library).

153 ANNUAL REPORT, 1863.

154 Malcolm C. McMillan, THE DISINTEGRATION OF A CONFEDERATE STATE: THREE GOVERNORS AND ALABAMA'S WARTIME HOME FRONT, 1861–1865 109 (1986).

155 *Id.*

156 Letter from Landon Cabell Garland, president, University of Alabama, to Thomas Hill Watts, governor, Alabama (March 29, 1864) (on file with the W. S. Hoole Special Collections Library).

There were some limits to the exemption, and the Army sought to persuade the government to impose more as the war progressed.[157] In 1863, the university agreed to stop admitting cadets over the age of eighteen.[158] Throughout the war, Garland battled attempts by the Army to conscript cadets who had turned eighteen while at the university, engaging in a near constant exchange of letters with state and military officials on the matter.[159] In May 1864, he confessed to the father of a cadet that he had written to the governor so frequently about the conscription controversy without receiving a response that he was "embarrassed to write again."[160]

Garland frequently faced accusations that he was using the university to shield wealthy young men from conscription.[161] It is certainly true that by successfully enabling them to stay at the university past their eighteenth birthdays, he was helping them avoid conscription, giving credit to his critics' allegations. Therein lay the inherent problem with Garland's third goal for the university's Military Department: by undertaking a move that would ensure future stability in the state, he, by default, had to help the cadets avoid conscription.

Garland's exchanges with cadets' parents do not detract from the argument that he was keeping their sons away from the war. In the letters, Garland sought to reassure parents of their children's safety and often speaks of the cadets as youths, rather than soldiers. To one father, he wrote, "I lose no time in relieving your mind concerning Albert's appointment."[162] Eighteen months later, he wrote the same father to address concerns about the son's potential conscription, adding of the cadet, "[w]e have no finer boy here."[163] He took it upon himself to write frequent letters to parents when their sons fell ill.[164] And, when discussing whether to use the cadets to defend Tuscaloosa against a potential 1862 Union attack, he wrote Gover-

---

[157] McMillan, THE DISINTEGRATION OF A CONFEDERATE STATE, *supra* note 154, at 109.

[158] *Id.*

[159] *E.g.*, Letter from Landon Cabell Garland, president, University of Alabama, to John Gill Shorter, governor, Alabama (Nov. 24, 1862) (on file with the W. S. Hoole Special Collections Library); Letter from Landon Cabell Garland, president, University of Alabama, to John Gill Shorter, governor, Alabama (Feb. 3, 1863) (on file with the W. S. Hoole Special Collections Library); Letter from Landon Cabell Garland, president, University of Alabama, to Thomas Hill Watts, governor, Alabama (April 13, 1864) (on file with the W. S. Hoole Special Collections Library).

[160] Letter from Landon Cabell Garland, president, University of Alabama, to Dr. A. G. Mabry, Selma (May 26, 1864) (on file with the W. S. Hoole Special Collections Library).

[161] Letter from Landon Cabell Garland, president, University of Alabama, to John Gill Shorter, governor, Alabama (Oct. 16, 1862) (on file with the W. S. Hoole Special Collections Library).

[162] Letter from Landon Cabell Garland, president, University of Alabama, to Dr. A. G. Mabry, Selma (Dec. 11, 1862) (on file with the W. S. Hoole Special Collections Library).

[163] Letter from Landon Cabell Garland, president, University of Alabama, to Dr. A. G. Mabry, Selma (May 26, 1864) (on file with the W. S. Hoole Special Collections Library).

[164] Letter from Landon Cabell Garland, president, University of Alabama, to Hon. W. L. Yancy, (Nov. 24, 1862) (on file with the W. S. Hoole Special Collections Library).

nor Shorter: "I am for it myself, but I doubt whether parents would approve of it, as it would result no doubt in the loss of life."[165]

One irony associated with Garland's efforts to keep the cadets ineligible for conscription is that many of them wanted to join the Army just as much as their parents wanted to keep them out of it. Cadets frequently petitioned Garland to allow them to leave the school to fight.[166] Massey remembered that when war broke out in 1861, so many of the cadets wanted to travel to the front that had they done so, there would not have been enough remaining cadets to sustain the school.[167]

> Dr. Garland's strong personal influence and his masterly arguments held most of us in place until the close of the year. If the war should close soon, he said, we would not be needed in the field, and our education could go on without interruption; but if the war should be prolonged, we could do more good where we were in preparing ourselves as drillmasters and thoroughly trained officers than we could by prematurely sacrificing ourselves in the field.[168]

Not all of Massey's peers were convinced, but most, he reported, remained at the university until the end of the school year.[169] Other times, the cadets attempted to avoid confrontation with Garland altogether. In 1864, a contingent of cadets petitioned Governor Watts for permission to leave the university to serve as a personal bodyguard unit to General Pillow.[170] Upon learning of the cadets' request, a perturbed Garland wrote to Watts that such an allowance would prevent the university from being able to provide the Army with a continual supply of officers and would undermine the schools' ability to impart rigor and discipline to its students because it would be forced to accept new students throughout the year to fill empty spots.[171]

In an effort to forestall such requests and to establish an institutional stance on them, in 1862 the university began to require that cadets remain enrolled for a full academic year.[172] "In organizing the present Corps every effort was made to secure its *stability*," Garland explained to the universi-

---

165 Letter from Landon Cabell Garland, president, University of Alabama, to John Gill Shorter, governor, Alabama (Oct. 20, 1862) (on file with the W. S. Hoole Special Collections Library).

166 *E.g.*, Massey, REMINISCENCES, *supra* note 101, at 154; Letter from Landon Cabell Garland, president, University of Alabama, to Thomas Hill Watts, governor, Alabama (March 29, 1864) (on file with the W. S. Hoole Special Collections Library).

167 Massey, REMINISCENCES, *supra* note 101, at 154.

168 *Id.*

169 *Id.*

170 Letter from Landon Cabell Garland, president, University of Alabama, to Thomas Hill Watts, governor, Alabama (March 29, 1864) (on file with the W. S. Hoole Special Collections Library).

171 *Id.*

172 ANNUAL REPORT, 1863.

ty's trustees.[173] "The year before, cadets could resign their commission at any time, with their parents' approbation. This right was taken away, and no cadet was admitted excepting under a pledge of honor, enlisting for twelve months."[174] Garland's plans for stability, however, produced mixed results. While most students did stay at school for one year,[175] they rarely returned for a second.[176] Although Garland did not report to the trustees how many of the matriculating students were returning from the previous year,[177] one former cadet remembered that in 1863 there was not a single senior at the university and only three juniors.[178] As the number of matriculates indicates, cadets flocked to the university, but once they completed their mandatory year of instruction, they left to fight.[179]

It was not uncommon for students to fail to remain at the university for even the requisite year. "I must confess that desertions of post have taken place much more frequently than I anticipated," Garland wrote to the trustees in 1863.[180] The most serious threat to the university posed by an attempted desertion came in February 1863, when a group of cadets devised a plan to lead more than half of the cadets away from the university to join the Army.[181] Garland mollified them by making a speech and allowing those over the age of eighteen to write to the governor and ask to be released from their year-long pledge of duty.[182] He also showed them a surprising degree of sympathy, given his normal stance on desertion, which he considered "a serious evil."[183] He suspected that the cadets had been subject to taunting by the residents of Tuscaloosa for their exemption from conscription, and also believed that enrolling officers for the Army had made false promises to the cadets about the rank they would be assigned and salary they would receive upon joining.[184]

---

173 *Id.*

174 *Id.*

175 *Id*; ANNUAL REPORT, 1864.

176 Wolfe, *supra* note 22, at 51.

177 ANNUAL REPORT, 1863; ANNUAL REPORT, 1864.

178 Samuel Will John, *Alabama Corps of Cadets, 1860–65*, 25 CONFEDERATE VETERAN, 12, 13 (Jan. 1917).

179 Wolfe, *supra* note 22, at 51.

180 ANNUAL REPORT, 1863.

181 Letter from Landon Cabell Garland, president, University of Alabama, to John Gill Shorter, governor, Alabama (Feb. 17, 1863) (on file with the W. S. Hoole Special Collections Library).

182 *Id.* It is not clear whether any of the cadets actually did write Governor Shorter, and if so, whether he granted their request.

183 Letter from Landon Cabell Garland, president, University of Alabama, to John Gill Shorter, governor, Alabama (Oct. 29, 1862) (on file with the W. S. Hoole Special Collections Library).

184 Letter from Landon Cabell Garland, president, University of Alabama, to John Gill Shorter, governor, Alabama (Feb. 17, 1863) (on file with the W. S. Hoole Special Collections Library).

It does not appear that any mass desertions occurred at the university during the war,[185] but individual students deserted regularly.[186] During the 1862–1863 school year, 46 of the 256 matriculating cadets deserted.[187] The following year, 62 of the 345 matriculating cadets deserted.[188] These numbers may be deflated. Forty-four additional students were also dismissed from the university during these two years, the majority for receiving excessive demerits,[189] and Garland suspected that some students did so deliberately: "Some [cadets] have even been known to [run] up their demerit list with a view to being discharged, judging very rightly that their . . . reputations would suffer less from discharge on account of excess of demerits than from the desertion of post," he reported to the university's trustees.[190]

The degree of understanding that Garland extended to the cadets who planned to participate in the mass desertion of 1862 was an anomaly; in general, he considered desertion a "violation of every principle of duty and honor."[191] Nor did he actually believe that most desertions occurred because the offending cadets planned to join the Army. As he wrote to governor Shorter:

> There are but few cases in which patriotism is the impelling motive. In most, the object is to *escape discipline*, thinking that desertion for the assumed purpose of joining the Army will be laid to the account of becoming ardor to serve the country, and that thus the discredit of dismission [sic] for delinquencies of duty may be escaped.[192]

Garland officially dismissed every cadet who deserted.[193] He also insisted on the publication of the name of every deserter in various materials released by the university, but wondered if such publication would be a deterrent because of the public perception that cadets deserted to serve in the Army.[194]

Along with desertion and the controversy surrounding the attempts to keep the cadets exempt from conscription, another significant challenge face by the university during the war was the struggle to obtain adequate provisions to feed, clothe, and train the cadets. The 1863–1864 school year was shortened by a month in response to rising food prices.[195] Garland's

---

185 ANNUAL REPORT, 1863; ANNUAL REPORT, 1864.

186 *Id.*

187 ANNUAL REPORT, 1863.

188 *Id.*

189 *Id.*; ANNUAL REPORT, 1864.

190 ANNUAL REPORT, 1863.

191 Letter from Landon Cabell Garland, president, University of Alabama, to John Gill Shorter, governor, Alabama (Oct. 29, 1862) (on file with the W. S. Hoole Special Collections Library).

192 *Id.*

193 *Id.*

194 ANNUAL REPORT, 1863.

195 *Id.*

wartime correspondence reads like that of a procurement officer. He sent out inquiries searching for thread,[196] brandy,[197] cannons,[198] cloth,[199] sugar,[200] molasses,[201] and many other supplies. Shoes posed a particular challenge. In 1862, he attempted to arrange for the state's convicts to cobble shoes for the cadets.[202] Later that year, he protested the Army's seizure of a local tannery because its proprietor produced shoes for the university,[203] and in 1863 he attempted to obtain an exemption from conscription for another local cobbler for the same reasons.[204] By the fall of 1863, the university faced such a food shortage that aspiring cadets were required to provide the school with 100 lbs. of bacon as a condition of their enrollment.[205] Judging by the volume of letters Garland wrote to parents of would-be cadets explaining this requirement, it produced considerable hardship.[206]

During the summer of 1864, the cadets finally skirmished with the enemy.[207] One group, composed of all of the cadets who happened to be near Montgomery during their summer furlough, chased a band of Union soldiers from Mount Cheaha to Auburn, before returning to Montgomery.[208] After the furlough in the fall of 1864, the entire cadet corps was sent to north Alabama, but the opportunity to engage with Union troops never materialized.[209] Although two cadets were wounded during the summer

---

196 Letter from Landon Cabell Garland, president, University of Alabama, to "Pat" (Nov. 23, 1862) (on file with the W. S. Hoole Special Collections Library).

197 *Id.*

198 Letter from Landon Cabell Garland, president, University of Alabama, to John Gill Shorter, governor, Alabama (Oct. 29, 1862) (on file with the W. S. Hoole Special Collections Library).

199 Letter from Landon Cabell Garland, president, University of Alabama, to John Gill Shorter, governor, Alabama (Nov. 11, 1862) (on file with the W. S. Hoole Special Collections Library).

200 Letter from Landon Cabell Garland, president, University of Alabama, to Messrs. Baskerville & Whitfield, Columbus, Miss. (Oct. 29, 1862) (on file with the W. S. Hoole Special Collections Library).

201 *Id.*

202 Letter from Landon Cabell Garland, president, University of Alabama, to John Gill Shorter, governor, Alabama (Sept. 2, 1862) (on file with the W. S. Hoole Special Collections Library).

203 Letter from Landon Cabell Garland, president, University of Alabama, to John Gill Shorter, governor, Alabama (Dec. 2, 1862) (on file with the W. S. Hoole Special Collections Library).

204 Letter from Landon Cabell Garland, president, University of Alabama, to Gideon J. Pillow, general, Confederate Army (Dec. 18, 1863) (on file with the W. S. Hoole Special Collections Library).

205 Letter from Landon Cabell Garland, president, University of Alabama, to Amos Jones, Es. (Sept. 19, 1863) (on file with the W. S. Hoole Special Collections Library).

206 *E.g.*, Letter from Landon Cabell Garland, president, University of Alabama, to R. Weaver, Eutaw (Oct. 29, 1862) (on file with the W. S. Hoole Special Collections Library).

207 Sellers, *supra* note 1, at 279.

208 *Id.*

209 *Id.*

skirmishes, and several fell gravely ill during the journey to and from north Alabama, the corps did not sustain any fatalities.[210]

The end of the war came suddenly and unexpectedly. Massey, who—after surviving a nightmarish experience at the Battle of Chickamauga—gratefully accepted Garland's offer to return to the university as an instructor, remembered that by April 1865, morale had sunk so low in Alabama that "[c]onditions were unfavorable for doing college work."[211] A contingent of cadets and the area's Home Guard alternated keeping a nightly watch over the bridge spanning the Black Warrior River, which allowed Tuscaloosa to be reached from the north; on the night of April 3, 1865, Massey made a point of noting, the Home Guard was on duty.[212] That evening, Union General John T. Croxton launched a surprise attack on Tuscaloosa.[213] The cadets assembled and engaged in a brief skirmish with Union forces;[214] three cadets were wounded, but all recovered.[215]

During a lull in the fighting, Garland was approached by a Confederate officer, whom Massey only identifies as "Captain Carpenter."[216] Carpenter had experienced a tumultuous night.[217] Earlier that evening, he had been married to the daughter of a Tuscaloosa family.[218] Union forces interrupted the wedding reception and took Carpenter prisoner.[219] Upon arriving at a Union encampment, he discovered that its commanding officer was an old friend (both men were natives of Lexington, Kentucky).[220] Carpenter was allowed to return under guard to his bride, and inform her that "though a prisoner, he was safe and would not be harmed."[221] On his return trip to the Union camp, Carpenter encountered Garland.[222] He told Garland that "the Federals were fourteen hundred strong, that they held the bridge and were fortified by cotton bales, that it would be a useless sacrifice of life to attack so large a force of seasoned soldiers with only three hundred young boys."[223] Unwilling to allow the cadets to embark on a suicide mission, Garland

---

210 *Id.*

211 Massey, REMINISCENCES, *supra* note 101, at 210.

212 *Id.* at 211.

213 *Id.*

214 *Id.*

215 *Id.* at 212-13.

216 *Id.* at 212.

217 *Id.*

218 *Id.*

219 *Id.*

220 *Id.*

221 *Id.*

222 *Id.*

223 *Id.* In actuality, the Union forces numbered around 2,600. Sellers, *supra* note 1, at 281.

ordered them to retreat from the city.[224] The advancing Union Army burned the University of Alabama to the ground.[225]

Initially, Garland planned to lead the cadets to join General Nathan Bedford Forrest, who was believed to be in Selma.[226] But when they arrived in Marion, they learned that Selma had fallen and Forrest had passed through Marion two days prior, destination unknown.[227] Garland had no choice but to furlough the cadets, with orders to reassemble at Auburn on May 12.[228] Before that date, however, news reached Alabama of the surrender at Appomattox.[229] The war was over.

---

224 Massey, REMINISCENCES, *supra* note 101, at 212.

225 *Id.*

226 *Id.* at 213.

227 *Id.* at 214.

228 *Id.*

229 Sellers, *supra* note 1, at 288.

ECONOMIC GROWTH IN BLOUNT COUNTY/ONEONTA: ATTORNEYS, COMPANIES, AND CASES

Eddie Lowe

Many of the same forces that drove economic expansion in Alabama as a whole during the late-nineteenth and early-twentieth centuries were also present in Blount County during that period. Rich natural resources lured pioneers of industry who simultaneously brought railroads to the area as well as a demand for secondary services for their mining and transportation outfits. One can scarcely expect such transformative economic development to occur without significantly affecting the market for legal services, and this period of growth in the southern part of Blount County held true to expectations. Eminent domain cases were litigated to clear rights-of-way for the railroad, the state legislature passed an act that allowed the county seat to be moved nearer to the newly opened railroad depot in Oneonta, and one of the titans of Alabama's coal and iron industry, himself a lawyer, took a risk and made a significant personal investment in the area.

In this chapter, I will outline what is arguably the most significant period of industrial growth in Blount County's history and highlight the legal maneuvering that took place to help make it all possible. First, I will recount the process that caused the county seat to be moved from Blountsville to Oneonta. Next I will detail William T. Underwood's efforts to open a mine in Altoona, and the impact it had on the area. Finally, I will examine the legal battles that bookended the productive life of Cheney Lime and Cement Company's Graystone plant.

I. The County Seat Moves to Oneonta

A county older than the state, Blount was officially declared a county by David Holmes, Governor of the Mississippi Territory, on May 9, 1817.[1] In 1820, the county commission declared that Blountsville would be the county seat.[2] However, that "crown" would lie uneasy in Blountsville for the next few decades. As will be discussed further below, the issue of moving the county seat elsewhere was an oft-debated topic. Many residents resented the fact that instead of holding a popular election to decide the location of the county seat, an unelected commission had made the decision for them.[3]

---

[1] Blount County Historical Society, THE HERITAGE OF BLOUNT COUNTY ALABAMA 5 (1989).

[2] *Id* at 16.

[3] *Id.*

Finally, around 1880, the industrial forces that were causing change throughout the state started to creep into Blount County. Particularly, Henry DeBardeleben and James W. Sloss made a crucial investment to open the "Champion Mines," which would not only feed the industrialists' ever-hungry new furnaces in Birmingham, but would also spark the growth of what was to become the city of Oneonta.

DeBardeleben and Sloss were giants of the Alabama mineral district. DeBardeleben inherited the Pratt Coal and Iron Company from his father-in-law, and managed the company with enormous success.[4] James Sloss, an equally prolific industrialist, started out as a railroad man, and eventually partnered with Debardeleben to purchase the land that would come to be known as the "Champion Mines."[5] The area was named for its brown iron ore, which was of the highest quality known in the world at that time. In 1889, the L & N Railroad extended its northern terminus to Oneonta, two miles west of the Champion Mines, to satisfy DeBardeleben's need for more ore to fuel the furnaces he had built in the Birmingham area.[6] With trains running to and from Birmingham daily, the area around the train station grew. The arrival of the mining industry and the railroad had such a profound impact on the community that by the end of 1889, the residents of Blount County voted to move the county seat from Blountsville to Oneonta.

The legal community in Blount County couldn't simply start going to work in Oneonta because it was suddenly a more prolific area of the county. None of the appurtenances attendant to a seat of justice existed in Oneonta at the time. The town of Oneonta was not even incorporated until 1891.[7] Meanwhile, a $16,000 courthouse had just been completed in Blountsville in 1888.[8] Moving the county seat would take an act of Alabama's General Assembly.

On Nov. 17, 1888, Blount County's state representative, Mr. J. H. C. Johnson, introduced "An act to provide for a vote of the people on the subject of a permanent location of the county seat of Blount County."[9] The bill was referred to Mr. Johnson's Committee on Counties and County Lines and Boundaries, and after being favorably read a second and third time in the house, it was passed by a vote of 68–4.[10] Things did not go as smoothly in the Senate, however, as Mr. W. E. Skeggs made the Act a special project of his. On December 4, 1888, Skeggs offered an amendment to the bill that added Blountsville to the list of potential sites.[11] This meant that one month

[4] Ethel Armes, THE STORY OF COAL AND IRON IN ALABAMA 239 (1910).

[5] *Id* at 107; *see also* Historical Marker, "Champion Mines," located at 33° 56.337 N, 86° 27.529 W, Oneonta, Alabama.

[6] Woodard and Gunter, CHAMPION MINES: OUR FATHER'S MINES 90 (2011).

[7] Available online: http://www.cityofoneonta.us/ (last visited July 13, 2015).

[8] Woodard and Gunter, CHAMPION MINES, *supra* note 6, at 91.

[9] ALABAMA HOUSE OF REPRESENTATIVES JOURNAL 47 (1889).

[10] *Id* at 146.

[11] ALABAMA SENATE JOURNAL 158 (1889).

after a majority of voters chose to remove the county seat from Blountsville, another election would be held, in which these same voters would have the opportunity to choose Blountsville as the "new" location. And if none of the proposed locations received a majority of votes in the second election, voters could *still* choose Blountsville in a runoff election between the two sites receiving the most votes. All this adds up to mean that, theoretically, it could have taken an act of the general assembly and three subsequent elections, just to decide that the county seat should stay where it was.

However, considering the fact that a brand new courthouse was sitting in Blountsville, Mr. Skeggs might not have been completely off base in giving voters every opportunity to leave the county seat alone. After all, holding three elections was probably much cheaper than building a new courthouse. Still, the House excepted to the Senate's amendment, and the bill was referred to a conference committee.[12] The bill that came out of conference ultimately included Blountsville as a potential county seat, in addition to Nectar, Anderton (now known as Cleveland), W. T. Wood's Store, Brooksville, Blount Springs, Bangor, Chepultepec (present-day Allgood), and "Oneonto."[13]

The misspelling of "Oneonta" is commonly attributed to a mapmaker's error.[14] However, the mistake survives to this day, with long-time residents of Blount County informally shortening the city's name to "Onto." For example, ". . . Haven't seen you in a while. When will you be getting back up to Onto?" The origin of these dueling pronunciations did not make it into the historical record. However, editorials from the weekly *Blount County News and Dispatch* indicate an abrupt and decisive change of heart, at least where the newspaper was concerned. On March 28, 1889 an editorial read, "Oneonto has now a post office, with Captain A. J. Ingram as postmaster."[15] About a month and a half later, the paper declared, "Oneonta is still improving. . . . It is not true, as reported, that the citizens anticipated its becoming the future capital of Alabama, but they are confident that it will be the future County seat of Blount."[16] From this point on, editorials in the *News and Dispatch* consistently referred to the town as "Oneonta."

In spite of this dual identity, Oneonta eventually won the runoff election held in October of 1889. A total of 3,052 votes were cast, and Oneonta won by a margin of 368 votes (about 8%).[17] Attempts to move the county seat constituted a favorite pastime of local landholders and politicians around the turn of the century. There was a failed vote on the issue of removal in 1883 (Blount Springs, the home to a popular resort, was the en vogue

[12] ALABAMA HOUSE OF REPRESENTATIVES JOURNAL 661 (1889).

[13] Acts of Alabama, 600 (1888-89); *see also* Blountsville *Blount County News Dispatch*, May 25, 1889.

[14] Woodard and Gunter, CHAMPION MINES, *supra* note 6, at 91.

[15] Blountsville *Blount County News and Dispatch*, March 28, 1889.

[16] *Id.*, May 9, 1889.

[17] *Id.*, October 10, 1889.

challenger in this contest).[18] And another in 1901.[19] By this time, the editorial staff at the *News and Dispatch* had had enough of the debate (and probably the threat of having to move the location of the newspaper again). They argued forcefully about the financial calamity that would come from having to build yet another set of public buildings, and urged voters, "ponder when you go cast your vote—and vote for Oneonta."[20]

The influence of the railroad and the newly opened Champion Mines in tipping public opinion towards Oneonta in the 1889 election cannot be overstated. The same year that the railroad came to Oneonta and the mines opened, an act of the general assembly and three elections shifted the location of the overwhelming majority of legal business in Blount County. Voters chose to move the county seat from a brand new courthouse in Blountsville to a town that was not even incorporated until over a year later, in 1891. However, besides being a windfall for Oneonta, this move was arguably a fortunate turn of events for preservation of the county's historical documents. A fire of unknown origin destroyed the Blountsville courthouse in 1895.[21]

II. Underwood Opens the Mines of Altoona

With DeBardeleben and Milton H. Smith having brought the L & N Railroad to Oneonta, a lawyer named William Thompson Underwood made the next developmental leap into Blount County. Underwood first became acquainted with industrial players like DeBardeleben through his practice based in Kentucky. He did work clearing titles for industrial ventures in Texas and Minnesota. He had a taste for investment and speculation, and he "[c]ame at last to see . . . that the West was not to be compared to the new growing South as an investment field, so he eventually concentrated at Birmingham."[22] He co-founded the firm of DeBardeleben and Underwood in 1882, whose first venture was to raise capital for the Mary Pratt Furnace (named after Debardeleben's second daughter, who would go on to marry a prominent Birmingham attorney, Walker Percy).[23]

After selling his interest in the Pratt furnace, Underwood bought 3,000 acres of what he considered the best of the coal lands of eastern Blount and Etowah Counties. In his words: "[I] wanted to open mines. I wanted it badly, but my lands were many miles from a railroad, and I was not able to

---

[18] Robin Sterling, PEOPLE AND THINGS FROM THE *BLOUNT COUNTY NEWS AND DISPATCH*, 1879–1889 90-97 (2006).

[19] Robin Sterling, PEOPLE AND THINGS FROM THE *BLOUNT COUNTY NEWS AND DISPATCH*, 1898–1903 79-80 (2006).

[20] *Id.*

[21] *Id* at 27.

[22] Armes, STORY OF COAL AND IRON IN ALABAMA, *supra* note 4, at 306-09.

[23] *Id.*

command one-third of the money needed."[24] Underwood attempted to persuade officials of the Alabama Great Southern Railroad to finance a track that would join with theirs, but they were not interested. Next, he approached Milton H. Smith, of the L & N Railroad about extending his track about twelve miles northeast from Oneonta to Underwood's land. Smith was receptive to the idea, and when Underwood explained that he could not finance the venture himself, he replied that if Underwood had the quality and quantity of coal that he thought he had, then he (Smith) would take care of building the railroad. Underwood hauled thirty wagonloads of coal to Champion to be tested in the furnace. After test results confirmed the quality of Underwood's coal, Smith had the new twelve-mile track extension completed within five months.[25]

The mining operation that resulted from this new construction spurred transformative development into an area of Blount County that Underwood had described as "almost a wilderness." Regarding this transformation, Ethel Armes writes:

> He [Underwood] operated these mines with success, developing one of the most valuable fields of coal in the State, and changing that little known region into a populous and prosperous community. He gave the people, both in and outside of his camp town, schools and churches, encouraged them to establish lodges of Odd Fellows and Masons, and helped them in many ways.[26]

William Underwood is an example of an attorney who helped change Alabama through investment and community development. Like the generations of attorneys before him who followed the money and tried to emulate their planter clients,[27] Underwood entered the industrial business of the clients for whom he spent his early career clearing titles. He adopted Alabama as his home, and was proud of the fact that most of the money for the project in Altoona came from outside the state and would remain invested in Alabama. Reflecting on his contributions, he wrote: "Though my part was not large as compared with that of others, yet it has been enough to entitle me to feel pride and a great interest in the Alabama mineral district . . . and anxiety for its welfare."[28]

---

[24] *Id* at 444.

[25] Woodard and Gunter, CHAMPION MINES, *supra* note 6, at 94.

[26] Armes, STORY OF COAL AND IRON IN ALABAMA, *supra* note 4, at 444.

[27] Paul M. Pruitt, Jr., *The Legal Profession in Antebellum Alabama, 1819–1861*, 43-47, in Paul M. Pruitt, Jr. and Tony A. Freyer, eds., "Alabama's Supreme Court and Legal Institutions: A History" (1999) [unpublished manuscript, filed at University of Alabama, Bounds Law Library].

[28] Armes, STORY OF COAL AND IRON IN ALABAMA, *supra* note 4, at 307.

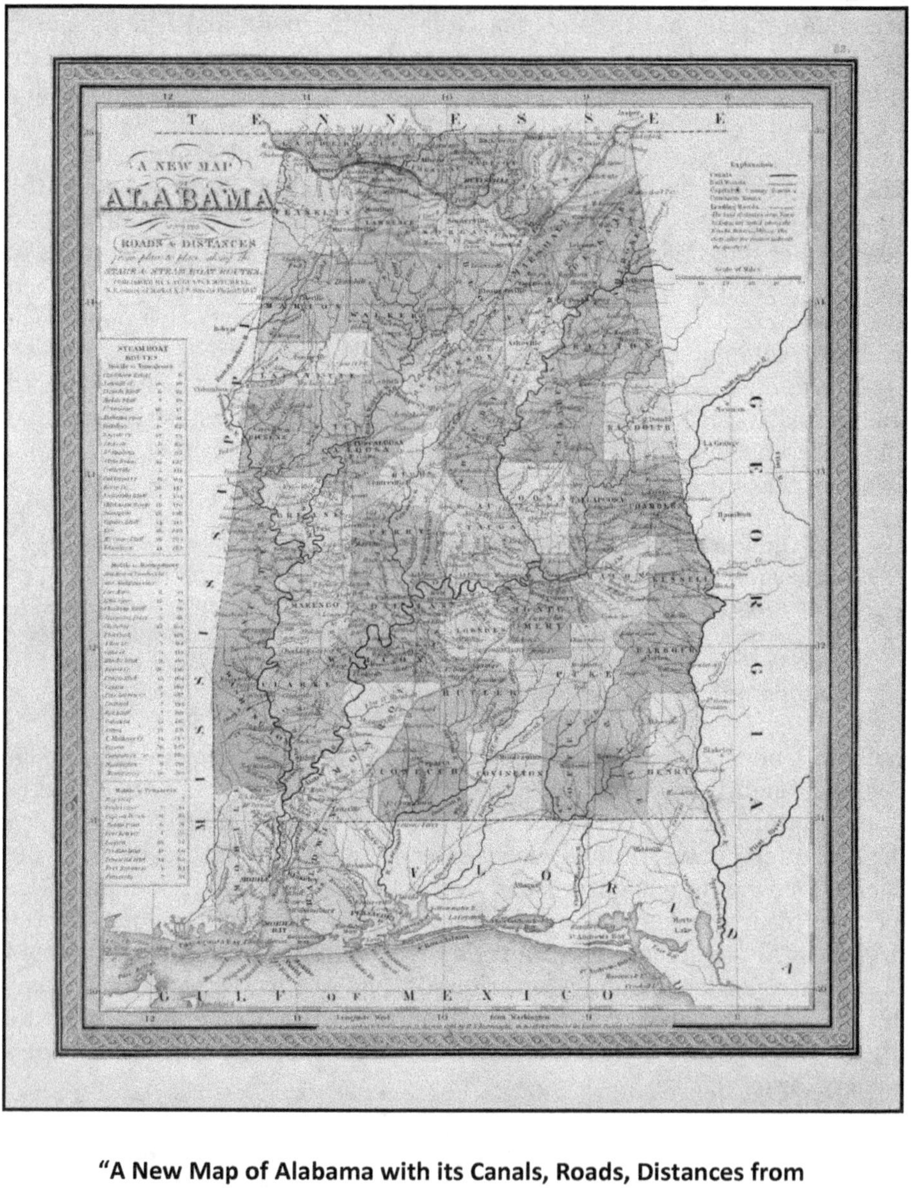

"A New Map of Alabama with its Canals, Roads, Distances from Place to Place, along the Stage & Steam Boat Routes . . ."

1847, published by Philadelphia mapmaker Samuel Augustus Mitchell

Early map of the state names two cities in Blount County: Blountsville and Brooksville. Blountsville was the county seat until 1889 when the government was moved to Oneonta.

Courtesy Barry Lawrence Ruderman Antique Maps, www.RareMaps.com, used by permission

III. Cheney Lime and Cement: Beginning and End in Court

Eminent Domain

The Cheney Lime and Cement Company's "Graystone" plant, in the town of Allgood, was an economic force in Blount County for almost 100 years. Like many industrial concerns in the early twentieth Century, the Cheney operation had a "company town" on site, and paid at least a portion of workers' wages in money minted by the company. In 1903, with DeBardeleben and Smith having brought the L & N Railroad to nearby Oneonta, company founder John A. Cheney recognized that the railroad would be crucial to the widespread distribution of his product. Ultimately, the viability of the company would turn on the ability to ship lime products from the factory by rail. With this in mind, Cheney set out to build a spur track that stretched from his plant in Allgood (at that time, the town was called "Chepultepec"), to the L & N line in Oneonta. This set the stage for the eminent domain and abandonment legal battles that would bookend the productive life of the Graystone plant.

Cheney Lime and Cement (hereafter referred to as "Cheney Lime") was not involved in many legal disputes, and especially few reported cases that made it above the circuit court level. Reflecting on this fact, John W. Cheney, whose grandfather founded the company, commented, "There wasn't a lot of conflict . . . We generally got along with our neighbors in the community."[29] The general absence of Cheney Lime and its ownership in the Blount County court records from the early 1900's bears out this fact. The one exception from that time period occurred right at the beginning of the Graystone plant's productive life. In 1903, John A. Cheney founded the company, and had a vertical kiln built for quicklime production.[30] Around that same time, Cheney brought five eminent domain proceedings against various property owners who were holding out against offers to buy strips of their land near the plant for purposes of constructing the spur line to connect with the L & N, in Oneonta.[31]

Even in 1903 the availability of eminent domain proceedings for railroad construction was an old and well-settled concept in Alabama. The oldest Alabama statutory provision giving corporations this power dates back to an act of the legislature in 1868. Titled "An Act to provide for the creation and regulation of railroad companies in the state of Alabama," the act was quite permissive, and stated that for purposes of constructing a railroad, a corporation was authorized to:

> [E]nter upon any land for the purpose of examining and surveying its railroad line, and . . . appropriate so much thereof as may be deemed necessary for its railroads, including necessary side tracks, depots

[29] Notes from Interview with John W. Cheney, October 2012, p. 1.

[30] Company History, http://www.cheneylime.com/ (last visited July 13, 2015).

[31] Probate Court Minutes, Blount County, AL, 169 (June 20, 1903).

> and workshops, and water stations, materials for construction, except timber, a right of way over adjacent lands, sufficient to enable such company to construct and repair its road . . . .[32]

However, in keeping with the constitutional requirement of just compensation, such construction could not occur until the owner was paid in full or a deposit was made to the owner, to ensure payment.[33] The process for determining just compensation was set forth long before being codified, and dates back to common law court decisions which read similarly to the 1868 statute.[34]

The eminent domain process for would-be railroad companies consisted of five steps: The corporation must first make a good faith offer to buy the land in question. If negotiations to buy the land were unsuccessful, the company could apply to the probate court to institute an eminent domain proceeding, and a hearing date would be set. On the hearing date, the court would hear evidence from both sides and make a determination as to whether the application was due to be granted. These hearings were often mere formalities, with the only serious potential hang-ups being if the owner of the property in question was an infant or incompetent, and if so, whether such a person was properly represented before the court. If the application was granted, a commission of three county residents who qualified as jurors was appointed to inspect the land in question, review the evidence, and make a finding as to just compensation. The judge would make an order awarding that amount to the current landowner and, upon payment, the railroad company could begin construction.[35] On this subject, one historian notes, "Railroad corporations derived extraordinary power from the law . . . and the railroad's right of eminent domain . . . punctuated nearly all property negotiations between railroad lawyers and southerners."[36]

While the power of eminent domain punctuated negotiations between lawyers and landowners, it also punctuated John Cheney's negotiations for his spur line. From the court records outlining the five separate eminent domain proceedings, it appears that none of the parties, Cheney included, was represented by counsel. The court documents list only the parties, with no one appearing on their behalf, along with County Probate Judge Tyre H. Davidson.[37] Even so, it appears that this process worked out well for all

---

[32] Acts of Alabama, 462-472, at 465(1868).

[33] *Id.*

[34] *See, e.g.*, Aldridge v. Tuscumbia, C. & D. R. Co., 2 Stew. & Port. 199 (1832); *see also* Davis v. Tuscumbia, C. & D. R. Co., 4 Stew. & Port. 421 (1833); Jones v. New Orleans & Selma Ry. & Immig. Ass'n, 70 Ala. 227 (1881); and Montgomery So. Ry. v. Sayre, 72 Ala. 443 (1882).

[35] *See id.*

[36] William G. Thomas, LAWYERING FOR THE RAILROAD: BUSINESS, LAW, AND POWER IN THE NEW SOUTH 10 (1999).

[37] *See, e.g.*, *J.A. Cheney vs. M.C. Allgood*, unreported: Probate Court Minutes, Blount County, AL, 173 (1903).

parties involved. With three-man juries interposed between the parties on the issue of valuation, landowners were more likely to get a fair assessment, rather than being snowed under by the influence of outside, moneyed interests. The three men charged with determining what amounted to just compensation were reputable neighbors who were probably more likely than the judge to imagine themselves in the shoes of the landowners being proceeded against.

In the end, Cheney benefited from the considerable power the law granted him to appropriate the land and construct the spur line that was so vital to his company's success, while the landowners were awarded almost five times the average value for an acre of land in Blount County at the time. For a strip of land consisting of 1.6 acres, M. C. Allgood was awarded $175.[38] For other, similar-sized strips of land, the court made awards of $125 and $150.[39] Meanwhile, an optimistic writer of the time was forecasting that the arrival of the L & N, with its attendant growth and development, would cause land values to skyrocket to perhaps $35 an acre in the near future.[40] Comparing the amount paid for the land with the average property value at the time, one might argue that the landowners received a windfall. However, an examination of the case law on this subject helps explain the rationale behind the system of evaluating just compensation in eminent domain cases like these.

An 1881 Alabama Supreme Court case is particularly illustrative. In *Jones v. New Orleans & Selma Railway & Immigration Association*, the Court discussed the concept of just compensation from both the railroad and the landowners' perspectives.[41] In this case, the railroad had begun construction of its line *before* paying the landowner or filing a condemnation petition with the local probate court. Once the petition was finally brought, the landowner argued that just compensation included the value of the newly constructed trackage, because the taking did not officially occur until the petition was filed. The landowner based this argument on a well settled point of common law which stated that any improvements made by a trespasser that become affixed to the land become part of the lawful owner's estate.[42] In other words, "it was the fraud, or the folly of the tortfeasor, to build, to plant, or to sow, on the lands of another, without his consent," and the landowner would be under "no legal or equitable obligation to make compensation for them, or to suffer them dissevered and removed."[43] However, the Court looked past this seemingly clear point of law,

---

[38] *Id* at 183.

[39] *J.A. Cheney vs. Rachel Bynum, et. al.*, unreported: Probate Court Minutes, Blount County, AL, 163 (1903); *J.A. Cheney vs. M.E. Harvy*, unreported: Probate Court Minutes, Blount County, AL, 167 (1903).

[40] Blount County Historical Society, THE HERITAGE OF BLOUNT COUNTY ALABAMA 11 (1989).

[41] Jones v. New Orleans & Selma Ry. & Immig. Ass'n, 70 Ala. 227 (1881).

[42] *Id.* at 232.

[43] *Id.*

holding that such a finding for the property owner would go beyond the "just" compensation prescribed by the Alabama Constitution.

Having discussed the concept of just compensation from the railroad's perspective, the Court went on to outline what would constitute a just outcome for the landowner; and in doing so, it shed some light on what the three-man commission in the Cheney cases probably considered when making its valuations. The *Jones* Court found that just compensation for the landowner did not just include payment for the land taken, but also the surrounding land that was injured by the taking.[44] For instance, if a newly built railroad line cut a cornfield in half, or cut off live-stock from access to a barn, this injury would be considered in addition to the right-of-way value of the comparatively small strip of land. Further, the assessed value of that strip of land would be assessed based on the use to which it would be put, rather than basing the valuation on the use to which it would be put if left in the landowner's possession. The Court quoted Michigan Supreme Court Justice Thomas M. Cooley, who nicely summed up these principles of valuation in his 1886 work, *A Treatise on the Constitutional Limitations Which Rest Upon the Legislative Power of the States of the American Union*:

> The question in these cases relates, first, to the value of the lands appropriated; which is to be assessed with reference to what it is worth for sale, in view of the uses to which it may be applied, and not simply in reference to its productiveness to the owner in the condition in which he sees fit to leave it. Second, if less than the whole estate is taken, then there is further to be considered, how much the portion not taken is increased or diminished in value in consequence of the appropriation.[45]

Understanding these principles, it is now easier to see how $150 constituted just compensation for less than two acres of land in turn-of-the-century Blount County. None of the parties appealed the decision, Cheney paid the landowners, and after quitclaiming his newly acquired interest to the L & N construction began on the spur line that would serve the Graystone plant.

The Abandonment Fight

With the spur line completed, Cheney Lime operated largely free of legal complications for 80 years. There were occasional small personal injury claims, as well as labor disputes, but again, nothing that made it into the courts of record. Then, in 1983, the L & N announced its intent to abandon the track that served the Graystone plant and to discontinue service along that line. As the U.S. Court of Appeals for the District of Columbia Circuit noted in a 1990 opinion that would come out of the resulting legal dispute:

---

[44] *Id.*

[45] *Id., quoting* Thomas M. Cooley, CONSTITUTIONAL LIMITATIONS 705-12 (1868).

"A limestone products factory without access to rail transportation is apparently not good for much. . . ."[46] John W. Cheney recounts learning of the L & N's decision one day at work:

> I had just graduated from college and went to work for the company. I hadn't been there six months, when one day, two guys come pulling up to the office in a sedan and ask to speak to my dad. They just went in, handed him this letter, and started walking away. . . .[47]

Thus began a decade long legal battle to keep the plant viable, which would bring the Cheneys before the Interstate Commerce Commission and the D.C. Circuit, and would ultimately result in Alabama's first and only acquisition of a railroad under the Staggers Rail Act of 1980.[48]

At first, Cheney attempted to negotiate the purchase of the line that served his plant. This was a drawn-out process. CSX acquired L & N's interest in the track during this period, and CSX did not believe Cheney could actually raise enough capital to purchase the line.[49] Once it became apparent that Cheney was a viable purchaser, CSX dropped plans to abandon the line and said that it would continue service. According to Cheney, CSX had no desire to allow Cheney to operate that section of track because this would lead to competition for "overhead freight."[50] This means that potential clients would be paying Cheney, rather than CSX, to ship their goods over that section of track. With this in mind, it is no surprise that in 1987 when CSX renewed its plans to abandon and discontinue service, it continued to fight off Cheney's attempts to purchase the track. Cheney, however, had a legal remedy.

The Staggers Rail Act of 1980 was an attempt to prune down over 90 years of accumulated railroad regulations overseen by the Interstate Commerce Commission.[51] The act provided for easier entries and exits from the railroad market, and contained a provision that allowed "financially responsible" parties to force railroad carriers to sell their abandoned lines.[52] Pursuant to this mandatory sale provision, Cheney filed an application for forced sale with the I.C.C. on March 19, 1987.[53] For simplicity's sake, the reader can imagine the 54.61 miles of track that Cheney was trying to buy as

---

[46] Cheney R. Co. v. I.C.C., 902 F.2d 66, 67 (D.C. Cir. 1990).

[47] Notes from Interview with John W. Cheney, October 2012, p. 2.

[48] 49 U.S.C.A. §10910.

[49] Notes from Interview with John W. Cheney, October 2012.

[50] Cheney R. Co. v. I.C.C., 902 F.2d 66, 68 (D.C. Cir. 1990).

[51] Kenneth R. Feinberg, DEREGULATION OF THE TRANSPORTATION INDUSTRY 602 (Practising Law Institute 1981).

[52] *See* 49 C.F.R. Part 1151 (1983); *see also* Cheney R. Co. v. I.C.C., 902 F.2d 66, 68 (D.C. Cir. 1990).

[53] Petition of Cheney R. Co., Inc., to Reopen Proceedings (unpublished) 6 (1993).

the vertical stem in an uppercase "I."[54] This section of track would allow Cheney to serve the Graystone plant, as well as other shippers located between the main CSX lines that made up the top and bottom of the "I."

The application looked like an easy victory for Cheney. All of the requirements for a forced sale were satisfied: CSX had abandoned the track, Cheney had sufficient capital to be deemed "financially responsible," and the application was properly submitted.[55] However, on April 20, 1987, the last day they could have possibly done so, Tyson Foods filed a competing application with the I.C.C. to purchase 1.46 miles of the same track, where the main line met the feeder line.[56] Tyson's purchase of this tiny section of track would cut Cheney off from the main line in the North, and redirect all of the plant's rail traffic southward, not to mention the lost ability to compete for overhead traffic along the feeder line. Once Tyson filed their competing application, Cheney went from having the law on its side to losing almost every court proceeding that would follow.

On May 28, 1987, the I.C.C. denied a motion filed by Cheney requesting that Tyson's competing application be rejected.[57] Cheney argued that the board lacked statutory authority to review competing applications, pointing to the fact that language specifically authorizing such review was deleted from the Act during conference committee.[58] The board disagreed, finding that the lack of explicit authority to review competing applications did not amount to a prohibition of such review.[59] This being a federal regulatory decision, Cheney's subsequent appeal was heard in the U.S. Court of Appeals for the District of Columbia Circuit.[60] The court affirmed, finding that Congress' silence with regard to how to deal with competing applications suggested not a prohibition, but simply a decision *not to mandate* a particular solution.[61] The court also agreed that simultaneous review of competing applications was consistent with the intended purpose of the forced sale act,[62] that purpose being to help shippers avoid loss of rail service when railroads decided to abandon their lines. First-come-first-served review could lead to delays if the first applicant (or two) did not pan out.

With the question settled as to whether the board could consider competing applications simultaneously, CSX was allowed to go forward with its plan to sell Tyson the roughly 1.5 mile northern section of track and leave Cheney without a northern interchange. Tyson subsequently operated the

---

[54] *Id.*

[55] *See* 49 C.F.R. Part 1151.1-4 (1983).

[56] Petition of Cheney R. Co., Inc., to Reopen Proceedings (unpublished) 7 (1993).

[57] Surface Transportation Board Commission Decision, 1987 [WL 98590], 1-2 (1987).

[58] *Id.*

[59] *Id.*

[60] Cheney R. Co. v. I.C.C., 902 F.2d 66 (D.C. Cir. 1990).

[61] *Id.* at 68.

[62] *Id.*

tiny section of track for just three years, the statutory minimum allowed under a forced sale, and then sold the track back to CSX.[63] To ship products North, Cheney was forced to use an approximately 60-mile detour, which rendered the Graystone plant economically non-viable.

The plant was decommissioned, but the company's general offices are still located in Allgood. (The "Landmark" plant near Alabaster, Alabama remains operational.)[64] Regarding "Graystone's" fate, John W. Cheney laments: "I wanted to keep the plant open, but I got out-voted. . . . If we had been able to buy that track and operate our railroad, there is no doubt in my mind that we would still be shipping lime out of the plant today."[65] Instead, the 109-year-old plant sits idle, barely visible from State Highway 75 when there are no leaves on the trees to obscure the view. It is a monument to Blount County's first era of industrial growth. And with eminent domain and federal regulatory actions playing major roles in the plant's birth and death, it is also a relic of Blount County's legal history.

IV. Conclusion

The Champion and Altoona Mines, as well as Cheney Lime and Cement Company's Graystone plant, are three of the most significant industrial landmarks—regardless of era—in Blount County history. There is a relatively large body of historical scholarship surrounding these landmarks (less so, Cheney Lime), but there is precious little treatment of this history from a legal perspective. I hope that this chapter has contributed to a more complete understanding of these episodes in Blount County's history by highlighting the legal battles, regulatory structures, and legislation that helped shape these otherwise well-documented historical landmarks.

---

[63] Petition of Cheney R. Co., Inc., to Reopen Proceedings (unpublished) 4 (1993).

[64] *See* http://www.cheneylime.com/ (last visited July 13, 2015).

[65] Notes from Interview with John W. Cheney, October 2012, p. 2.

Pioneers in Alabama Legal History: A Firm Understanding of the History of Alabama

Mike Dodson

I. Introduction

Perhaps no other occupation is as reflective of the society in which it operates as the law. As a natural consequence of the profession, lawyers are tied to the social and business interactions of the clients they serve; the overall structure, profile, and spirit of the legal profession are patterned after the prevalent sociocultural environment. In other words, where the money is, the lawyers are.

To that end, Southern lawyers are creatures of the local spheres in which they work. In times of agrarian dominance, legal evolution in the South had a distinctively rural tint. When industry began its advent, the legal dynamic shifted considerably towards a discussion about labor and big business. Even in the modern era, as civil rights and a "great society"[1] have taken a dominant place in the social consciousness, the law has followed. In this way, lawyers closely track the evolution of society, and "[t]he life of the law has not been logic: it has been experience."[2]

Alabama is an excellent example of this gradual evolution, and one story in particular is especially illustrative: the story of the Burr and Forman law firm in Birmingham, Alabama. From roots in antebellum rural Alabama and Mississippi, Burr and Forman has created a lasting legal presence that has tracked, and in some ways shaped, the landscape of the state. Because of its unique bloodline running from rural agrarian society to the modern-day cosmopolis of Birmingham, Burr and Forman stands as a particularly helpful study of the underlying cultural, social, and economic trends of Alabama and the South as a whole.

This chapter proceeds in four main parts. The first part will examine the roots of Burr and Forman from its origins with the Mississippi-based legal practice of Colonel William Alexander Percy. Colonel Percy, a native of Huntsville, was a Civil War hero and an accomplished practitioner in the Yazoo Delta city of Greenville, Mississippi. The second part examines the exodus of Walker Percy, the grandfather of the esteemed novelist of the same name. Walker began in Birmingham, fresh out of law school, and would become one of the first partners of the firm that would later become Burr and Forman. The third part will examine the other name partners of

1 President Lyndon B. Johnson, Remarks in Athens at Ohio University (May 7, 1964).

2 O. W. Holmes, Jr., THE COMMON LAW 1 (1881).

Burr and Forman with a focus on the involvement of these men with the rise of industrialism in Birmingham, as well as a number of other major historical events and concepts with which the firm was involved. Finally, the paper will conclude with an examination of Burr and Forman in more recent years, including a brief overview of modern Alabama in the 1990s and early 2000s and how the firm has once again tracked the development of the state.

II. Gray Eagle

The antebellum South was a largely agrarian society, with the vast majority of the population living in rural isolation.[3] In fact, in certain plantation districts of the Deep South, with Alabama as a particular paradigm, white residents were significantly outnumbered by their black slaves.[4] Particularly in regions like the Black Belt, where the cash crop of cotton was king and white planters were amassing tremendous wealth, large swaths of land were owned by a very small number of persons, and white population density was minimal at best.[5]

During this time, lawyers were especially interested in agriculture-related law.[6] Examples abound of rural property cases that served as the central focus of the legal profession during that era.[7] Lawyers at this time were involved in cases over injuries to hogs by dogs,[8] actions concerning slaves,[9] and losses of cotton.[10] Thus, as the local society was dominated by agricultural interests, so too were the local attorneys.

Practicing law at this time could also be a difficult proposal. With the wide geographical separation of land holdings came a wide physical separation of legal practice.[11] While one client might be close to a centralized town

---

[3] *See* Paul M. Pruitt, Jr. and Tony A. Freyer, "Alabama's Supreme Court and Legal Institutions," 2 [hereinafter ASCLI] (unpublished manuscript, on file with author) (stating that the "proportion of rural to urban population" in 1860 was 94.9).

[4] Janet Duitsman Cornelius, SLAVE MISSIONS AND THE BLACK CHURCH IN THE ANTEBELLUM SOUTH 23 (1999) ("In the 1840s blacks outnumbered whites along the Alabama and lower Tombigbee Rivers, in the Tennessee Valley, and in the central Black Belt.").

[5] *See The Cotton Economy of the Old South*, AM. AGRIC. HISTORY PRIMER, http://rickwoten.com/CottonEconomy.html (last visited July 6, 2015) (discussing the concentration of lands in white planters' hands).

[6] *See* Pruitt and Freyer, ASCLI, *supra* note 3, at 14.

[7] Property cases, especially related to slavery, abounded in antebellum Alabama. For one example of these cases and the property law precedents they set, see Rowan v. Hutchisson, 27 Ala. 328 (1855). For more such cases, see *infra* note 9.

[8] Smith v. Causey, 28 Ala. 655 (1856).

[9] Rowan v. Hutchisson, 27 Ala. 328 (1855); Thomas v. De Graffenreid, 27 Ala. 651 (1855); Lanier v. Branch Bank at Montgomery, 18 Ala. 625 (1851); Beall v. Ledlow, 14 Ala. 523 (1848); *see also* Wolfe v. Parham, 18 Ala. 441 (1850) (relating to a disputed contract for transport of slaves); Lanier v. Rainey, 15 Ala. 667 (1849) (discussing implications of a trust with a slave).

[10] Jones v. Sims & Scott, 6 Port. 138 (Ala. 1837).

[11] *See* William P. Trent, SOUTHERN STATESMEN OF THE OLD RÉGIME 208 (1897) (discussing how

or village, another client might be significantly farther away, and traveling was necessary to garner a sufficient living.[12] Adding to this need for mobility, access to courts could also be limited by distance: although Alabama counties were authorized to have local courts beginning with the Constitution of 1819,[13] many of the state's present counties were nonexistent at that time.[14] Thus, the state of Alabama, today divided into sixty-seven counties,[15] was in 1819 only composed of twenty-two counties,[16] meaning large swaths of land with few courthouses. Furthermore, access to federal jurisdiction was extremely limited: federal circuits were notoriously difficult to travel to, exacting significant hardships from the judges.[17] But, of course, on the other side of the bench were the lawyers who had to ride to meet the judges.[18]

All of these factors combined to create a unique framework with which the legal profession could evolve during this era. Lawyers, impressed by wealth when visiting their landholding clients, sought to emulate the aristocratic lifestyles of rural society.[19] Furthermore, the relative distance and resultant concentration of lawyers led to a system of camaraderie and home rule within the courts.[20] Thus the foundation for legal society in Alabama was born.

Colonel William Alexander (W. A.) Percy—the father of Burr and Forman's first attorney, Walker Percy—was a rural lawyer, similar to those seen

---

"[a] circuit was really a circuit in Georgia; for the lawyers rode on horseback from one county-seat to another").

12 *Id.* (stating that circuit-traveling ensured lawyers could get "an immense number of new cases, and charge[] heavy fees").

13 ALA. CONST. of 1819, art. V, §1.

14 *See Delegates to the Constitutional Convention Held at Huntsville July 5–August 2, 1819*, ALA. STATE LEGISLATURE, http://www.legislature.state.al.us/aliswww/history/constitutions/1819/1819delegates.html (last visited July 6, 2015) (listing only twenty-two counties at the delegation).

15 *Alabama Counties*, ALA. DEP'T OF ARCHIVES & HISTORY, http://www.archives.state.al.us/counties.html (last visited July 6, 2015).

16 *Delegates to the Constitutional Convention*, *supra* note 14.

17 Eric J. Gribbin, Note, *California Split: A Plan to Divide the Ninth Circuit*, 47 DUKE L.J. 351, 359 (1997) ("Although each Congress was peppered with complaints from Justices about the time-consuming and exhausting travel schedules precipitated by the circuit-riding requirement, these duties remained . . . a part of the judicial system until 1891."); *see also* Stephen P. Brown, JOHN MCKINLEY AND THE ANTEBELLUM SUPREME COURT: CIRCUIT RIDING IN THE OLD SOUTHWEST 129-42 (2012).

18 *See also* TONY A. FREYER & TIMOTHY DIXON, DEMOCRACY AND JUDICIAL INDEPENDENCE: A HISTORY OF THE FEDERAL COURTS OF ALABAMA, 1820–1994 23-31 (1995) (discussing the legal working culture between the relatively small number of attorneys admitted to the federal bar and the judges with whom they worked).

19 *See* Pruitt and Freyer, ASCLI, *supra* note 3, at 45 ("It is hardly surprising that prosperous lawyers should identify with the social classes which make up their clientele. . . .").

20 *See* Trent, SOUTHERN STATESMEN, *supra* note 11, at 208 (discussing how "in the . . . State of Alabama at this time, where, if we may trust Judge Baldwin, it was highly unusual, if not improper, for a judge to insult a 'young probationer and candidate' for legal honors by asking him a single question [before admission to the bar]" (internal footnote omitted)).

throughout the South, who pursued multiple land-related cases during his career. A native of Huntsville, Alabama, the Colonel was born into a distinctly Mississippi family: his grandfather had settled in the early Natchez province following service in the British royal navy, and his father had been born in the same area—Adams County, Mississippi.[21] From an early age, Percy was familiar with the trappings of land ownership in the rural South: his father, Squire Thomas George Percy, owned a plantation in Madison County, Alabama and, in 1829, bought land on Deer Creek in Mississippi for the establishment of a plantation that would be known as Percy Place.[22]

The area chosen for Percy Place was an excellent location to settle a plantation and begin the practice of law, and Percy's choice reflected the agricultural preference of antebellum society. Though a small stream, Deer Creek is a tributary of the Yazoo River and thus contributes to the waters of the Mississippi Delta region.[23] The Yazoo River, which flows down a significant portion of western Mississippi, was bordered by a fertile cotton-producing region.[24] It was in this area that Thomas Percy sought to settle upon leaving Huntsville, but the patriarch of the Percy family would never call Deer Creek his home. After buying the land in 1829, Squire Thomas died in Huntsville.[25] Thereafter, Squire Thomas's widow moved with her three sons to Deer Creek and settled down for the rest of her life.[26] By this time, the future Colonel Percy had graduated from college.[27]

W. A. Percy received his undergraduate degree from Princeton University before studying law at the University of Virginia.[28] While at Virginia, he was so successful at his studies that a professor remarked that he would surely be in the forefront of his profession.[29] However, after law school, he showed little inclination to practice law, and instead focused on the planter life established by his father.[30] It was around this time that Percy married Nannie Armstrong, uniting his Mississippi lineage with a prestigious eastern Tennessee family.[31]

---

[21] BIOGRAPHICAL AND HISTORICAL MEMOIRS OF MISSISSIPPI, VOL. II, at 581 (The Reprint Co. 1978) (1891).

[22] Bertram Wyatt-Brown, THE HOUSE OF PERCY: HONOR, MELANCHOLY, AND IMAGINATION IN A SOUTHERN FAMILY 175 (1994).

[23] Sec. of War, REPORT FROM CAPTAIN ERIC BERGLAND, CORPS OF ENGINEERS, OF A PRELIMINARY EXAMINATION OF DEER CREEK, MISSISSIPPI (1885).

[24] *Id.*

[25] Wyatt-Brown, THE HOUSE OF PERCY, *supra* note 22.

[26] *Id.*

[27] Lewis Baker, THE PERCYS OF MISSISSIPPI: POLITICS AND LITERATURE IN THE NEW SOUTH 4 (1983).

[28] BIOGRAPHICAL AND HISTORICAL MEMOIRS OF MISSISSIPPI, *supra* note 21.

[29] *Id.*

[30] Baker, THE PERCYS OF MISSISSIPPI, *supra* note 27.

[31] *Id.*

The first years of marriage to Nannie in Deer Creek were not easy: although Deer Creek and the Yazoo Delta were extremely fertile grounds for crops, natural obstacles impeded the newly settled family's efforts.[32] In the end, however, the efforts struck pay dirt, and the Percys prospered; their hospitality and wealth garnered an admirable reputation throughout western Mississippi.[33]

As with many Southerners, the arrival of the Civil War prompted substantial changes for Colonel Percy. Although against secession, Percy would be responsible for fielding the Mississippi Swamp Rangers, the first company to depart from Washington County for the Confederate cause.[34] These beginnings of wartime service ultimately led him to participation in the Siege of Vicksburg, to the battles in Virginia, and, of course, to win the ultimate rank of colonel.[35] His service was considered to be so illustrious and respectable that he earned the nickname "the Gray Eagle of the Delta," a respectful moniker that would follow him for the rest of his life.[36]

After the war, Percy returned home to the Mississippi Delta.[37] Percy Place had suffered greatly during the war and, although he did not abandon the plantation, Percy packed up his family and moved to Greenville, Mississippi to start anew.[38] Once settled in the small town, Percy began a new practice of law and quickly set about becoming involved in the local political scene.[39]

Politics in the Reconstruction Era arose from a very tumultuous time in the South. The local population was under constant strain from a variety of civil disturbances, including riots and Ku Klux Klan violence, not to mention widespread poverty.[40] Faced with Republican rule and African American suffrage, many white Democrats sought to preserve "white supremacy" by seeking new representation in the state house: specifically, and especially in the devastated Yazoo Delta, the call arose for a "redemption" of home rule by Southerners.[41] Colonel Percy was one example of a politician who answered this call, entering into the political sphere quite successfully. From 1870–1888, he was widely considered to be the lead politician on the

---

[32] *Id.* at 5.

[33] *Id.*

[34] BIOGRAPHICAL AND HISTORICAL MEMOIRS OF MISSISSIPPI, *supra* note 21.

[35] Wyatt-Brown, THE HOUSE OF PERCY, *supra* note 22.

[36] Baker, THE PERCYS OF MISSISSIPPI, *supra* note 27, at 7.

[37] BIOGRAPHICAL AND HISTORICAL MEMOIRS OF MISSISSIPPI, *supra* note 21.

[38] Baker, THE PERCYS OF MISSISSIPPI, *supra* note 27.

[39] *Id.*

[40] For a study of the complex pressures on the nation during the Reconstruction Era, see Eric Foner, RECONSTRUCTION: AMERICA'S UNFINISHED REVOLUTION, 1863–1877 (1988). As one example of the sort of rumors prevalent during Reconstruction, both substantiated and fictional, see *id.* at 434-36 (providing a sample of both black and white-inspired violence in the South during the Reconstruction).

[41] BIOGRAPHICAL AND HISTORICAL MEMOIRS OF MISSISSIPPI, *supra* note 21.

"race question," and in 1875, he was appointed to a "committee of seven" that "issued a call for the reorganization of the state democracy preliminary to the profound struggle which resulted in the overthrow of base and alien rule."[42] Thus, Percy was instrumental in orchestrating Mississippi's "redemption" from Republican control, assisting with the continuation of white dominance in local culture.

The ongoing stress from both his political and legal careers was not without its negative consequences. The loss of productivity at the plantation as well as the demands of his family began to have a taxing effect on the Colonel's finances.[43] At this point, his sons were all arriving at college age.[44] Deciding that Princeton, his alma mater, was too expensive, he instead opted for the more affordable University of the South in Tennessee.[45] One son, Walker Percy, heeded his father's wishes and attended the University of the South before going to the University of Virginia for law school.[46] But with these tuition bills and related expenses multiplying, and with the expenses of normal home life remaining substantial and sustained, the Colonel was faced with severe money shortages.[47] Thus, towards the end of his life, Colonel Percy was drastically overworked, ultimately leading to his death at the age of 53.[48]

The story of Colonel Percy represents the earliest stages of agrarian Deep South attorneys. His ultimate goal was to have a law practice that was ancillary to his position of gentleman planter, and for a while his dream seems to have been fulfilled. His military service in the Civil War compounded his honor and military prestige, qualities to which the mythology of the Deep South is so deferential. In terms of clients, Percy was also representative of agrarian society. His law practice seems to have been structured around the local plantations and lands of the Yazoo Delta,[49] and at times he extended attention to his personal land holdings and contracts.[50] Based on these characteristics, the first chapter of the Burr and Forman law firm closely mirrored the overall agricultural society in which it operated.

---

[42] *Id.*

[43] Wyatt-Brown, THE HOUSE OF PERCY, *supra* note 22, at 177.

[44] *Id.*

[45] *Id.*

[46] *Id.*

[47] *Id.*

[48] *Id.*

[49] *See, e.g.*, Fox v. Miller, 71 Miss. 598 (1893) (providing one example, albeit later in the 1800s, of a land transaction with which Percy was involved).

[50] *See, e.g.*, A.B. Carson v. W.A. Percy, 57 Miss. 97 (1879) (providing one example of Percy's personal-life practice, in this case involving a landing on a plantation riverfront).

III. A Move to Birmingham

The time immediately following the Civil War was a tumultuous time for all Southerners. The previously profitable agricultural economy was turned on its head, and thus much of the old wealth that had been consolidated in plantations and the land-related economy was diverted to other pursuits.[51] In addition, profit-seeking Northerners traveled to the South for enterprise opportunities,[52] opening the way for new power structures that would reshape Alabama's cultural and political landscape.[53] The influx of new entrepreneurialism and shifting investment, coupled with a massive industrial revolution and post-war building process, led to perhaps the largest development in modern Alabama history: Birmingham.

Although Birmingham became the largest city and industrial center in Alabama, following the Civil War the city was nothing more than a remote valley inhabited by a few landholding families.[54] However, during the post-war industrial boom, Birmingham rapidly gained prominence as the only location in the world where all materials necessary for steel production could be procured in such close proximity.[55] As the importance—and price—of steel rose, so too did the importance of production.[56] Thus, Birmingham went from a small, relatively uninhabited place in 1871 to a booming metropolis virtually overnight.[57] By the Census numbers, for example, Birmingham grew from a population of about 38,000 in 1900[58] to a population of about 133,000 in 1910[59]—a growth rate of nearly 250% in just ten years.

The new and prospering steel industry naturally led to other growth. Apart from steel-related production, other support businesses were created to profit from the new population. Commercial banking began to gain ground in Birmingham, beginning with First National Bank in 1872 (later to become AmSouth)[60] and extending to the Exchange Security Bank in 1928

---

[51] *See* Pruitt and Freyer, ASCLI, *supra* note 3, at 8.

[52] James Wilford Garner, Reconstruction in Mississippi 135 (1902) (discussing the immigration of Northerners to the South for profit-making opportunities).

[53] *See, e.g.*, Freyer & Dixon, Democracy and Judicial Independence, *supra* note 18, at 78 (discussing the influence of the so-called Big Mules coalition).

[54] *The Founding of Birmingham*, Alabama Dep't of Archives & History, http://www.alabamamoments.alabama.gov/sec29qs.html (last visited July 6, 2015) (calling the Birmingham site "a corn field in a poor hill country valley with no navigable river").

[55] W. David Lewis, *Birmingham Iron and Steel Companies*, in Encyclopedia of Alabama, http://www.encyclopediaofalabama.org/face/Article.jsp?id=h-1597 (last visited July 6, 2015).

[56] *Id.*

[57] *See The Founding of Birmingham*, *supra* note 54.

[58] Population of the 100 Largest Urban Places: 1900, U.S. Bureau of the Census, http://www.census.gov/population/www/documentation/twps0027/tab13.txt (June 15, 1998) (listing Birmingham city as the 99th largest urban place, with a population of 38,415).

[59] Population of the 100 Largest Urban Places: 1910, U.S. Bureau of the Census, http://www.census.gov/population/www/documentation/twps0027/tab14.txt (June 15, 1998) (listing Birmingham city as the 36th largest urban place, with a population of 132,685).

[60] *AmSouth History*, Regions, http://www.regions.com/about_regions/amsouth_info.rf (last

(later to become Regions Bank).[61] Buffalo Rock Company—today, a regional beverage manufacturer—derived from the Alabama Grocery Company, which was founded by a Mississippian who relocated to Birmingham to take advantage of the boom economy.[62] The Parisian department store, owned today by Belk, opened in 1887 as a milliner and general purveyor of dry goods, thus supplying the growing demand for retail.[63] All over the city, new business interests were expanding and evolving, making Birmingham one of the most impressive metropolitan areas in the nation.

Behind a significant amount of this growth and prosperity was the dominance of the Tennessee, Coal, Iron, and Railroad Company (TCI), particularly through its strategy of regional integration. The largest and most important steel and mining company in Birmingham, TCI would become the second largest steel producer in the United States.[64] Before being sold to U.S. Steel in 1907, TCI would absorb a large number of localized steel production outfits in and around Birmingham,[65] including the important DeBardeleben Coal and Iron Company.[66] This integration would provide the personal and economic connections necessary for the birth of the Burr and Forman law firm.

The founder of the DeBardeleben Coal and Iron Company, Henry DeBardeleben, was a leading New South industrialist from Autauga County, Alabama[67] and was responsible for founding the city of Bessemer.[68] After serving in the Civil War, DeBardeleben moved to Birmingham and began the Pratt Coal and Coke Company with two other well-known industrialists—Truman Aldrich, a Northerner and esteemed Congressman, and James Sloss, founder of the fabled Sloss Furnaces near First Avenue North.[69] DeBardeleben would ultimately earn the name "King of the Southern Iron World,"[70] and his massive acquisition of $13 million in Birmingham proper-

---

visited July 6, 2015).

[61] *Regions History*, REGIONS, http://www.regions.com/about_regions/regions_history.rf (last visited July 6, 2015).

[62] *History of Buffalo Rock Company*, BUFFALO ROCK COMPANY, http://www.buffalorock.com/about-us/history (last visited July 6, 2015).

[63] Ted Pratt, *Parisian History Stitched into City's Fabric*, BIRMINGHAM NEWS, Mar. 17, 2002, at 34.

[64] Gregory D. L. Morris, *Still They Ride*, FIN. HIST., Winter 2004, at 20.

[65] *See id.*

[66] Patrick Samway, *The Union of the DeBardeleben and Percy Families*, MISS. Q., Winter 1997, at 20. [For a general history of TCI's impressive growth and acquisitions in late-nineteenth century Alabama, see also Ethel Armes, THE STORY OF COAL AND IRON IN ALABAMA 420-35 (1910).]

[67] *Id.* at 16-17.

[68] *Id.* at 21.

[69] *Id.* at 19.

[70] *Id.*

ty would make his DeBardeleben Coal and Iron Company "the largest industrial undertaking in the South at that time."[71]

Henry DeBardeleben and Walker Percy's paths crossed and finally united on April 17, 1888 when Percy married DeBardeleben's second daughter, Mary Pratt, in the Church of the Advent in downtown Birmingham.[72] From this union, the city of Birmingham would not only get one of its most talented local artists (the son of Walker Percy was LeRoy, who would ultimately father Walker's namesake grandson/author)[73] but also one of the greatest business-legal relationships the city had ever seen. Beginning with Percy's admission to the Alabama State Bar in 1893, Henry DeBardeleben would ensure that his son-in-law was never short of legal work from TCI Company, which had formally taken over DeBardeleben Coal in 1892.[74]

Walker Percy represents the next chapter in the Burr and Forman history. Having grown up in Greenville, Mississippi and Percy Place, Percy left rural Mississippi to attend college at the University of the South before studying law at the University of Virginia.[75] Upon graduating, Percy opted to move to Birmingham rather than returning to his father and brother's practice in Greenville.[76] Seeing Birmingham as a boomtown,[77] and no doubt having become acquainted with young society (and young society women) during his college years,[78] Percy would quickly blend in and settle down in his legal career in Birmingham. When Henry DeBardeleben purchased a seat as the Vice President of TCI, Walker was awarded with the position of chief counsel for the entire company.[79] This position, understandably one of high power in Birmingham, would lead to numerous other experiences, opportunities, and positions of importance. He would become a leading attorney for a large number of industrial interests throughout the city: he would serve as the president of Berney National Bank in 1890 (later absorbed by First National, which would in turn become AmSouth),[80] and he would also represent important entities like the city waterworks.[81] In sum, Percy was able to gain a strong foothold in the industrial capital of Birmingham and from that point was able to launch an impressive legal empire.

---

[71] *Id.* at 21.

[72] *Id.* at 22.

[73] *Id.* at 23. In addition, attorney Walker Percy was the grandfather to another notable member of the Percy family: author Walker Percy's brother, Billups Phinizy Percy, who was a long-standing and much-admired member of the faculty at Tulane University Law School.

[74] *Id.* at 24.

[75] Wyatt-Brown, THE HOUSE OF PERCY, *supra* note 22, at 247.

[76] *Id.*

[77] *Id.*

[78] Samway, *Union of the DeBardeleben and Percy Families, supra* note 66, at 22.

[79] Wyatt-Brown, THE HOUSE OF PERCY, *supra* note 22, at 247.

[80] Samway, *Union of the DeBardeleben and Percy Families, supra* note 66, at 28.

[81] Carl V. Harris, POLITICAL POWER IN BIRMINGHAM 128 (Dewey W. Grantham ed., 1977).

Percy was also prominent in local affairs, both socially and politically. A marriage to the wealthy DeBardeleben family alone carried significant baggage, but Percy independently "pursued a life that merged his interests with those of the other elite of Birmingham."[82] He was a member of the Roebuck, Southern, and Birmingham Country Clubs, having helped form the latter in 1898[83] and eventually serving as its president in 1909.[84] It was in these environments that Percy seemed particularly well-suited: as an avid golfer, he was credited with being an original golf course dealmaker, orchestrating and finalizing plans for any number of his private business interests.[85]

Percy's contributions to the political and business realms of Alabama seem to have been substantially driven by a vehement protection of industrialism. At the time of his peak in Birmingham society, Birmingham was in a continuing storm of racial tension. Many white citizens of Birmingham were convinced that the city's black population was lazy, leading to a push for vagrancy laws.[86] Percy himself is documented as having condescendingly referred to the "excessively irregular work habits" of black laborers in Birmingham, complaining that "the ordinary Negro . . . works the least percentage of time" and that "[t]hey want to squander their money. The chief use they have for it is for three purposes—craps, women and whiskey. I do not believe anybody will deny that. They work for two or three days—just long enough to get money to shoot craps."[87] Thus, Percy could unquestionably be accused of racist views demeaning to his black laborers.

But was this racism or just industrialism? If the two were possibly separable during this period, Percy could have made a case for the latter. As evidence, Percy's arguments against the county fee system would evidence industrialist tendencies over outspoken racism. The local business elite detested this system, which consisted of providing per-incident fees to county officials for arrests, services of process, and commencements of proceedings in lieu of salaries.[88] In particular, "Walker Percy denounced 'the disorganization of labor by indiscriminate arrests of working negroes for trivial offenses.'"[89] It is not clear whether Percy's fairness towards the laborers was early twentieth-century industrialism devoid of racism or simply racism conquered by monetary interests, but in any event Percy did seem to prioritize business over a social agenda.

---

[82] Samway, *Union of the DeBardeleben and Percy Families, supra* note 66, at 30.

[83] Wyatt-Brown, THE HOUSE OF PERCY, *supra* note 22, at 248.

[84] Samway, *Union of the DeBardeleben and Percy Families, supra* note 66, at 30.

[85] Wyatt-Brown, THE HOUSE OF PERCY, *supra* note 22, at 248.

[86] *See* Harris, POLITICAL POWER IN BIRMINGHAM, *supra* note 81, at 198.

[87] *Id.*

[88] *Id.* at 207-08.

[89] *Id.* at 211.

Percy's protection of business interests against social agendas did not stop with the vagrancy laws. Local religious and progressive groups had seized on the political winds to seek the closure of "saloons" in the Birmingham area.[90] Seen as dens of sin and depravity, and thus contributing to the "allegedly unreliable and menacing behavior of blacks," a law was passed to inflict severe penalties on saloons that operated during Sundays.[91] To Percy, such a law represented a devastating shift in precedent: shortages of both skilled and unskilled labor were rampant across the nation, and closing saloons would only encourage the best laborers to leave Birmingham.[92] Fearing a mass exodus of workers and thus fearing for his own profitability, Percy took to the stands, even going so far as to speak at anti-prohibition rallies throughout the city.[93]

It is unsurprising that this background would serve as the perfect platform from which Percy could become a state legislator, and the opportunity soon arose for him to act on this potential. The original system of government in Birmingham consisted of an aldermanic group renowned for significant graft within the city.[94] Such corruption was unpopular for the profit-maximizing firms of Birmingham, so many local leaders began to push for a more independent city commission.[95] Walker Percy agreed with this group, contending that a city like Birmingham should be run by a group of sophisticated businessmen, much like a corporation.[96] These arguments positioned him as the spokesperson for the new concept, and he soon emerged as the leader for the movement.[97] Beginning with local challenges, Percy would be elected to the state legislature and there would oversee the successful transition of Birmingham to a "city commission" form of government in 1911.[98]

All throughout these periods of personal prosperity, Percy's firm began to gain significant local prestige, maintaining the traditional partnership format while undertaking highly sophisticated work. In 1905, Percy joined Augustus Benners to form a two-man law partnership, and in 1909 Borden Burr of Talladega joined the firm.[99] Thus, the law firm of Percy, Benners, and Burr was formed—and one of those names lives on in the firm masthead to this day. Built initially and primarily on TCI business, the new firm would develop a long list of illustrious industrial clients. As a 1944 issue of

---

90 *Id.* at 193.

91 *Id.*

92 *Id.*

93 *Id.* at 193-94.

94 *Id.* at 82-87.

95 *Id.*

96 *Id.* at 82.

97 *Id.*

98 *Id.* at 91; Samway, *Union of the DeBardeleben and Percy Families, supra* note 66, at 31.

99 Samway, *Union of the DeBardeleben and Percy Families, supra* note 66, at 29.

Alabama Lawyer would reveal, the firm (then known as Benners, Burr, Stokely, and McKamy) oversaw the "[c]onsolidation of various companies into [the] Tennessee Coal, Iron, & Railroad Company," the "[f]ormation of [the] Bessemer Coal, Iron & Land Company for [the] development of [the] City of Bessemer," the "[o]rganization of [the] Southern Railway System in Alabama," and the "[c]onsolidation of [the] South & North Alabama Railroad Company with [the] Louisville & Nashville Railroad Company."[100] Of these representative cases, one can fairly see the impact of both DeBardeleben specifically and the steel industry generally on the early development of the firm.

The end of Walker Percy's life was as storied as his rise to prominence in local Birmingham society. Following a life full of fast-paced and rigorous work, Percy suffered from a complete nervous breakdown in 1911.[101] He was subsequently treated at Johns Hopkins University Hospital in Baltimore, Maryland before returning to Birmingham.[102] For six more years, Percy would continue to live an active and prosperous life in the Birmingham social sphere until his life was cut short by a mysterious tragedy. On February 7, 1917, Walker's son LeRoy (an attorney with his father's firm and the father of the famous novelist) decided to visit his parents' stately Arlington Avenue mansion to discuss an upcoming duck-hunting trip.[103] Seemingly, Walker was in decent spirits, excited about the trip, and not perceptibly depressed.[104] However, soon after 3:00 P.M., LeRoy heard the sound of a "muffled report" from the upstairs of the house.[105] Rushing to the sound, LeRoy found the lifeless, crumpled body of his father, apparently killed by self-inflicted gunshots from a .12 bore shotgun.[106] Debate still remains as to whether the fateful incident of February 7 was a suicide or just a tragic accident. One local newspaper, the Birmingham *Age-Herald*, would attribute the death to suicide, while the other newspaper, the Birmingham *News*, would defend the death as an accident.[107] Ultimately, and in keeping with past family history, the Percy family would declare the death a suicide.[108]

Walker Percy's legacy is a strong example of the post-Reconstruction, New South industrialism that swept through Alabama. He was acquainted with the finest members of the Birmingham business elite, intertwined with the rise of the largest industrial concerns, and at least partially responsible

---

[100] Note, *History of Benners, Burr, Stokely and McKamy of Birmingham, Ala.*, 5 ALA. LAW. 98, 101 (1944).

[101] Samway, *Union of the DeBardeleben and Percy Families*, *supra* note 66, at 32.

[102] *Id.*

[103] Wyatt-Brown, THE HOUSE OF PERCY, *supra* note 22, at 248.

[104] *Id.*

[105] *Id.*

[106] *Id.*

[107] *Id.*

[108] *Id.*

for much of the development that has led to modern Birmingham. In that way, his life and his legal practice mirror the overarching sociocultural evolution of the state in general at this time.

But even more than the superficial similarities between Percy and his contemporaries, Percy represents a potentially much deeper metaphor for the conflicted nature of turn-of-the-century Southern society as a whole. As the son of a Southern planter and Civil War veteran, Percy had been raised according to a certain "code of honor"—a glorification of Southern ideals and perspectives that were inculcated from an early age.[109] Later, when he became involved with Henry DeBardeleben, he was marrying into a family that was not marked just by wealth and success: instead, he was becoming intertwined with a family that had shed the embarrassment of Southern military defeat to become prominent economic leaders.[110] But Percy did not achieve such high Southern aspirations; rather, he arguably achieved the exact opposite. By arranging for the sale of TCI to U.S. Steel, Percy orchestrated what he might have viewed as the ultimate betrayal: selling a unique example of Southern pride to a group of Northern investors.[111] In this light, was Percy one of any number of Southerners who felt some form of remorse for selling out to the Carpetbaggers? At least one author has contended that this psychological tension may have contributed to Percy's suicide.[112] In any event, what seems apparent is that Percy was an excellent example of his fellow Southerners, torn between allegiance to the past and the desire for future success. Today, through his legacy of both Burr and Forman and Birmingham generally, Walker Percy lives on as an illustration of the crossroads between the Old South and the New South: the intersection of quiet agriculture with hurried industry, perceived gentility with hard-minded capitalism, and recalcitrant adherence to old methods with ultimate capitulation to new ideas.

IV. New South Industrialists

Birmingham at the turn of the century was a booming metropolis, full of potential and promise for anyone who settled in its city limits. Despite a number of financial and social setbacks in the late 1800s, Birmingham would become "the 'Magic City' of the New South,"[113] characterized by substantial urban expansion, technological improvements, and economic prosperity.[114] Success and pride were so widespread that one commenter was driven to call Birmingham "the 'Magic City of the World, the marvel of the South, the miracle of the Continent, the dream of the Hemisphere, the

---

[109] *Id.* at 249.

[110] *Id.* at 249-50.

[111] *Id.*

[112] *Id.*

[113] Zane L. Miller, *Foreword to* Harris, POLITICAL POWER IN BIRMINGHAM, *supra* note 81, at vii.

[114] *Id.*

vision of all Mankind,'" reflecting an optimistic and excited society.[115] Unsurprisingly, much of this progress was mirrored in the legal profession: lawyers played an integral part in the formation and development of these businesses, served on municipal committees devoted to regional development, and contributed vastly to the evolution of the city over the years.

The fledgling Percy and Benners firm would morph alongside the city, eventually holding nine total names, including the firm's current moniker.[116] The firm would be named Percy and Benners from 1904–1909 before changing to Percy, Benners, and Burr (1909–1929); Benners, Burr, McKamy, and Forman (1929–1943); Benners, Burr, Stokely, and McKamy (1943–1950); Burr, McKamy, Moore, and Tate (1950–1955); Burr, McKamy, Moore, and Thomas (1955–1960); Moore, Thomas, Taliaferro, Forman, and Burr (1960–1965); Thomas, Taliaferro, Forman, Burr, and Murray (1965–1986); and finally, Burr and Forman (1986–today).[117] In addition, the firm has occupied several prestigious addresses within Birmingham, including the Woodward Building,[118] the Brown Marx Tower,[119] and, today, the Wells Fargo Tower, the tallest building currently in Birmingham.[120] The remainder of this section is an evaluation of several of the partners named in the firm's masthead over the years, including a few illustrative stories of those individuals' involvement with Alabama history.

Augustus H. Benners

Augustus H. Benners was the original partner of Walker Percy in the firm that would ultimately become Burr and Forman.[121] A native of Greensboro and the son of the chancellor for the Northwestern Division of Chancery for Alabama, Benners would join Percy in 1905.[122] Understandably, Benners was a renowned TCI attorney as well, and much of his reputation hinges on his association with that company.

Benners was also a prominent local politician. At the turn of the century, local governments were largely controlled by the state: the state legislature had complete authority to add and remove municipal bodies and governments, and for any type of civic change, the legislature had to be

---

[115] *Id.*

[116] *Burr & Forman LLP — Office Profile*, MARTINDALE, http://www.martindale.com/Burr-Forman-LLP/25882-law-firm-office.htm (last visited July 6, 2015).

[117] *Id.*

[118] Samway, *Union of the DeBardeleben and Percy Families, supra* note 66, at 24.

[119] Letter from A.H. Woodward to Borden Burr (Oct. 25, 1927), *available at* http://acumen.lib.ua.edu/u0003_0001577_0014735#item%3Du0003_0001577_0014735%3B (addressed to Brown-Marx Tower).

[120] *See* http://www.emporis.com/buildings/125536/wells-fargo-tower-birmingham-al-usa (last visited July 6, 2015) ("This is the tallest building between Dallas and Atlanta."). Previously the building was named The Wachovia Tower and SouthTrust Tower; it is 454 feet high. *Id.*

[121] Samway, *Union of the DeBardeleben and Percy Families, supra* note 66, at 29.

[122] *Id.*

petitioned.[123] Access to the legislature, however, was not open to everyone: instead, one had to go through the county's legislative "delegation" in order to petition the state government.[124] Consisting of one state senator and the county's several members of the House of Representatives, these delegations held a substantial amount of power in municipal government.[125] Benners, along with Percy, was a member of the Jefferson County legislative delegation.[126] In fact, and as opposed to Percy's single term, Benners held that position for three terms.[127] Moreover, Benners' position was more than that of just an ordinary legislator: as a corporate lawyer, he was in the upper rank of representative economic groups, a position held by only 8% of the delegates during the entire lifespan of legislative delegations.[128] Thus, Benners likely held a certain level of economic power over decisions lobbied for or acted upon by the legislative delegation.

Despite Benners' power within the delegation, it is not clear that the power extended to a statewide level. At that time, rural Alabama was in comfortable control of the state legislature: cities, including Birmingham, had about 21% of the state's total population during this time, but only had 13% of seats in the House and 9% of the seats in the Senate.[129] Thus, "[r]ural representatives who had no ties to large cities dominated the legislature."[130] Despite this daunting reality, however, Benners would exercise significant power locally, particularly during an episode involving Borden Burr.

Borden Burr

Borden Burr was one of the more political members during the early days of the firm. Apart from his involvement in city affairs, Burr would garner state attention through his alleged run-ins with both the Klan and the Big Mule Movement.[131] Overall, however, he is best known for anti-labor advocacy and defense of large business interests throughout the state.

A native of Talladega, Burr joined Walker Percy and Augustus Benners in 1909 after leaving the firms of Knox, Dixon, and Burr in his hometown and Knox, Bowie, Acker, and Blackmon of Anniston.[132] He was a graduate of

---

123 Harris, POLITICAL POWER IN BIRMINGHAM, *supra* note 81, at 91-92.

124 *Id.* at 92.

125 *Id.*

126 *Id.* at 92 n.69.

127 *Id.*

128 *Id.* at 92.

129 *Id.*

130 *Id.*

131 Glenn Feldman, POLITICS, SOCIETY, AND THE KLAN IN ALABAMA, 1915–1949 165, 271 (1999). For a definition of Big Mule, see Freyer & Dixon, DEMOCRACY AND JUDICIAL INDEPENDENCE, *supra* note 18, at 78 (describing the Big Mule group as "[a] conservative coalition including a business group known as Big Mules (because of their 'pull') centered in urban areas").

132 Samway, *Union of the DeBardeleben and Percy Families*, *supra* note 66, at 30.

the University of Alabama, having played quarterback for the football team from 1894–1895.[133] During this time, he "laid claim to the invention of the football huddle," a claim that perhaps sheds some light on his overall personality.[134]

Borden was involved in a number of political controversies during his life in Birmingham. One famous incident concerned a highly contested proposal to split Birmingham into a separate county from Jefferson County.[135] The logic stemmed from the need for additional property tax revenues for the city: Birmingham residents were paying a total of 2.5 mill, only to see the corresponding benefits go to residents outside of the city limits.[136] Thus, the proposal sought to increase revenues through the retention of those exported 2.5 mills.[137] Big business, however, and especially the mining operations, did not like this plan. Publicly, these companies argued against the change because it would be cost-prohibitive to have two separate corps of lawyers for the two different counties.[138] In reality, however, their reluctance was likely attributable to potential tax increases in newly cash-strapped unincorporated areas, where desperation for funding might lead to higher mineral taxes.[139] Regardless of the reason, the large Birmingham corporations were displeased with the proposal, and Benners and Burr were enlisted as attack dogs to defeat the measure.

Focusing on the Chamber of Commerce, the state legislature, and various other public groups, Burr rallied against the division of "imperial" Jefferson County.[140] Backed by substantial business interests and the attendant political power, Burr was very successful in Birmingham, and this success was soon followed by a similar victory in the state legislature.[141] The proposal was defeated in a close vote during the 1919 session of the Alabama state legislature, and Burr returned to Birmingham with his laurels.[142]

Burr's political connections and influence defeated labor as well. From 1919 to 1921, a major coal conflict between labor and management arose that threatened the profitability of many of the major industrial outfits in

---

[133] *See 1894 Season Recap, available at* http://grfx.cstv.com/photos/schools/alab/sports/m-footbl/auto_pdf/1894-season.pdf; *1895 Season Recap, available at* http://grfx.cstv.com/photos/schools/alab/sports/m-footbl/auto_pdf/1895-season.pdf.

[134] Peter Brandwein, *Deaths of John Cobb and Briggs Saddened Sports World in 1952*, N.Y. TIMES, Dec. 21, 1952, at 4S ("Borden Burr, Alabama quarterback in 1899 [sic], who laid claim to the invention of the football huddle.").

[135] Harris, POLITICAL POWER IN BIRMINGHAM, *supra* note 81, at 137.

[136] *Id.* at 135.

[137] *Id.* at 136.

[138] *Id.*

[139] *Id.*

[140] *Id.* at 137.

[141] *Id.*

[142] *Id.*

the city.[143] By this time, however, Birmingham had become much more labor-friendly than it had been during similar conflicts in the past, and the city leadership was more accommodating to mass meetings of the United Mine Workers in the main city park.[144] Once again, Burr attacked: first relying on an order from the commander of the mine district's militia that would ban such mass meetings,[145] Burr argued for the revocation of the mass meeting permit.[146] Though this effort initially failed, Burr was forced once again to turn to his political connections, this time to the governor of Alabama, Thomas Kilby, who was especially friendly towards industry and hostile towards organized labor.[147] Through the combined efforts of Burr and Kilby, the coal miners' strike was weakened and ultimately broken, and production continued.[148]

Despite these victories, Burr did not point to those experiences as his most "exhilarating" experience as a trial lawyer. Instead, that honor went to "[d]efense of [the] 'mosquito cases' against Alabama Power Company, in which General [William Crawford] Gorgas was the principal witness."[149] In that case, the newly-incorporated utility was sued by malaria-stricken residents of the Coosa River region for the alleged "negligent causing and maintenance of the impounded waters to serve as a breeding place of an invading army of mosquitoes."[150] In that "crowded courtroom of Shelby County,"[151] Borden Burr received his "greatest thrill"—he called General Gorgas as "an unsuspected surprise witness."[152] Gorgas, Surgeon General of the United States at the time and renowned for efforts in fighting malaria and yellow fever in Central America, had visited and inspected the lands around the river and testified as to the "sanitary conditions surrounding the impounded waters."[153] Thus, upon this spectacular courtroom experience, of which Burr was so proud, Burr received testimony from an excellent witness and walked away with a verdict for the power company.

Perhaps the most interesting aspects of Borden Burr, however, concern his ideological struggles. A man "whose compact stature and scrappy behavior gave him the reputation of a junkyard bulldog,"[154] Burr was frequently on

---

143 *Id.* at 222-23.

144 *Id.*

145 *Id.* at 222.

146 *Id.* at 223.

147 *Id.*

148 *Id.*

149 Note, *History of Benners, Burr, Stokely and McKamy*, *supra* note 100, at 100.

150 Borden Burr, *A Trial Lawyer's Greatest Thrill—"Mr. Sheriff, Call for the Defense General William Crawford Gorgas,"* 8 ALA. LAW. 363, 363 (1947).

151 *Id.*

152 *Id.* at 365.

153 *Id.* at 367.

154 Steve Suitts, HUGO BLACK OF ALABAMA: HOW HIS ROOTS AND EARLY CAREER SHAPED THE GREAT CHAMPION OF THE CONSTITUTION 86 (2005).

the attack for different sides. Through his connections with TCI, he was a professed industrialist,[155] but this did not stop him from being a rabid prohibitionist—despite Walker Percy's well-reasoned, pro-business warnings to the contrary.[156] In addition, despite at times using racial prejudice in trials,[157] he openly rallied against the power structure of the Ku Klux Klan.[158] Finally, as a union-busting lawyer he often fought plaintiff's attorneys like later Supreme Court Justice Hugo Black,[159] at times with unfavorable outcomes,[160] but would put aside any differences to defend Black's honor in a prohibition case.[161] As with Percy, Burr's internal battles shed light on the psychological struggles of his contemporaries and reflect a world grappling with conflicting views.

Borden Burr was representative of elite culture during his time in Birmingham. His experiences with the University of Alabama football team, his involvement with the fledgling utility company, and his anti-labor efforts were all reflections of the overall mentality among high society. Even his racial views, which he at times tried to obfuscate in terms of passion for "home rule" and the attendant freedom from Northern oversight,[162] echoed the same "racial questions" experienced by Walker Percy. Burr's time as a legal professional in Birmingham, just as much as Percy or Benners' time, represented the clash of two separate eras.

Brief Notes on the Other Name Members

What follows are a few notes of special interest that highlight the political, social, and cultural involvement of the "name attorneys" at Burr. As with the other aforementioned attorneys, the men described below were decidedly creatures of the environments in which they operated, not only shaped by the world in which they lived, but also creators of the sociocultural landscape of Birmingham and Alabama.

---

[155] *Id.* at 316 (describing one example of Burr's pro-industrialist work, concerning an order from the Alabama Supreme Court permitting mining companies to evict striking workers' families from company grounds with one day's notice).

[156] *Id.* at 135 (stating that Burr and Percy were on opposite sides of the liquor debate).

[157] *Id.* at 372-74 (describing Burr's racially charged strategy in a personal injury case).

[158] *Id.* at 391 (discussing Burr's protest of Klan activities, especially floggings).

[159] *Id.* at 128 (citing one example of Black winning a case against Percy and Burr's client, U.S. Steel).

[160] *Id.* at 374 (describing a series of collapsed settlement talks and a subsequent jury verdict in which Burr's client lost more money than had originally been requested by Hugo Black).

[161] *Id.* at 219-20 (recounting an episode of Burr acting as attorney for the Jefferson County sheriff, and, through association, defending Black's honor, in a case that was both a challenge to prohibition and an episode in a long-running feud between County Solicitor Hugo Black and Circuit Solicitor Joseph Tate).

[162] *See* Borden Burr, THE SOUTH'S SERIOUS, AND PECULIAR POLITICAL PLIGHT: SPEECH BEFORE KIWANIS CLUB OF BIRMINGHAM, JULY 27, 1948 (1948).

James R. Forman is the other named attorney on the current masthead for the firm. A native of St. Clair County, Forman joined the firm in 1918 after leaving a practice in Gadsden.[163] Before arriving in Birmingham, he attended the University of Alabama, and, according to one article, "was one of the greatest athletes ever produced at the University of Alabama," becoming "an All-Southern player both at baseball and football."[164] Indeed, this sentiment seems to have been echoed by the 1902 season recap, where Forman was listed as "outstanding for Alabama."[165] During that season, he would be listed as an excellent player for his performances in both the Georgia Tech and Mississippi A&M games.[166]

Frontis Moore and J. T. Stokely were both fairly prominent government appointees. Moore, who arrived at the firm in December of 1936, acted as the "Assistant Attorney General in charge of tax matters" for the state of Alabama before joining.[167] He also seems to have enjoyed some reputability as a corporate, banking, and business lawyer, having delivered a talk about creditors' rights and bankruptcy at the American Bar Association's Deep South Regional meeting in 1956.[168] Meanwhile, Stokely, who had acted as a city judge, organized a separate firm, later to merge with Percy's firm, in 1913.[169] After serving as the United States General Solicitor in charge of valuations for certain railroad properties in 1923, Stokely would return to Birmingham to his practice.[170]

Greye Tate joined the firm in 1942.[171] During the early 1950s, Tate was called to serve on a citizens' committee investigating allegations of corruption and graft in the city's police department.[172] The main focus of the investigation was none other than Bull Connor, the police chief who would be made infamous for his cruel treatment of blacks during Civil Rights protests in Birmingham.[173] The committee ultimately rebuked the police chief and the department he headed,[174] but they left the ultimate punishment to be determined by other ongoing proceedings.[175] One note of inter-

---

163 Note, *History of Benners, Burr, Stokely and McKamy*, *supra* note 100, at 99.

164 *Id.*

165 *See 1902 Season Recap*, *available at* http://www.rolltide.com/auto_pdf/p_hotos/s_chools/alab/sports/m-footbl/auto_pdf/1902-season (last visited July 6, 2015).

166 *Id.*

167 Note, *History of Benners, Burr, Stokely and McKamy*, *supra* note 100, at 99.

168 *Deep South Regional Meeting a Great Success*, A.B.A. J., Jan. 1956, at 34.

169 Note, *History of Benners, Burr, Stokely and McKamy*, *supra* note 100, at 100.

170 *Id.*

171 *Id.* at 99.

172 Glenn T. Eskew, BUT FOR BIRMINGHAM: THE LOCAL AND NATIONAL MOVEMENTS IN THE CIVIL RIGHTS STRUGGLE 99 (1997).

173 *Id.*

174 *Id.* at 100.

175 *Id.* at 101.

est, however, is that the committee advocated the hiring of black police officers, a suggestion that was consistent with other political tides during that time period.[176]

Of Mark Taliaferro, Andrew Thomas, and D. K. McKamy, not much is reported in prominent literature of their personal legacies. Other than a record of McKamy joining the firm in 1917 after leaving Dalton, Georgia,[177] and a note of Taliaferro and Thomas being stationed at Sheppard Field in Texas and Maxwell Field in Montgomery, respectively, during World War II,[178] their story remains to be told. Without a doubt, however, their names were placed on the firm masthead for major contributions to the firm,[179] and as a result these attorneys symbolically represent a large group of under-recognized professionals who have shaped current society.

V. Conclusion: Alabama Today

Just as it has throughout the antebellum and New South years, Burr and Forman continues to represent the cultural evolution of Alabama. A major Southeastern firm that has offices in nine cities across five states, Burr represents the new extraterritorial sense of the South. In addition, Burr's clients have been responsible for several major economic developments, including the development of the Mercedes plant in Vance and the construction of the largest private development in United States history—the Thyssen Krupp steel plant near Mobile.[180] However, despite this progress, Burr retains strong ties to clients from its roots: from its representative clients list, names such as U.S. Steel, Regions (the ultimate acquirer of the old First National Bank through AmSouth), and Buffalo Rock continue to be among those represented.[181] As has been the case ever since its founding, Burr stands for the intersection of the "old way of doing things" with the drive that defines Alabama's economic progress over the past two hundred years.

But what relevance is a firm's history if it doesn't contribute anything to our understanding? As has been illustrated in this chapter, Burr and Forman's history reflects a much greater social change, both in Alabama and in the Southeast generally. It is a history that derives from the alluvial soils of rich agrarian life on the South's river deltas, but which merged in a tumul-

---

176 *Id.*

177 Note, *History of Benners, Burr, Stokely and McKamy*, *supra* note 100, at 99.

178 *Id.* at 101.

179 Although no biographical information was readily available, several cases mention these three men. Of particular note, Taliaferro appears to have been adverse to unions in several important cases, including one case alongside former FDIC chairman George LeMaistre. NLRB v. Newton, 214 F.2d 472 (5th Cir. 1954).

180 Lauren B. Cooper, *Industrial Deals: Burr's Thuston Sits on the Other Side of the Table*, BIRMINGHAM BUS. J., Aug. 5, 2007 (discussing both projects).

181 Sample Client List, BURR, http://www.burr.com/About-Burr/Client-list.aspx#.UIo_NI5wbnY (last visited July 6, 2015).

tuous fashion with the harsh black soot of the Birmingham steel mills. Today, it is embodied in a glistening skyscraper in the heart of a cosmopolitan city center, surrounded and bolstered by the new corporate giants of banking and finance. It is a reflection of where we have been and what we have to look forward to—in short, it is a firm understanding of the history of Alabama.

A MAN IN A BOY'S COAT: THE EVOLUTION OF ALABAMA'S CONSTITUTIONS

Courtney Cooper[1]

I. Introduction

Thomas Jefferson once wrote that he was no fan of changing laws and constitutions, but he understood the importance of keeping pace with the times: "We might as well require a man to wear still the coat which fitted him when a boy as civilized society to remain ever under the regimen of their barbarous ancestors."[2] Consequently, one must know the government of their ancestors to understand the burdens on their present society.

Alabamians carry a unique burden—the longest constitution in the world.[3] The Alabama Constitution of 1901 was likely illegally ratified and was the offspring of decades of undemocratic politics. Alabama's Constitution was motivated by race in an effort to strip blacks from their right to vote, and since blacks were still voting, they were manipulated into endorsing their own disfranchisement.[4] Instead of rewriting the constitution and freeing the state of its ancestral regimen, Alabama has found itself in the habit of amending its constitution to the point of absurdity.[5] While the "era of using the Constitution and laws of Alabama to foster and protect a particular, white-dominated system"[6] came to an end in the 1960s, by simply

---

[1] To paraphrase the introduction to Professor Rob Riser's thesis, as an undergraduate I was an "idealistic twenty year-old" appalled by what my constitution writers did and even more discouraged that my country, one promoted to liberty and justice for all, would permit Alabama to distort our nation's ideals. While, at heart, I am still the "idealistic twenty-year old," this paper was not written to advocate constitutional reform. However, I believe any discussion on the problems of our past should motivate Alabama's citizens and future leaders to consider petitioning for a change, and the conclusion leaves the reader with this invitation. See Robert Volney Riser II, "Between Scylla and Charybdis: Alabama's 1901 Constitutional Convention Assesses the Perils of Disfranchisement," 8 (Nov. 14, 2000) (unpublished M.A. thesis, University of Alabama) (on file with Gorgas Library, University of Alabama).

[2] Letter from Thomas Jefferson to Samuel Kercheval (July 12, 1816), *available at* http://www.let.rug.nl/usa/presidents/thomas-jefferson/letters-of-thomas-jefferson/jefl246.php (last visited July 20, 2015); *see* J. Michael Allen III & Jamison W. Hinds, *Alabama Constitutional Reform*, 53 ALA. L. REV. 1 (2001).

[3] Alabama has the longest constitution in the world, with single amendments longer than the entire U.S. Constitution. *See id.* at 4.

[4] William H. Stewart, THE ALABAMA STATE CONSTITUTION 6 (1994).

[5] *Id.* at 2 (explaining that the "piecemeal constitutional change Alabama has experienced since 1901 has been facilitated because of the ease with which the document may be formally amended").

[6] *Id.* at 7.

patching its wounds through amendments, Alabama continues to create laws in its undemocratic shell.

This chapter serves as a compilation of extensive research on Alabama's government from 1819–1903. First, I will briefly explain the history of Alabama's constitutions with a more in-depth analysis of the politics surrounding the ratification of three constitutions arising after the Civil War: the Constitutions of 1868, 1875, and 1901. Because the Constitution of 1901 reflects "continuity with all preceding state constitutions,"[7] it is imperative to understand the evolution of constitutional development in Alabama. Next, this chapter will question the federal government's role during the period of disfranchisement when Southern states were eliminating the newly freed black man from the electorate. After the Civil War, the federal government was the key player in "reconstructing" Southern states, such as Alabama. They enforced military control and divided the state into military districts. For years, the federal government monitored the state and its politics. Over time, however, the federal government became more and more apathetic to the problems of the South. Therefore, Alabama seized the moment and created the government it had long desired.

II. The Fraudulent Road to 1901

In the preface to arguably the best resource for Alabama's constitutional history, Malcolm McMillan observes that "[f]rom 1819 to 1901, constitution making in Alabama was a never-ending process."[8] In eighty-three years, Alabama organized six constitutional conventions.[9] To fully comprehend the Constitution of 1901, it is crucial to understand the evolution of these previous constitutions. The Civil War would re-orient the focus of the conventions and political parties. After the war, the federal government would have military control of the state, and the Republican Party would gain influence and glorify black suffrage. Consequently, the Democratic Party would make it their duty to "redeem" the state by returning it to white Southern supremacy.[10] As Professor Harvey Jackson emphasized, "[y]ou need to understand that if anything else is to make sense."[11] Jackson was referring to the period of "redemption" when some Alabamians believed carpetbaggers, scalawags, and blacks[12] were taking their state away from them.

---

[7] *Id.* at 3.

[8] Malcolm Cook McMillan, CONSTITUTIONAL DEVELOPMENT IN ALABAMA, 1798–1901: A STUDY IN POLITICS, THE NEGRO, AND SECTIONALISM vii (The Reprint Co. 1975) (1955).

[9] *Id.*

[10] Harvey H. Jackson III, INSIDE ALABAMA: A PERSONAL HISTORY OF MY STATE 107 (2004).

[11] *Id.* at 114-16.

[12] I first remember learning the word "carpetbagger" in my fourth grade Alabama History class. It's a traditional Southern word used to reference Northerners who came down after the Civil War "with all they owned stuffed into a carpetbag." *Id.* at 109. Some "carpetbaggers" did come down to exploit the black vote and take advantage of a defeated state. *Id.* However, Jackson

Furthermore, this "evil trinity"[13] is exactly how the President of the Constitutional Convention of 1901, John Knox, justified the goal of legalizing white supremacy, including excusing past corrupt practices that had ensured Democratic rule.[14] Knox described the history of Alabama as he and others believed it to be:

> After the war, by force of Federal bayonets, the negro was placed in control of every branch of our government. Inspired and aided by unscrupulous white men, he wasted money, created debts, increased taxes until it threatened to amount to confiscation of our property. While in power, and within a few years, he increased our State debt from a nominal figure to nearly thirty millions of dollars.[15]

Unfortunately, Knox's party would develop a more troubling reality: in less than 100 years, Alabama was transformed from "one of the most democratic states in 1819 to one of the least democratic a century later."[16]

A. The Build-Up to a Failed Democracy: 1901 Constitution's Predecessors

On the same day Mississippi became a state, December 10, 1817, Alabama became a territory.[17] The Alabama Territory grew rapidly as times were good and cotton prices were high.[18] Planters and their slaves settled along the Tennessee and Tombigbee River valleys while farmers inhabited the Northern Hill Country and Wiregrass Region of the southeast.[19] Because of this rapid growth, the Alabama Territory had only been in existence for fifteen months when Congress passed an enabling act for Alabama to become a state.[20]

On July 5, 1819, delegates convened in Huntsville, Alabama to write the first constitution of the state, the Constitution of 1819.[21] The convention was led by the developing aristocrats, the planters, but was balanced out by the

---

explains that most came to invest. *Id.* "Scalawag" is also a commonly understood word in Alabama that references the white Alabamians who supported black suffrage. McMillan, *supra* note 8, at 133. Alabama history, especially as told by McMillan, uses these words as descriptive terms without negative connotation. *See id.*

[13] Jackson, *supra* note 10, at 109.

[14] JOURNAL OF THE PROCEEDINGS OF THE CONSTITUTIONAL CONVENTION OF THE STATE OF ALABAMA 12-13 (1901) [hereinafter JOURNAL OF PROCEEDINGS].

[15] *Id.*

[16] Wayne Flynt, *Alabama's Shame: The Historical Origins of the 1901 Constitution*, 53 ALA. L. REV. 67, 76 (2001).

[17] McMillan, *supra* note 8, at 24.

[18] Jackson, *supra* note 10, at 44.

[19] *Id.* at 52-53; McMillan, *supra* note 8, at 46.

[20] McMillan, *supra* note 8, at 28-29.

[21] *Id.* at 31.

"plain men" to create an honest and democratic constitution.[22] One of the major controversies that began the divide between North and South Alabama regarded the apportionment of the legislature: whether representation should include letting five slaves equal three white men.[23] This ratio of three-fifths was introduced by the United States Constitution in 1787.[24] The counties where black slaves were in the majority favored using the federal ratio of three slaves to one white man because they desired the value of the added representation.[25] However, these "black" counties were outvoted by the "white"[26] counties who would not benefit from the black population.[27] This disagreement was the predecessor of what would become an all-out political war, during the Reconstruction period, centered on which party could manipulate the black vote to its advantage.[28]

In order to vote under the Constitution of 1819, one had to be a white, male, United States citizen who was at least twenty-one years of age.[29] In fact, this constitution was slightly more liberal than those of other Southern states because Alabama did not have a property, tax-paying, or militia qualification to its suffrage laws.[30] Also, Alabama was one of the first in the United States to permit its citizens to directly participate in amending its constitution.[31] However, the constitution itself was not submitted to the people for ratification.[32] Its enabling act, like those of the original Southern states, did not require a vote for acceptance.[33]

After thirty-three years, Alabama newspapers began hinting that it was time for a new constitution, and part of their reasoning was that the legislature had too much power.[34] In 1852, the legislature submitted this idea for a

---

22 McMillan, *supra* note 8, at 46 ("To the 'plain men,' those who came mostly from the 'white counties,' must go the credit for amending the document into an even more democratic constitution.").

23 *Id.* at 36-37.

24 U.S. CONST. art. 1, §2, para. 3.

25 McMillan, *supra* note 8, at 36-37.

26 McMillan distinguished the state by "black" counties and "white" counties based on which race made up the majority of the county's population. McMillan, *supra* note 8.

27 *Id.* at 36-37.

28 *See* Jackson, *supra* note 10, at 113 ("Whoever controlled the black vote won the election.").

29 McMillan, *supra* note 8, at 35.

30 *Id.*

31 To amend the constitution, the legislature had to pass a proposed amendment by a two-thirds vote and submit it to the voters. If the amendment was approved by a majority of the voters it would be presented to the following legislature where it had to gain three-fourths of the vote. *Id.* at 43.

32 *Id.* at 44.

33 *Id.*

34 *Id.* at 71 ("By a review of the acts of the last few sessions of the legislature it will be seen that they have assumed in great measure the administrative and executive as well as the legislative department of the state government. They pass general laws and then legislate an exception for almost every county, town, and village in the state.") (quoting MONTGOMERY ADVERTISER, May

new constitution to the people.[35] Every county voted against it.[36] Their objection was based on fear that the power to convene would be abused.[37] Efforts to replace the constitution failed in the 1850s, but by 1860–1861, the state was distracted by the events leading up to the Civil War.[38] A secession convention was called, and in addition to the obvious goal of creating an independent state, the convention made constitutional reform an important issue.[39] A committee composed of seven secessionists and two cooperationists,[40] most of whom were lawyers from the Black Belt,[41] organized to recommend certain changes to the constitution.[42] However, the constitution was not changed more than the convention believed necessary because of the impending war.[43]

After the Civil War, in order to regain citizenship and the right to vote, one had to take an amnesty oath to support the Union, including acceptance of the emancipation of slaves.[44] The Constitution of 1865 was a necessary document passed to end slavery and create a provisional government.[45] However, there is no evidence that this constitution was actually ratified by an electorate or otherwise.[46] While Alabamians were urged to make the best

---

22, 1852).

[35] *Id.* at 73.

[36] *Id.*

[37] *Id.*; *see also* MILLS J. THORTON, POLITICS AND POWER IN A SLAVE SOCIETY 80-87 (1978) (explaining that Alabama's electorate believed that its legislators were often overcompensated for legislative sessions that convened longer than necessary).

[38] McMillan, *supra* note 8, at 75 (explaining that the amendment process broke down because of the section crisis and the tendency of voters to completely ignore proposed amendments).

[39] *Id.* at 76-77.

[40] Secessionists were those who favored seceding from the Union. Cooperationists varied in their beliefs. Some cooperationists believed in "unconditional unionism" while others desired an overt act against the South before seceding. The latter believed they should make one last demand to the North for Southern rights before seceding. Also, there were some cooperationists who advocated secession only if Alabama cooperated with other Southern states to ensure an alliance if Alabama seceded. *Id.* at 76-77 n.4.

[41] The Black Belt is a section of Alabama made up of approximately nineteen counties in the middle to southern part of the state. It is known for its rich soil, and during the 1800s, planters, or mostly their black slaves, made up the population of this area.

[42] McMillan, *supra* note 8, at 85.

[43] Most of the proposed alterations to the constitution were struck down. Among the changes were banking regulations and limitations on the legislature's power to incur debt. *Id.* at 86.

[44] *Id.* at 90 n.2 (Amnesty Oath: "I, ____, do solemnly swear (or affirm) in the presence of Almighty God, that I will henceforth faithfully, support, protect, and defend the Constitution of the United States, and the Union of the states thereunder; and that I will, in like manner, abide by and faithfully support all laws and proclamations which have been made during the existing rebellion with reference to the emancipation of slaves: So help me God.").

[45] *Id.* at 90.

[46] ALABAMA CONSTITUTION OF 1865 RATIFICATION, http://www.legislature.state.al.us/aliswww/history/constitutions/1865/1865rat.html (last visited July 13, 2015) ("The Constitution of 1865 was not submitted to the electorate for ratification, and no document can be found, declaring such ratified. Such submission to the people was not stipulated in President Andrew

of the situation and vote, few did: less than 30,000 Alabamians voted for the 1865 convention.[47] Consequently, the convention was made up mostly of those who had been opposed to secession.[48] But like other conventions, most were lawyers or planters and had been involved in Alabama politics before.[49] Additionally, the convention was reluctant to extend civil rights to blacks.[50] This constitution did not give blacks suffrage.[51] Instead, the Reconstruction Acts of 1867, and later, the Fourteenth and Fifteenth Amendments, would extend civil liberties to blacks, including the cherished right to vote.

Therefore, Republicans were able to take advantage of this newly acquired privilege. To their benefit, the Reconstruction Act of 1867 required an "iron-clad" oath be taken before Alabamians could vote, swearing that one had "never been disfranchised for participation in the rebellion."[52] Thus, more black Alabamians registered than whites, and they were being courted by the Republican Party.[53] A constitutional convention was again proposed in 1867, and for the first time, African-Americans were able to exercise their newly acquired right to vote on it.[54] A total of 71,730 African-Americans voted in favor of the convention, while only 18,553 whites voted affirmatively.[55] Interestingly, there were allegations that these black votes were manipulated into favoring the convention. The newspapers supported these allegations, including the correspondent of the *New York Herald*, who wrote:

> The day before election, Radical agents travelled through Montgomery County and summoned the blacks to come to the city and vote,

---

Johnson's letter, appointing Lewis E. Parsons as Provisional Governor of Alabama, nor in Governor Parsons' Proclamation, calling for a constitutional convention.").

47 McMillan, *supra* note 8, at 91; *see* Jackson, *supra* note 10, at 106.

48 McMillan, *supra* note 8, at 92 (explaining that in the presidential campaign of 1860, eighteen delegates had voted for secessionists candidates and the other eighty-one voted for cooperationists).

49 *Id.*

50 *Id.* at 97.

51 *Id.*

52 McMillan, *supra* note 8, at 110 n.2 ("One had to swear that he had never been disfranchised for participation in the rebellion and had never been a state or federal official who had taken an oath of loyalty to the United States and later engaged in the rebellion."); Lynch v. State, No. 5:08-cv-00450-CLS, slip op. at 493 n.952 (N.D. Ala. Nov. 7, 2011).

53 McMillan, *supra* note 8, at 113 (explaining that before the election for a convention, 104,518 blacks were registered and 61,295 whites were registered). Many whites were disfranchised by the oath requirement, and many who were not disfranchised "chose not to participate because they believed that the federally-mandated government under congressional reconstruction in Alabama was illegitimate." Lynch v. State, No. 5:08-cv-00450-CLS, slip op. at 494 (N.D. Ala. Nov. 7, 2011); *id.* slip op. at 494 n.955 (explaining that as many as 53,409 whites did not register—"either because they made no effort to register or because they were rejected and disfranchised for wartime activity").

54 McMillan, *supra* note 8, at 112-13.

55 *Id.* at 113.

> telling them that General Swayne had ordered them to do so, and would punish them if they did not . . . they acted simply in obedience to the instructions of the Bureau agents; and without the faintest glimmering of an idea of what they were doing.[56]

Consequently, a convention was called made up of a most unusual group of delegates.[57] This was the only convention in Alabama's history in which the delegates were mostly laymen with little property; it was not a lawyer's convention.[58] There were also a number of black delegates and Northerners, but the most compelling statistic is that there were ninety-six Republican delegates and only four of the "rebel influence," who had supported secession.[59] For the delegates, "the real issue in the convention was the disfranchisement of more whites."[60] White disfranchisement was not what the blacks necessarily promoted, but it was what the white Republican delegates required.[61]

The Constitution of 1868 was also never legally ratified.[62] The Second Reconstruction Act required that state constitutions be ratified in an election where at least half of the voters participated.[63] Because of Democratic boycott and terror tactics, less than half the electorate voted; and ratification failed.[64] A total of 70,812 voted for the constitution and 1,005 voted against it.[65] The constitution needed 85,000 votes.[66] However, the Fourth Reconstruction Act became law a month later, March 11, 1868, which changed the requirement to a majority vote.[67] Therefore, under this new law, the constitution could have been ratified. The United States Congress, over President Johnson's veto, readmitted Alabama into the Union with its new constitution, and thus, the Constitution of 1868 came into being essentially under a retroactive law.[68] Despite its undemocratic maneuvers and suffrage requirements, the Constitution of 1868 was possibly one of the best

---

56 *Id.* at 113 n.21 (quoting the NEW YORK HERALD, Nov. 10, 1867).

57 *Id.* at 114-22.

58 *Id.* at 116.

59 *Id.* at 114.

60 *Id.* at 124.

61 According to McMillan, "on the issue of further proscription of the whites [blacks] were victims of circumstances—forced in the final vote into a coalition with their Carpetbag superiors and extreme Scalawags." *Id.* at 132.

62 ALABAMA CONSTITUTION OF 1868 RATIFICATION, http://www.legislature.state.al.us/aliswww/history/constitutions/1868/1868rat.html (last visited July 13, 2015); McMillan, *supra* note 8, at 169-74.

63 McMillan, *supra* note 8, at 169.

64 *Id.*

65 *Id.*

66 *Id.*

67 *Id.* at 171-72, especially 171 n.98.

68 *Id.* at 174.

Alabama ever had. It created a democratic public school system, improved women's rights, abolished imprisonment for debt, and protected poor men's property from sale.[69] It was a constitution dedicated to economic development, education, and a government for the citizens' well being.[70] Nevertheless, it would be short-lived.

Many Bourbon Democrats[71] blamed the carpetbaggers and scalawags for the problems facing the South,[72] and maybe the Bourbons were partially right in this respect. The Republicans, at both the state and federal level, set an example of how to develop laws that could subtly remove from a race their right to vote, and there is some evidence that Alabama's Republicans manipulated the black vote.[73] The Constitution of 1868 was the first to enact a poll tax requirement,[74] and its suffrage clauses were vague.[75] Prohibited from registering were those who "violated the rules of civilized warfare;" those who had been disqualified under the Fourteenth Amendment or the acts of 1867; and those convicted of "treason [regardless of whether they had been pardoned], embezzlement of public funds, malfeasance in office, crime punishable by law with imprisonment in the penitentiary, or bribery."[76] Also, all "idiots and insane persons" were not allowed to vote.[77] Additionally, the Constitution of 1868 enforced its own registration oath, which required that electors swear, among a list of other affirmations, that they "accept the civil and political equality of all men."[78]

Of course, if individuals had simply taken the oath to honor black suffrage, more whites would have been able to vote. Nevertheless, Bourbons might not have felt the need to disfranchise, primarily members of the opposing party, were it not for the fear of radical disfranchisement of themselves. Therefore, in many ways, the Democrats were acting on the defensive side to protect themselves. However, as Jackson pointed out, this idea of a need for redemption may have been more a facet of Southern folklore than fact.[79] Many Alabamians, particularly farmers, had begun to switch to the Republican Party because they felt disconnected from the Democrats, whose leaders spoke primarily for planters and lawyers.[80]

---

[69] *Id.* at 150.

[70] Flynt, *supra* note 16, at 67.

[71] Democrats preferred the nickname "Redeemers." However, they became known as "Bourbons" after the French ruling family whose members worked to restore the "Old Regime" following their revolution. Jackson, *supra* note 10, at 122.

[72] *See id.* at 107.

[73] McMillan, *supra* note 8, at 113-14.

[74] ALA. CONST. of 1868, art. XI, §12.

[75] *Id.* art. VII.

[76] *Id.* §3; *see* McMillan, *supra* note 8, at 125 n.78.

[77] ALA. CONST. of 1868, art. VII, §3.

[78] *Id.* §4.

[79] Jackson, *supra* note 10, at 106-07.

[80] *Id.* at 109.

And so, in retaliation to the Republicans, the Bourbon Democrats did everything within their power to win back "their" state. They believed it was necessary for them to come into power to redeem Alabama from the black and carpetbagger Republican empire.[81] As mentioned above, the Republican Constitution of 1868 made this easier. Alabamians were living under a constitution that had been ratified contrary to current law. It was a constitution ratified primarily by blacks, and this opened the door for the Democrats to create a popular platform based on white supremacy.[82]

Nevertheless, the Bourbon Democrats faced numerous challenges throughout the mid-to-late 1800s in Alabama. In 1870, the Democrats fell back on the basic tactic of using violence, particularly Klan[83] violence, to scare blacks away from the polls, primarily in the Black Belt counties.[84] The federal troops returned in 1872 to guard the polls, and Republican power was restored.[85] But in 1873, the nation fell into an economic recession known as the Panic of 1873.[86] Cotton prices fell[87] and Northern "carpetbaggers," who had been members of the Republican Party, "left the states that they turned over to the Redeemers impoverished or bankrupt."[88] By 1874, the Alabama Republican Party fell apart and made way for the Democrats to rebound.[89] By this time, Democrats were aware that they needed to compose a new constitution to protect themselves, and thus, they constructed the Constitution of 1875. The Constitution of 1875 aimed to reduce the size of government and curtail the newly acquired political power of blacks.[90] However, the delegates refrained from disfranchising voters for the time being because they feared the federal government would intervene.[91] Nevertheless, the constitution did separate state and federal elections.[92] This kept

---

[81] *See id.* at 107.

[82] *See* Harvey H. Jackson III, *"Supremacy" and the Stolen Vote: Bourbon Democrats Solidified Power in 1901 with the Highly Suspect Election Approving a New Constitution*, MOBILE REGISTER, Dec. 11, 1994 ("Branding native Alabama Republicans as 'scalawags,' condemning outsiders as 'carpetbaggers' and issuing dire warnings about 'black rule,' Democrats offered themselves as true Southerners who would end corruption in Montgomery...."), *available at* http://www .constitutionalreform.org/archive/news/mobile/supremacy.html.

[83] The "Klan" refers to the Southern terrorist organization, the Ku Klux Klan, that used violence and fear to "keep things as they had been in the South through slavery." Southern Poverty Law Center, KU KLUX KLAN 5 (1997). The Klan was used to help white Southerners regain control of the government. *Id.* at 14. One of the Klan's strengths was its respectable members, including editors, ministers, former Confederate officers and political leaders. *Id.* at 12.

[84] Jackson, *supra* note 10, at 114.

[85] *Id.*

[86] *Id.* at 113.

[87] *Id.*

[88] C. Vann Woodward, ORIGINS OF THE NEW SOUTH 30 (9th vol. 1995).

[89] *Id.*

[90] Flynt, *supra* note 16, at 68.

[91] *Id.*

[92] Jackson, *supra* note 10, at 115.

federal officials away from the polls during the more important, state vote.[93] And, of course, the delegates at the 1875 Convention abolished the registration oath and disfranchising clauses of the 1868 Constitution.[94]

Between 1875 and 1901, the Democrats fought a hard battle to maintain control of Alabama's government. The economy was unpredictable. After the Panic of 1873, the price of cotton again slid in the late 1880s, but "the price of everything associated with [cotton] seemed to rise."[95] Consequently, the Democratic Party began to divide because their "core constituency," the farmer, was unhappy.[96] No longer were the Democrats only fighting the Republicans, but a number of independent movements, including the Jeffersonian Democrats and Populists, were threatening the Bourbon Democrats' power.[97] Alabama was in an all-out political war in an "era of political corruption and violence."[98] The forms of corruptive tactics that these political parties, primarily the Bourbon Democrats, developed were almost endless:

> [B]allot box stuffing; theft of ballot boxes; removal of polls to unknown places; burning ballots before elections; illegal arrests on election day; importation of voters who did not live in the precinct; calling off names wrongly; fabricating reasons to refuse to hold elections in precincts populated with blacks; the voting of dead or fictitious persons; ensuring that poll watchers and ballot counters became drunk while votes were counted; and, organizing 'disorderly demonstrations' to intimidate voters.[99]

---

[93] *Id.*

[94] McMillan, *supra* note 8, at 201. In a footnote, McMillan observes that the Constitution of 1868 would gradually reinstate the white vote that it sought to remove. This was partly responsible for the Democrats regaining their power in the 1870s. *Id.* at 201 n.86.

[95] Jackson, *supra* note 10, at 126.

[96] *Id.* at 127.

[97] Flynt, *supra* note 16, at 69.

[98] *Id.*

[99] Lynch v. State, No. 5:08-cv-00450-CLS, slip op. at 539 (N.D. Ala. Nov. 7, 2011). Professor Wayne Flynt testified during this case about the methods used to control the black vote before the Kolb-Jones election of 1892: "One is basically simply returning [a] total vote count that is no relation whatsoever to the number of people who voted. So, for instance, no matter how an African-American may vote, whoever counts the votes and turns in the electoral returns to the secretary of state is the one who's going to determine the total head count in that county. So just simply misrepresenting the count is one easy way to do it. Another easy way of doing it is to simply tell sharecroppers on your plantation that if Rueben Cobb [sic: Kolb], the populist candidate in 1890's carries the counties there's no point in showing up because he is not going to renew your contract. That's another way to do it. Another way is to haul everybody from your plantation in, in a single wagon and putting them all in one precinct, so you can know how that precinct goes and how it should go. That's another way of doing it. So there are all sorts of unethical and illegal methods of controlling the ballot. The most extreme examples actually had ballots of different colors. You might have a Republican of one color and Democrat of another color. That really sealed the issue." *Id.* slip op. at 539-40 n.1118; McMillan, *supra* note 8, at 219 (explaining that in the late seventies and eighties, methods to control the

But the most disheartening evidence was the 177 lynchings committed in Alabama during the 1890s, more than in any other state.[100]

These forms of corruption would be utilized in one of Alabama's most controversial gubernatorial elections, the Kolb-Jones election of 1892.[101] An odd man for the position of Bourbon governor, Thomas Goode Jones was a moderate Democrat.[102] He believed that it was the white man's job to make African-Americans "feel that we intend to be just to him, to be his friend,"[103] but he followed racist beliefs during this election.[104] Governor Jones was loyal to the Democratic Party "even if it meant further corrupting an already corrupt political process,"[105] and he believed suffrage limitations would purify politics and eliminate political enemies.[106] Unfortunately, a year later he signed into law the destructive act that helped make the 1901 Constitution possible.[107]

The Sayre Act of 1893 set the stage for complete disfranchisement of African-Americans. This Act legalized some of the most clever corruptive practices, one of the most powerful of which required registration only in May, the busiest month for farmers.[108] Additionally, the governor would appoint registrars who followed his political beliefs, and the common ticket (Australian ballot) was introduced.[109] Under the common ticket, one voted in secrecy on a ballot that listed all of the candidates' names in alphabetical order.[110] If illiterate, a voter could only be aided by an election official.[111] Illiterate voters were now at the mercy of the ballot worker and could not

---

vote had moved from intimidation and violence to clever practices such as "[t]heft, exchange of ballot boxes, removal of polls to unknown places, false certification, illegal arrests on the day of election, importation of voters, purloining of ballots, the use of fictitious names, and the systems of 'counting out' and 'counting in'"). However, my personal favorite was "refusing to hold an election in precincts where the opposition vote was heavy because of a case of the smallpox." *Id.* at 220.

100 Flynt, *supra* note 16, at 70.

101 McMillan, *supra* note 8, at 229 n.66 (explaining that Jones received a majority of 26,246 of the Black Belt vote as contrasted with Kolb's majority of 14,811 in the rest of the state).

102 *See* Jackson, *supra* note 10, at 130; Paul M. Pruitt, Jr., TAMING ALABAMA: LAWYERS AND REFORMERS, 1804–1929 66-73 (2010).

103 Pruitt, *supra* note 102, at 67. It is also interesting to note that Booker T. Washington and Thomas Goode Jones were friends and confidants throughout life. With Washington's backing, Jones was appointed federal judge of Alabama's Middle and Northern districts. *Id.* at 63, 72.

104 *Id.* at 70.

105 Jackson, *supra* note 10, at 130.

106 Pruitt, *supra* note 102, at 71.

107 *See id.* at 70.

108 Jackson, *supra* note 10, at 133 (explaining that poor white and black farmers would not be able to leave their farms to come into town and register).

109 McMillan, *supra* note 8, at 223-24.

110 *Id.* at 223.

111 *Id.* at 223 n.48 (explaining that under previous Alabama law, an illiterate voter could be aided by a friend).

effectively vote. Oddly enough, the same government that stripped their right because of illiteracy also destroyed any chance of redemption because the Constitutions of 1875 and 1901 essentially demolished the education system.[112]

B. The Constitution of 1901

By the 1890s, Alabama citizens were well aware of what was going on in their state. They knew that their vote was not being counted correctly, and the government itself knew it needed to reform its behavior. The solution was a new constitution, but this time the primary purpose would be to disfranchise African-Americans and poor whites.[113] Both of these groups were a threat to Democratic supremacy.

Throughout the South, disfranchisement had been accomplished by constitutional conventions.[114] In 1890, Mississippi was the first Southern state to create an example of disfranchisement laws.[115] It implemented suffrage restrictions, including a literacy test, good character provision, poll tax, and understanding clause.[116] Following Mississippi's model was South Carolina in 1895, Louisiana in 1898, and North Carolina by means of an amendment in 1900.[117] The process of disfranchisement quickly became a Southern effort as state conventions began borrowing ideas from each other.[118] This combined effort led to an evolution of complex suffrage requirements.[119] Therefore, Alabama had a powerful set of examples to mold into the creation of its own constitution.

---

112 *See* Flynt, *supra* note 16, at 68 (explaining that the 1875 Constitution abolished the State Board of Education and reduced funds for public schools); McMillan, *supra* note 8, at 325-26 (explaining that the 1901 Constitution allocated a statewide tax for education but did not adopt a much needed special municipal tax for schools or reestablish the Board of Education); *see id.* at 353 ("Many illiterate whites were disfranchised on reaching 21 years, because, although Alabama leaders linked the suffrage provisions with increased education, time as well as a good school system was necessary in order to reduce Alabama's high illiteracy rate.").

113 *See generally* William H. Stewart, *The Tortured History of Efforts to Revise the Alabama Constitution of 1901*, 53 ALA. L. REV. 295, 296 (2001–2002) ("It could be argued that Alabama has not had comprehensive constitutional reform since 1875 because, except for the black disenfranchising provisions, the 1901 Constitution is so similar to the one adopted a quarter-century earlier."); Bailey Thomson, *Conceived in Fraud*, MOBILE REG., Dec. 11, 1994, at C2 ("The great industrialists of Birmingham and the mighty planters of the Black Belt wrote a constitution that was even more perniciously devoted to protecting their interests than had been the 1875 predecessor, itself a product of reaction and white supremacy.").

114 Woodward, *supra* note 88, at 321.

115 *Id.*

116 R. Volney Riser, DEFYING DISFRANCHISEMENT: BLACK VOTING RIGHTS ACTIVISM IN THE JIM CROW SOUTH, 1890–1908 39 (2010).

117 Additionally, Virginia set up a disfranchisement constitution in 1901–1902, followed by Georgia by amendment in 1908, and Oklahoma in 1910. WOODWARD, *supra* note 88, at 321.

118 *Id.* at 334.

119 *Id.*

After a decade of discussion on a constitutional convention,[120] an enabling act was passed in the Alabama legislature, and the convention was presented to the people for a vote.[121] The Democrats made the convention a party issue and believed it their duty to campaign for the convention's favor "by raising the Negro issue and by assuring the whites of the hill counties that no white man would be denied the franchise."[122] Additionally, Bourbons outside of the Black Belt were campaigning for honest elections, which they argued would be "possible only if 'corruptible voters' . . . were removed from the polls."[123] Essentially, they were arguing that "whites would stop stealing only when blacks had nothing to steal."[124]

On April 23, 1901, 70,305 votes were cast for a convention and 45,505 against.[125] In the twenty-one Black Belt counties, which were predominately African-American, the convention won 32,202 to 5,273 (a margin of 26,929).[126] In the counties where white voters were in the majority, the convention lost 40,232 to 38,103 (a margin of 2,129).[127] Because the Democrats had made it well known that the goal of the convention would be to disfranchise black voters, it is highly unlikely that blacks would have voted in the majority for this convention. Consequently, it is reasonable to assume that the vote was thwarted again by the political parties. If the numbers are not themselves telling,[128] two weeks before the election, members of the Democratic Party admitted to each other that they intended to manipulate the black vote.[129]

In the first hours of the convention, after the President, John Knox of Calhoun County,[130] was presented by the Chief Justice, Knox introduced the

---

120 McMillan, *supra* note 8, at 249-51.

121 *Id.* at 259-60.

122 Joseph H. Taylor, *Populism and Disfranchisement in Alabama*, J. OF NEGRO HIST. 410, 420 (1949); *see* McMillan, *supra* note 8, at 259-60. Poorer whites were skeptical of the Democrats' disfranchising campaign: "No doubt, it was the opposition of the poor whites, especially of North Alabama, which proved to be the greatest barrier to a constitutional convention." *Id.* at 254.

123 Jackson, *supra* note 10, at 135.

124 *Id.*

125 McMillan, *supra* note 8, at 261.

126 Taylor, *supra* note 122, at 422.

127 *Id.*

128 McMillan, *supra* note 8, at 262. Two Black Belt counties give a great indication of the value of the black vote. Dallas County had 45,372 blacks and 9,285 whites living in the county at the time of the election. In Dallas County, 5,668 votes were cast for the convention and only 200 against. In Lowndes County, there were 5,500 black voters and 1,000 white voters, but the convention won with 3,226 votes in favor and 338 against. *Id.*

129 *Id.* at 261 n.93 ("In the privacy of the State Democratic Executive Committee meeting, about two weeks before the election, some Democratic leaders frankly admitted they intended 'to vote' or 'count out' the Negro.").

130 In a speech by President Knox's Secretary, Neil Stern, Knox was described as a kind man who loved blacks, exemplified by his substantial bequests to "an old colored draymen who had been his friend since boyhood," a faithful servant, and "a hospital ward for colored patients."

delegates to the importance of the issue at hand, and the *Journal of the Convention* divides this speech up into sections. The first four section headings are: "Importance of the Issue," "Northern Interference," "The Attitude of the Southern Man Towards the Negro," and "White Supremacy by Law."[131] In the beginning hours of this convention, the President made clear that what ignited the convention (blacks, scalawags, and carpetbaggers) would also be defused by the ensuing constitution.[132]

President Knox argued that the Northerners were just as much to blame for racism, because "race prejudice exists at the North in as pronounced a form as at the South."[133] However, he praised the South for its congeniality towards black men and women but believed that blacks were not yet fitted for participation in the government.[134] And so, the time had come to develop white supremacy by law:

> I submit to the intelligent judgment of this Convention that there is no higher duty resting upon us, as citizens and as delegates, than that which requires us to embody in the fundamental law such provisions as will enable us to protect the sanctity of the ballot in every portion of the State.[135]

Ironically, President Knox reiterated that fraud was not the answer, but if it were not for fraud, the Constitution of 1901 and its predecessors might have never emerged. Nevertheless, President Knox explicitly stated that white supremacy must be established by "law—not by force or fraud."[136] Because corruption and fraud were known problems, President Knox addressed the issue with the justification that "whatever manipulation of the ballot that has occurred in this State has been [in response to] the menace of negro domination."[137] And thus, he reaffirmed the idea that had it not been for the "Radicals,"[138] disfranchisement would not be necessary; the

---

Neil Stern, ADDRESS BEFORE THE SURVIVORS OF THE CONSTITUTIONAL CONVENTION OF ALABAMA OF 1901 7 (Nov. 4, 1937) (transcript available in the W. S. Hoole Special Collections Library). Stern expressed his wish that Northerners "could read the lesson to be found in the life of this leader of Southern thought who bore the foremost role in taking suffrage from the negroes, because they were not qualified to exercise it, but who throughout his life was unceasingly their friend and benefactor." *Id.* at 8.

[131] JOURNAL OF PROCEEDINGS at 8-12.

[132] *Id.*

[133] *Id.* at 9.

[134] *Id.* at 11 ("The Southern man knows the negro, and the negro knows him. The only conflict which has, or is ever likely to arise, springs from the effort of ill-advised friends in the North to confer upon him, without previous training or preparation, places of power and responsibility, for which he is wholly unfitted, either by capacity or experience.").

[135] *Id.* at 12.

[136] *Id.*; Flynt, *supra* note 16, at 71.

[137] JOURNAL OF PROCEEDINGS at 12.

[138] The term Radical referred to the carpetbaggers and scalawags who made up the 1868 convention and regime. *See* McMillan, *supra* note 8, at 362.

manipulation of the ballot would not be necessary; and the manipulation of the ballot to ensure that disfranchisement resulted would be justified because of what those "Radicals" did, or at least, this is how the Democrats would see it. Furthermore, Knox defended any sort of "stratagem," possibly referencing intimidation and violence, because "such a course might be warranted when considered as the right of revolution, and as an act of necessity for self-preservation."[139] However, he urged that "stealing" was not the answer for the future because our sons would believe that it is not only right to steal votes, but "to steal whatever [they] may need or greatly desire."[140] With unintentional irony, he warned that this influence would infect all branches of society.[141]

As with the conventions of 1868 and 1875, the delegates to the 1901 Convention were not balanced with regard to political affiliation. For example, the 1901 Convention consisted of 155 white delegates: 141 Democrats, 7 Populists, 6 Republicans, and 1 Independent.[142] Sixty-three of the delegates were from the Black Belt counties,[143] and, "[t]o the everlasting shame of [the] profession," the convention has been termed a "lawyer's convention."[144] President Knox had the power to appoint all committees, and the Suffrage and Elections Committee would be made up of twenty-five members.[145] Every member of this "all powerful" committee was a Democrat.[146]

After much debate, the Suffrage Committee settled on a smorgasbord of disfranchising clauses. First, there were residency requirements, which included that a person must have resided "in the State at least two years, in the county one year, and in the precinct or ward three months, immediately preceding the election."[147] Next, those who were to be grandfathered in were listed under the "descendents" and understanding clauses.[148] All of those who had served in or had descendants who had served in any major war from the American Revolution to the Spanish-American War could register before December 20, 1902.[149] Additionally, those who were of "good character" and understood "the duties and obligations of citizenship under

---

139 *Id.* at 13.

140 *Id.* at 12.

141 *Id.*

142 Flynt, *supra* note 16, at 73.

143 Taylor, *supra* note 122, at 422.

144 Lynch v. State, No. 5:08-cv-00450-CLS, slip op. at 579-80 (N.D. Ala. Nov. 7, 2011) (explaining that ninety-six of the members were lawyers).

145 RULES OF THE CONSTITUTIONAL CONVENTION, 1901 14 (The Brown Printing Co. 1901).

146 Taylor, *supra* note 122, at 423 (explaining the composition of the Suffrage and Elections Committee). "Sixteen of the 22 counties represented on the Committee were carried by Jones and Oates in 1892 and 1894." *Id.* And the Black Belt counties had one more representative than the white counties (thirteen versus twelve). *Id.*

147 ALA. CONST. of 1901, art. VIII §178.

148 *Id.* §180.

149 *Id.*

a republican form of government," could register before December 20, 1902.[150] However, the statute did not define good character or the duties and obligations of citizenship.[151] Anyone who was lucky enough to register under these two clauses would remain registered for life.[152] Everyone else would have to renew their registration annually.[153]

Those who registered after January 1, 1903 had to be able to read and write any "article of the Constitution of the United States in the English language" unless unable "solely" because of a physical disability.[154] Also, voters had to be lawfully employed for the year preceding registration unless physically unable.[155] There were property requirements of real or personal property taxable for $300 or more, and those taxes must have been paid.[156]

Additionally, no Alabama voter, whether temporarily or permanently registered, could be an "idiot or insane person[]."[157] And, no Alabama voter could be convicted of a long list of crimes, including vagrancy (a crime frequently charged against blacks), "any infamous crime or crime involving moral turpitude" (vague enough for liberal interpretation), and manipulation of the ballot.[158] Everyone between the ages of twenty-one and forty-two was required to pay an annual and cumulative $1.50 poll tax.[159] Therefore, if a voter failed to pay the poll tax one year, he would be required to pay $3.00 the next year to vote. The price-tag could easily add up.

The grandfather, "descendants," clause proposed by Alabama was different from that utilized in other Southern states. Louisiana and North Carolina had chosen to grandfather in everyone who was eligible to vote in

---

150 *Id.*

151 *Id.*

152 Riser, *supra* note 116, at 121.

153 *Id.*

154 ALA. CONST. of 1901, art. VIII §181.

155 *Id.*

156 *Id.*

157 *Id.* §182.

158 *Id.* The full list of crimes included: "those who shall be convicted of treason, murder, arson, embezzlement, malfeasance in office, larceny, receiving stolen property, obtaining property or money under false pretenses, perjury, subornation of perjury, robbery, assault with intent to rob, burglary, forgery, bribery, assault and battery on the wife, bigamy, living in adultery, sodomy, incest, rape, miscegenation, crime against nature, or any crime punishable by imprisonment in the penitentiary, or of any infamous crime or crime involving moral turpitude; also any person who shall be convicted as a vagrant or tramp, or of selling or offering to sell his vote or the vote of another, or of buying or offering to buy the vote of another, or of making or offering to make a false return in any election by the people or in any primary election to procure the nomination or election of any person to any office, or of suborning any witness or registrar to secure the registration of any person as an elector." *Id.*; *see* Jackson, *supra* note 10, at 136-37 (explaining that many of the crimes listed were frequently charged against blacks).

159 *Id.* §194.

any state prior to the Reconstruction Act, mandating black men's enfranchisement, before January 1, 1867.[160] Alabamians believed this would be a risky endeavor as it would essentially exclude all blacks, and thus, chose a clause that appeared racially equitable. Because African Americans had fought in wars, including the Spanish American War, it appeared that some blacks would be grandfathered in. Therefore, as will be explained further, Alabama's grandfather clause would not conflict with the Fifteenth Amendment. It did not discriminate based on race because both races were qualified to be grandfathered into enfranchisement.

Nevertheless, the Boards of Registrars held the power to enfranchise or disfranchise. Every county had a board of registrars consisting of three "reputable and suitable persons" appointed by a committee of the Governor, State Auditor, and Agriculture Commissioner.[161] Obviously, these appointed members would be faithful to the dominant party of the state. As Professor Rob Riser observed, the boards ruled at their own whim: "Through official foot dragging, arbitrary denial of applications, and general malfeasance, the boards could prevent anyone from registering before January 1, 1903."[162]

The Constitution of 1901, on its face, appeared to provide justice to those unfairly denied their suffrage.[163] Section 186 created an appeals process for "any person to whom registration is denied."[164] However, as Riser explained, this appeals process was a "fiction."[165] Following the advice of South Carolina's delegate and U.S. Senator, Ben Tillman,[166] Alabama's delegates had intentionally created a costly and time-consuming appeals process.[167] A discouraged citizen could file a petition with the Circuit Court, and after the jury's decision, an appeal would automatically go to the Alabama Supreme Court.[168] If the Supreme Court favored the petitioner, then, and only then, could he be registered.[169] Alabama had obeyed Tillman's warning that disfranchisement would not be safe "unless we put in the Constitution a provision that will give the people the idea that we are going

---

[160] Riser, *supra* note 116, at 106.

[161] ALA. CONST. of 1901, art. VIII §186.

[162] Riser, *supra* note 116, at 123.

[163] ALA. CONST. of 1901, art. VIII §186.

[164] *Id.*

[165] Riser, *supra* note 116, at 123.

[166] Benjamin Tillman dominated South Carolina's disfranchising convention. McMillan, *supra* note 8, at 266 n.21. As U.S. Senator, he advocated ratification of Alabama's 1901 Constitution by explaining that no white men had been disfranchised by the South Carolina Constitution of 1895. *Id.* at 346. He maintained regular correspondence with the delegates to the 1901 Convention. *Id.* at 275. As U.S. Senator, he was the leader in opposing the Treaty of Paris, which was signed at the close of the Spanish-American War, and its resulting American imperialism. R. Volney Riser, *The Burdens of Being White: Empire and Disfranchisement*, 53 ALA. L. REV. 243, 258 (2001).

[167] Riser, *supra* note 116, at 123.

[168] ALA. CONST. of 1901, art. VIII §186.

[169] *Id.*

to have fairness."[170] To further this illusion, the constitution's writers created a provision that prohibited individuals involved in election scams from voting.[171] Unfortunately, these promising provisions did not eradicate Alabama's corrupt elections.[172]

C. Ratification of the Constitution of 1901: Fraud's Final Victory

Based on the returns, it seemed blacks were in favor of returning their new independence back to their old white superior.[173] In fact, this constitution seems to owe its existence to those willing blacks who endorsed their own disfranchisement. The Black Belt returned a vote of 36,224 to 5,471 for ratification,[174] and it was late in reporting this vote.[175] For the rest of the state and the majority of whites, it was a close question, but the constitution was rejected by 76,263 to 72,389.[176] In these counties, blacks voted against the constitution.[177] The *Bessemer Weekly* cried that a "'fraud of the grossest' character had been committed . . . and the explanation that the 'colored voters through ignorance voted for ratification . . . is . . . far from plausible or correct.'"[178] Recently, Judge Lynwood Smith stated that "those numbers stink like rotten fish."[179] Why the outrage? Many of the purported voters were never seen: "[I]n some counties almost every eligible Negro was 'voted' although thousands never appeared at the polls."[180]

---

170 Riser, *supra* note 116, at 123.

171 ALA. CONST. of 1901 art. VIII §182.

172 In concluding his article on disfranchisement in Alabama, Joseph Taylor cited an editorial from the August 11, 1940 *Montgomery Advertiser*, which was obviously a cry for help: "There are several old vices prevalent in many parts of Alabama: gambling, drunkenness, prostitution and stealing. But the greatest single vice in Alabama, the greatest menace to our social and political order, is vote-selling. . . . Evil reports from every section of the state have been published. The reports are true. Every practicing politician in Alabama, every alert newspaper, every sophisticated fireside sitter knows that the reports are true." Taylor, *supra* note 122, at 426.

173 In Dr. Bailey Thomson's words, "What an irony that the planters stole votes from the very black men that the convention proposed to disfranchise." Bailey Thomson, *Conceived in Fraud*, MOBILE REG., Dec. 11, 1994, at C2.

174 Riser, *supra* note 116, at 137. In the Black Belt counties of Dallas, Hale, and Wilcox, with only 5,623 white male voters combined, 17,475 votes were cast for the constitution and only 508 against it. McMillan, *supra* note 8, at 350. Similarly, the Black Belt County of Lowndes had a population of 1,000 white and 5,600 black adult male voters. In this county, the constitution received 5,326 votes for ratification and only 338 against. Flynt, *supra* note 16, at 75.

175 McMillan, *supra* note 8, at 350.

176 Riser, *supra* note 116, at 137.

177 Lynch v. State, No. 5:08-cv-00450-CLS, slip op. at 617 (N.D. Ala. Nov. 7, 2011).

178 Riser, *supra* note 116, at 136-37 (quoting BESSEMER WEEKLY, Nov. 16, 1901).

179 *Lynch*, No. 5:08-cv-00450-CLS, slip op. at 616.

180 McMillan, *supra* note 8, at 351; *see* Jackson, *supra* note 10, at 139 ("If you didn't know better, it would seem that nearly 12,000 black Alabamians had gone to the polls, some unseen by anyone, and voted for their own disfranchisement.").

The result was disfranchisement en masse. In 1900, there were approximately 181,315 eligible black voters, but by 1903, only 2,980 black males were registered.[181] Despite the assurance that no white man would be disfranchised,[182] over 40,000 white males had lost their right to vote between 1900 and 1903.[183] Many whites could not afford to pay the poll tax, and as it accumulated each year, the possibility of enfranchisement became more difficult for them.[184] Therefore, the Black Belt planters were successful in disfranchising "the uneducated and propertyless whites in order to legally create a conservative electorate."[185] All along, white supremacy had been a euphemism for white *elite* supremacy.

III. Where was the Anticipated Justice? Role of the Federal Government before the 1901 Constitution

In 1868, the United States Congress ratified the Fourteenth Amendment, and in 1870, the Fifteenth Amendment was ratified.[186] Both amendments purported to guard the rights and privileges of Americans, including the right to vote.[187] Yet, the federal branches would permit Southern governments to thwart the entire purpose of these novel amendments.

For example, the Fourteenth Amendment makes it a political crime to withhold the right to vote to any male over twenty-one.[188] If a state is found in violation of this rule, its representation is supposed to be cut.[189] Despite a Republican federal government, Alabama's representation was not curtailed and thus called into question the power of the Fourteenth Amendment.[190] President Knox noted in his opening speech to the Constitutional Convention that the federal government, particularly United States President William McKinley, was "fast yielding to reason" and had not cut Alabama's

[181] McMillan, *supra* note 8, at 352.

[182] Riser, *supra* note 116, at 134 (describing the Democratic Campaign Committee's effort to quell the fears of white voters and persuade them to vote for ratification).

[183] Flynt, *supra* note 16, at 75.

[184] McMillan, *supra* note 8, at 353.

[185] *Id.* at 269.

[186] U.S. CONST. amend. XIV-XV.

[187] *Id.*

[188] U.S. CONST. amend. XIV §2.

[189] *Id.* ("But when the right to vote at any election for the choice of electors for President and Vice President of the United States, Representatives in Congress, the executive and judicial officers of a state, or the members of the legislature thereof, is denied to any of the male inhabitants of such state, being twenty-one years of age, and citizens of the United States, or in any way abridged, except for participation in rebellion, or other crime, the basis of representation therein shall be reduced in the proportion which the number of such male citizens shall bear to the whole number of male citizens twenty-one years of age in such state.").

[190] *See* McMillan, *supra* note 8, at 232, 290-91.

representation, implying that such was warranted under the United States Constitution.[191]

> While we may differ from him politically, there is not an enlightened and patriotic Southern man who fails to see that much of this result is due to the honorable and statesmanlike policy of the present Chief Executive of these United States, who, by the consideration he has shown our section in many ways, notably in the Spanish-American war, and by refusing to lend his approval to any movement looking to the reduction of our representation in Congress or in the Electoral College; has shown himself capable of being President of the whole country.[192]

Unfortunately, all three branches of the federal government influenced the South's disfranchisement movement. The sections, North and South, had become allies during the Spanish-American War, and Congress found itself confused with the race issue as the United States expanded. But it was America's highest Court that "made a clear path for the Southern doctrine of a white man's government."[193]

A. Delegates No Longer Fear the Federal Government

By 1901, "America was of one mind with the South regarding Negro inferiority."[194] Members of the federal government, including the United States Supreme Court, shared in this belief, but their motivations were divided between paternalism and racism.[195] The delegates at the 1901 Convention understood that the federal government was not likely to intervene in their process of disfranchisement. Three key events encouraged this belief: the Spanish-American War, American expansion, and the Supreme Court's liberal interpretation of the Fourteenth and Fifteenth Amendments.

First, the Spanish-American War of 1898 had somewhat reunited the North and South. The sections had joined together for a common purpose, and "a sense of nationality had been rediscovered, based upon consciousness of national strength and unity."[196] In his opening speech, Knox praised

---

[191] JOURNAL OF PROCEEDINGS at 10.

[192] *Id.* at 10-11.

[193] *Three Constitutional Questions Decided by the Federal Supreme Court During the Last Four Months*, 37 AM. L. REV. 503, 503 (1903).

[194] Flynt, *supra* note 16, at 70.

[195] Two U.S. Supreme Court Justices express this divide. Justice David Josiah Brewer expressed a racial tone when he spoke disapprovingly of granting statehood to new United States territories, "Who can tell how many centuries must pass before the savage and semi-civilized races of these islands become fit to assume the responsibilities of self-government? . . . In the South we have the rapidly increasing colored population . . . elevated in ignorance to citizenship." R. Volney Riser, *supra* note 166, at 254-55. However, Justice John Marshall Harlan "conceived of a paternalistic, republican mission for the Anglo-Saxon race and believed that Hawaiians, Puerto Ricans, and Filipinos could be prepared for U.S. citizenship." *Id.* at 257.

[196] Paul H. Buck, THE ROAD TO REUNION 306 (1937).

President McKinley for "a reunited people . . . to place our government in the very front rank with the nations of the world."[197]

Second, America had begun expanding its territory, partly as a result of the Spanish-American War and the acquisition of Hawaii. The United States government was unsure what to do with these new people.[198] In a speech praising the report of the Suffrage and Elections Committee, President Knox cited Illinois' Senator Shelby Cullom, chairman of the Hawaiian Commission, for his stand on this issue.[199] His report on the Hawaiian Islands to Congress explained that a concern of Hawaii was "the adaptability of the several races of the people who inhabit the islands for American citizenship and their ability to sustain the obligations which attach to the right of suffrage."[200] Senator Cullom worried that the Hawaiians were not a body of educated people who could appreciate the responsibilities of free suffrage.[201] Similarly, some Alabamians, even without regard to politics, were concerned that blacks did not possess the requisite knowledge to effectively vote.[202] However, President Knox cited Cullom's section of the report to justify the descendants clause, which was never suggested as a suffrage limitation for Hawaii.[203] The suffrage limitations initially imposed on Hawaii included a literacy test and, to vote for senators, possession of a minimum amount of property.[204] Senator Cullom was an advocate for stricter disfranchising clauses.[205] He "proposed using property and economic status to regulate suffrage," but the House of Representatives struck the entire text of Cullom's disfranchising bill.[206] Therefore, despite President Knox's implications, Congress was not on par with the South's disfranchisement plan.

---

197 JOURNAL OF PROCEEDINGS AT 11.

198 McMillan, *supra* note 8, at 231 ("As the United States acquired subject races overseas, the people of the North were forced to consider the race problem objectively, without any sentimental prejudices growing out of the Civil War.").

199 REMARKS OF HON. JNO. B. KNOX IN SUPPORT OF THE MAJORITY REPORT OF THE COMMITTEE ON SUFFRAGE AND ELECTIONS 20-21 (July 26, 1901) (pamphlet available at W. S. Hoole Special Collections Library) (5,000 copies were printed in pamphlet form).

200 *Id.*

201 *Id.* ("The American idea of universal suffrage presupposes that the body of citizens who are to exercise it in a free and independent manner have, by inheritance or education, such knowledge and appreciation of the responsibilities of free suffrage, and of a full participation in the sovereignty of the country as to be able to maintain a republican government.").

202 *See id.*

203 *Id.*

204 *See* Robert Volney Riser II, "Between Scylla and Charybdis: Alabama's 1901 Constitutional Convention Assesses the Perils of Disfranchisement," 88-89 (Nov. 14, 2000) (unpublished M.A. thesis, University of Alabama) (on file with Gorgas Library, University of Alabama). Riser observes that the property requirements might have been difficult to obtain, but most of Hawaii's population was well educated and literate. *Id.* at 89.

205 *Id.* at 90-91.

206 *Id.* at 92-93.

Nevertheless, the federal government was debating the race issue and had begun to consider the South's concerns.

B. The Highest Court Posed No Threat

Regardless of the attitudes of the other branches, the federal courts are to blame for their apathy. Several Supreme Court cases were cited during discussions of the Suffrage and Elections Committee. These cases would give the committee comfort that their actions would not be dismantled by the federal courts. For example, *Minor v. Happersett* was cited for the proposition that the "Constitution of the United States does not confer the right of suffrage upon anyone."[207] In this case, a woman attempted to claim her right to vote under the Fourteenth Amendment's privileges and immunities clause, and the Court held that while women were citizens, citizenship did not necessarily make them voters.[208]

Likewise, in *United States v. Reese*, the Court stated that the Fifteenth Amendment also "does not confer the right of suffrage upon anyone."[209] In this case, the Court struck down two sections of the 1870 Civil Rights Act for being overly broad because they protected suffrage beyond race discrimination and exceeded the scope of the Fifteenth Amendment.[210] Consequently, as the statutes were deemed limitless, the Court dismissed the charges against two white election officials in Kentucky for refusing to count the vote of a black citizen.[211]

On the same day *Reese* was decided, the Court came down with an even narrower decision in *United States v. Cruikshank*.[212] In this case, nine members of a white mob had been convicted for murdering over a hundred black men after a disputed gubernatorial election in Louisiana.[213] The Court reversed the convictions for a number of reasons, including that the indictments had not explicitly stated that they were motivated by race, an apparent requirement of the 1870 Civil Rights Act.[214] In response to the allegation that defendants had hindered the black citizens' right to vote, the Court held that this right derives from state power.[215] "Concerned with congressional efforts to expand the powers of the federal government,"[216] the Court ob-

---

207 Minor v. Happersett, 88 U.S. 162, 178 (1874).

208 *Id.* at 173-74.

209 United States v. Reese, 92 U.S. 214, 217 (1875).

210 *Id.* at 215.

211 *Id.* at 220-22; *see also* Brent J. Aucoin, A RIFT IN THE CLOUDS 10 (2007) (explaining that the Court's decision to allow these "racist" election officials to go free sent a message that it was "determined to find ways to avoid sanctioning the spirit of the Reconstruction amendments and laws").

212 92 U.S. 542 (1875).

213 *Id.*; *see* Aucoin, *supra* note 211, at 10-11.

214 *Cruikshank*, 92 U.S. at 555.

215 *Id.* at 556.

served that states have separate powers from the nation, and after summing up the aforementioned cases, the Court concluded that the right to vote does not derive from United States' citizenship and is not secured by the United States Constitution.[217]

These three cases fueled President Knox's conclusion that discrimination would not be scrutinized under any sort of reasonableness standard. Knox stated before the Suffrage Committee:

> It seems clear to me, both upon principle and authority, that while the State cannot discriminate against the voter on account of his race, color or previous condition of servitude, it may discriminate against him on any other ground, and it is not material whether the discrimination made is reasonable or unreasonable.[218]

However, the paramount decision that freed the convention of its federal fears was *Williams v. Mississippi*.[219] When Mississippians convened in 1890 to create their disfranchising constitution, they made clear, like Alabamians, that they wanted "to eliminate as many black voters as possible."[220] Also, like Alabama, Mississippians had targeted "illiteracy, poverty, and criminal proclivities," and the result was that both blacks and whites were essentially disfranchised.[221] Consequently, the Supreme Court ruled that Mississippi's constitution did not target blacks, because it "reach[es] weak and vicious white men as well as weak and vicious black men, and whatever is sinister in [the constitution's] intention, if anything, can be prevented by both races by the exertion of that duty which voluntarily pays taxes and refrains from crime."[222] Essentially, the Court was blaming the victim, and it concluded that Mississippi's constitution and its statutes "do not on their face discriminate between the races, and it has not been shown that their actual administration was evil; only that evil was possible under them."[223]

---

216 Riser, *supra* note 204, at 110.

217 *Cruikshank*, 92 U.S. at 555-56.

218 REMARKS OF HON. JNO. B. KNOX IN SUPPORT OF THE MAJORITY REPORT OF THE COMMITTEE ON SUFFRAGE AND ELECTIONS 7 (July 26, 1901) (pamphlet available at W. S. Hoole Special Collections Library) (5,000 copies were printed in pamphlet form).

219 170 U.S. 213 (1898); *see* JOURNAL OF PROCEEDINGS at 14. In his opening speech, President Knox identified Mississippi as the "pioneer State in this movement." Mississippi had a poll tax requirement, registration requirement, and an understanding clause that was exclusively determined by registrars. While he warned that adopting the understanding clause would pervert the goal of eliminating corruption, Knox acknowledged that *Williams v. Mississippi* understood Mississippi to discriminate against the characteristics of blacks and not of their race. *Id.* at 15.

220 Riser, *supra* note 116, at 70.

221 *Id.*

222 *Williams*, 170 U.S. at 222.

223 *Id.* at 225.

The Court left unnoted what evidence might have proven racial discrimination or an "evil administration."[224]

Because Alabama had the audacity to hire a stenographer to record verbatim the convention's proceedings, the delegates must have been confident that they were not going to be punished for their actions. While many expressed their reluctance to speak openly at first,[225] the convention of well-educated persons accepted the risks and were praised by the state for their open disclosure.[226] Despite the fears of a minority, the United States Supreme Court would not be quick to use the convention's notes to the constitution's disadvantage. And no group was more surprised than blacks themselves: "Although the Court had historically been no friend to the Negro, this turn of events was nevertheless a bit perplexing to blacks because their closest white allies—northern Republicans—dominated the Court at the time."[227]

V. Conclusion

In 1915, Governor Emmet O'Neal met before the legislature to beg for a new constitution.[228] He had been a delegate at the 1901 Convention, and his father, Edward, had been a delegate at the 1875 Convention. Governor O'Neal explained to the legislature that the 1875 Constitution had been adopted to prevent the recurrence of the conditions of Reconstruction.[229] In 1901, when "the danger of federal interference no longer existed," reforming suffrage was the "paramount issue" and "little consideration was given to other matters of reform."[230] Therefore, the Constitution of 1875 had essentially been readopted.[231] One hundred years ago, before Alabama's law-

---

[224] *See* Riser, *supra* note 116, at 71.

[225] *Id.* 112-14. Delegate John Ashcraft warned that the convention might be judged, possibly by the Supreme Court, "by the bitterness which the sense of our ever pressing injury will be seen to infect our debates." *Id.* at 113. Delegate Thomas Long begged for a "record of what we do" but not "a record of what we say." *Id.*

[226] *Id.* at 114.

[227] Aucoin, *supra* note 211, at 1-2. However, it is important to point out that the Republican Party, while anti-slavery, was divided between those who favored giving freed slaves individual freedoms and those who did not. Interview with Tony A. Freyer, Professor, University of Alabama School of Law, in Tuscaloosa, Ala. (Nov. 15, 2012); *see also* R. Volney Riser, *supra* note 166, at 254-58 (explaining that members of the U.S. Supreme Court, including Justice Edward Douglas White and Justice John Marshall Harlan, were divided between racists and paternalists).

[228] Emmet O'Neal, "Constitutional Convention – Necessity for New Constitution –Message of Emmet O'Neal Governor to the Legislature of Alabama" (Jan. 15, 1915) (transcript available in the W. S. Hoole Special Collections Library).

[229] *Id.* at 1.

[230] *Id.* at 4.

[231] *Id.*

makers, Governor O'Neal made the bold statement that the law was "antiquated."[232] How would he define our law now?

Today, as in years before, the threads are continuing to unravel. The coat that Jefferson spoke of, the young boy's coat, is not only too tight, but it is an old, worn coat that is incessantly tugged. Reminders of the discomfort, such as when an Alabama voter flips over his or her ballot, as they did in the recent election, to see not only a long list of proposed amendments, but one in particular that asks voters whether they would like to repeal portions of an amendment relating to segregation of schools and poll taxes,[233] are all too frequent. Cases sometimes arise on the docket attacking the constitution and its provisions.[234] Recently, in 2010, a group of plaintiffs challenged the validity of the constitution, but the Alabama Supreme Court denied their claim based on standing.[235] In order to have standing to bring the case, the Court stated that the plaintiffs must have been voters at the time of ratification.[236]

However, Judge Lynwood Smith invites such a case to be brought in federal court.[237] In one of his recent cases, *Lynch v. State*, plaintiffs were not challenging the legitimacy of the 1901 ratification election, but they were challenging the property tax structure of Alabama, alleging that it had a racially-discriminatory intent and racially-disproportionate effect on the state's public school system.[238] Precedent and the rational basis standard of review required Judge Smith to rule against the plaintiffs, but instead of simply stating the law, Judge Smith wrote an 804-page opinion.[239] Judge Smith wrote at length to explain the constitution that Alabamians survive under, its history, and its setbacks. Because the plaintiffs did not base their challenge on the legitimacy of the constitution, Judge Smith stated that the issue is left "for another day, and another forum."[240] He concluded with the words of folk singer Bob Dylan in his famous song, "Blowin' in the Wind":

---

[232] *Id.* at 1.

[233] *See* Public Affairs Research Council of Alabama, *PARCA Analysis of Proposed Statewide Amendments for the November 6th General Election* (Oct. 19, 2012), *available at* http://parca.samford.edu/parca2/perspective/Statewide%20Amendments.pdf (last visited July 20, 2015).

[234] *See, e.g.*, Lynch v. State, No. 5:08-cv-00450-CLS, slip op. at 620 (N.D. Ala. Nov. 7, 2011); *Ex parte* King, 50 So. 3d 1056 (Ala. 2010); State v. Manley, 441 So. 2d 864 (Ala. 1983).

[235] *Ex parte* King, 50 So. 3d 1056 (Ala. 2010).

[236] *Id.* at 1062.

[237] Lynch v. State, No. 5:08-cv-00450-CLS, slip op. at 620; *see also* Bob Blalock, *1901 Constitution Fraudulent, 'Criminal,' and Ours* (Oct. 30, 2011, 5:43 AM), http://blog.al.com/bblalock/2011/10/bob_blalock_1901_constitution.html ("Smith practically begs for a federal lawsuit that challenges the validity of the Alabama Constitution because, as has been well-documented, supporters stole the referendum that approved it."), last visited July 20, 2015.

[238] *Lynch*, No. 5:08-cv-00450-CLS, slip op. at 797.

[239] *Id.*

[240] *Id.* at 200.

> How many times can a man turn his head, and pretend that he just doesn't see? How many ears must one man have, before he can hear people cry? The answer my friend is blowing in the wind, the answer is blowing in the wind.[241]

Because of Judge Smith's advocacy, to cite another Bob Dylan song, there is hope that "the times they are a-changing.'"[242] Only when Alabamians understand the history of their forefathers, the writers of their laws, will they be able to hang up their coats, and rid themselves of an "antiquated" burden.

---

[241] *Id.* at 804; Bob Dylan, *Blowin' in the Wind*, on THE FREEWHEELIN' BOB DYLAN (Sony Records).

[242] Bob Dylan, *The Times They Are A-Changin'*, on THE TIMES THEY ARE A-CHANGIN' (Sony Records).

The Uniform Beneath the Robe

Deirdra Drinkard

I. Introduction

"Uncontrolled and uncontrollable liberty is an enemy to domestic peace."[1] These words resonated with Supreme Court Justice Abe Fortas as he read Justice Hugo Black's dissent in *Tinker v. Des Moines Independent Community School District*.[2] Shocked by the statements, Fortas noted in the margins next to this statement, "Hugo Black!!"[3] The disbelief that Black would write such things in his opinion is apparent by Fortas's continued use of exclamation marks throughout his copy of Black's dissent.[4]

Fortas, who delivered the majority opinion, was not the only one Black managed to shock with his dissent. In fact, Chief Justice Earl Warren, who joined the majority, even said, "Old Hugo really got hung up in his jock strap on that one."[5] With his blistering dissent against the majority's ruling that the First Amendment afforded protection to students wearing black armbands to school in opposition to the Vietnam War, Black shocked the nation[6] by taking an unusual stance in favor of the government—or in this case, the school officials in *Tinker*—and against the speaker.[7]

What happened to Hugo Black, a civil libertarian[8] and a defender of the First Amendment,[9] to cause him to write such a strongly worded opinion in opposition to the students' symbolic speech against the Vietnam War? Had his age affected or altered his views over time?[10] Was his disappointment

---

1 *Tinker v. Des Moines Indep. Cmty. School Dist.*, 393 U.S. 503, 524 (1969) (Black, J., dissenting).

2 *See* John W. Johnson, The Struggle for Student Rights 179 (1997).

3 *Id.*

4 Johnson, *supra* note 2, at 178.

5 *See* Roger K. Newman, Hugo Black: A Biography 592 (1997).

6 *See Armbands Yes, Miniskirts No*, New York Times, February 26, 1969 (describing Black's opinion as a "peppery dissent," which did not "rightly" draw the line between symbolic speech and disorderly conduct) [hereinafter *Armbands Yes*].

7 *Tinker*, 393 U.S. at 524 n.1 (1969).

8 Newman, *supra* note 5, at back cover.

9 *See* Wilson Ray Huhn, *In Defense of the Roosevelt Court*, 2 Fla. A & M U. L. Rev. 1, 14 (2007) (recognizing that Black was well known for his defense of the First Amendment, specifically pointing to Black's opposition to obscenity laws).

10 *See* David J. Garrow, *Mental Decrepitude on the U.S. Supreme Court: The Historical Case for a 28th Amendment*, 67 U. Chi. L. Rev. 995, 1050 (2000) (noting that advanced age and mental capacity of the Justices has troubled the Supreme Court, citing Justice Black as one of

with children—particularly his own grandchildren[11]—a reason for his suggestion that children should be seen and not heard?[12] Various academics have attempted to answer these questions,[13] but one possible reason has remained largely untouched. Perhaps the lack of acknowledgment has suppressed the idea,[14] but before Justice Hugo Black was a Supreme Court Justice, he served as a Captain of the U.S. Army in World War I.[15]

After reviewing principal works on Hugo Black, it appears to me that previous scholars have not considered whether Black's prior military background affected his decisions while on the U.S. Supreme Court. This chapter will consider whether Black's military experience and his views on the military affected his decisions while serving on the Court, particularly those decisions involving symbolic speech in opposition to the government's war efforts. Part II of this chapter will examine Black's service in the military as an essential part of his life that shaped and molded his personal views on the U.S. military and war. Part III will consider whether Black's opinions in particular cases during his tenure on the Court shed light on his personal opinions biasing his decisions in favor of the military. Part IV will focus on Black's dissent in *Tinker*, and the theories behind his opposition to the students' symbolic speech against the Vietnam War. Part V will conclude by piecing together Black's past military experience with his opinions while on the Court suggesting that the soldier within never left the mind of Justice Hugo Lafayette Black.

II. The Man Before the Robe

A. The Fight to Serve

Before he was appointed to serve on this nation's highest court, Hugo Black voluntarily joined the military so he could serve his country.[16] At a time when the nation was at war in World War I, the ambitious young man from Clay County, Alabama[17] decided to step away from a legal career[18] and

---

the Justices who became mentally incapacitated while serving on the Court).

[11] Newman, *supra* note 5, at 592 (noting that Hugo Black's grandson, Sterling, Jr. had recently gotten in trouble at school for the production and distribution of an underground newspaper).

[12] *Tinker,* 393 U.S. at 522 n. 1 (1969).

[13] Newman, *supra* note 5, at 589-93. Newman provides theories supporting both age and familial strains as reasons for Black's dissent in *Tinker*.

[14] *Justice Black Dies at 85; Served on Court 34 Years,* THE NEW YORK TIMES, September 25, 1971, at 1 [hereinafter *Justice Black Dies at 85*].

[15] *See* Hugo L. Black & Elizabeth Black, MR. JUSTICE AND MRS. BLACK: THE MEMOIRS OF HUGO L. BLACK AND ELIZABETH BLACK 52 (1986).

[16] *Id.* at 51.

[17] *Id.* at 3.

[18] *Id.* at 48 (detailing his career at the time, Black explained he would have served as Solicitor for Jefferson County until January of 1919; however, he resigned before the expiration of his term).

join the military. The decision was a difficult one for Black: he felt the need to consult with others, so he spoke with a colleague, Judge Fort, about the idea of enlisting in the military.[19] "I told him I was undecided as to whether I should enlist, even though I was exempt from the draft on account of both my job and my age."[20] Black recounted that his colleague "emphatically" rejected Black's idea of joining the military,[21] pointing to Black's job as a prosecuting attorney as an "essential activity" of war and peacetime.[22]

Black's colleague was not alone in this viewpoint. Black later admitted that even Army personnel told him he should not enlist.[23] However, Black soon learned of a way he could serve his country: as an officer. With few college-educated soldiers,[24] the military needed more officers.[25] This led to Black taking a training course, applying to a training school and then being assigned to train at Fort Oglethorpe, Georgia.[26]

His training at Fort Oglethorpe required Black to be knowledgeable in mathematics, particularly trigonometry in order to be an officer of the Field Artillery.[27] Despite his high intellect displayed by his higher education of one year studying medicine[28] and graduation from the University of Alabama School of Law with all high marks,[29] Black said he felt his knowledge of math was inadequate.[30] As a result, Black suggested to his commanding officer that he would better serve his country in the Infantry.[31] No argument would change the mind of his commanding officer, though. Instead, he was instructed by his commanding officer, "You are in the army now and you will go where you are assigned. The Field Artillery needs officers."[32] This order silenced Black's protests of joining the Infantry, and for the next three months he said he worked harder than he ever had before.[33] "Some years before, when I made the honor roll and graduated from the University of

---

19 *Id.* at 51.

20 *Id.*

21 *Id.*

22 *Id.*

23 *Id.*

24 *Id.* Although never college educated, Black had earned his law degree from the University of Alabama School of Law. This education seemingly qualified him to seek an officer position in the U.S. Army.

25 *Id.*

26 *Id.*

27 *Id.*

28 *Id.* at 15 (describing his reasoning for going to medical school, Black pointed to his "affection" toward his brother Orlando—who attended medical school—encouraged Black to follow in Orlando's footsteps and go to medical school at the age of 17).

29 *Id.* at 52.

30 *Id.* at 51.

31 *Id.*

32 *Id.* at 52.

33 *Id.*

Alabama School of Law, I felt I had merely been given that which I earned. When . . . I received a Commission of Captain in the Field Artillery, my feeling of gratitude could not be expressed in words."[34]

B. A Captain that Never Saw War

Hugo Black overcame adversity, including going against others' opinions, when it came to serving in World War I. Yet, there was one thing Black could not argue his way around. With his officer training, higher military staff found that Black was of better use at training rather than serving overseas.[35] In November of 1917, Black was assigned to the 81st Field Artillery Unit,[36] but when his unit reached the battlefront in September of 1918, Black was not with his unit.[37] Both he and his colonel had been left behind to train a new brigade in Fort Sill, Oklahoma.[38] "Mad as hell with me, aren't you?" Black's Colonel asked him.[39] To this Black replied, "Maybe not quite that mad, Sir, but certainly not happy."[40]

Instead of fighting, Black was thought to be more efficient at his job safely within the shores of the United States.[41] His primary duties were "keeping the War Department's bureaucrats from interfering with the Colonel's job of making capable soldiers. . . ."[42] This duty of running interference between the policy makers and the military was something Black knew how to do, and something he likely decided to do in a case involving the military's belief that Japanese-Americans posed a threat to the United States during World War II.[43]

Black's former unit reaching the battlefront was as close as he ever got to the frontline of war. Soon after receiving orders to train a new brigade, Black remembers hearing that the "Armistice rolled around."[44] Never did he hear the noise of battle or smell the smoke of rounds fired at an enemy; he was disappointed.[45] Black later summed up his hard work, training, and

---

[34] *Id.*

[35] Steve Suitts, HUGO BLACK OF ALABAMA: HOW HIS ROOTS AND EARLY CAREER SHAPED THE GREAT CHAMPION OF THE CONSTITUTION 239 (2005) (noting that Black's Colonel, Colonel Littebrandt, was reassigned to train a new brigade; Colonel Littebrandt insisted "his old adjutant," Black, was needed to assist him with training).

[36] Black & Black, *supra* note 15, at 52.

[37] *Id.* at 55.

[38] *Id.*

[39] *Id.*

[40] *Id.* (detailing the vivid memories of conversations he had while Black was serving in the military)

[41] Suitts, *supra* note 35, at 239.

[42] *Id.*

[43] Korematsu v. United States, 323 U.S. 215 (1944).

[44] Black & Black, *supra* note 15, at 55.

[45] *Id.* at 56.

attempts to reach the battlefront: "Captain Black . . . tried to serve his country in war."[46]

Strong emotions were evident as Black described his thoughts about not being able to serve on the frontline. However, in a moment of realization he added that there was no glamour in the war of which he had fought so hard to be a part.[47] He went on to say that his hope one day was that there would be no more war,[48] but he made no effort to sum up his view of a world constantly torn by war—a world as it actually existed then and still does today. One can only be guided by his words of reverie and gratitude for the people and the experiences which helped him on his journey to becoming Captain Black of the 81st Field Artillery.

C. The Need to Remember

Wishing to shed light on a long and eventful life, Black began a memoir while in his seventies.[49] Information pertaining to his childhood, military service and early career was closely chronicled in Black's memoirs. However, he was never able to complete his entire life story. Upon his death, Black had only written 12 chapters, which accounted for his life from his birth until 1921.[50]

Although these 12 chapters only touch a fraction of Black's life, they expose a new side of the Justice. These writings reveal many of the factors that made Black the man he was. They also give evidence of what Black found to be truly important in his life—what was worth remembering. In his memoir, Black freely described memories and events that occurred during his first 35 years of life. What is interesting is the emphasis and space he placed on certain events. For example, Black dedicated three chapters to his service in the military.[51] To get a better idea of the important role the military played in his life, Black dedicated one-fourth of the chapters covering his first 35 years of life to discussing an experience in his life that covered a little more than one year. In comparison, only one chapter details Black's one year at medical school and his entire education at the University of Alabama School of Law, combined.[52] For someone who went on to become a Supreme Court Justice, law school would seem to be an important step in the journey to the bench. However, Black uses little space to discuss his legal education.

---

[46] *Id.*

[47] *Id.*

[48] *Id.*

[49] Black & Black, *supra* note 15, at 3.

[50] Black & Black, *supra* note 15, at 6-61. These first 12 chapters cover the first 35 years of Black's life.

[51] Black & Black, *supra* note 15, at 48-59 (titling those chapters covered, "August, 1917—I resign as Solicitor and Go to World War I," "Captain Black of the Field Artillery," and "Armistice Day: I return to Birmingham to Practice Law").

[52] *Id.* at 15 (titling the chapter of professional education as "I go to Medical School, then to Law School, and Then to Practice Law").

Whether the decision to expand on his military background was made subconsciously or not, the space Black dedicated to it further demonstrates how the military played an important role in his early life, more than 40 years earlier. Black could still recall conversations with his commanding officer, the desire to serve overseas and the disappointment he felt when he was kept in the United States. He could still remember the call to serve and his feeling of duty to protect his nation.

III. The Man Who Wore Many Uniforms

A. A Nation at War

Almost two decades after retiring his army uniform, Black began wearing new attire—a judge's black robe.[53] Although he never made it to war as a soldier, the evidence of wars presented themselves to him as a sitting justice of the Supreme Court. In the more than 30 years Justice Hugo Black served on the Supreme Court, he witnessed, from the high bench, three wars and his nation at war with its own people. World War II, the Korean conflict, the Vietnam War and the Civil Rights Movement all took place during Black's tenure on the Court.[54] Black's opinions involving cases dealing with war reveal a sharp departure from his "civil libertarian" views.[55] Considering Black's military background, perhaps there is no departure in his views, only a confirmation of his feelings on the military.

B. Outlying Decisions

Age can change a man, and arguably his mind. As he advanced in age, Hugo Black became subject to criticisms that his mind was not the same.[56] Decisions such as his dissent in *Tinker*, which were thought to fall outside his normal views,[57] provided ammunition for Black's critics to attack him concerning his age.[58] While a plausible argument can be made that his mental capacity declined during his later years on the court as the result of a stroke in 1968,[59] this argument does not solve the issue concerning other outlying decisions. Scattered throughout his 34-year career serving on the

[53] *See* Huhn, *supra* note 9 (providing the years President Roosevelt's appointees reached the Supreme Court, with Hugo Black documented as ascending to the Court in August of 1937).

[54] Black served on the court from 1937 until 1971, during which time the United States became involved with three wars and the Civil Rights Movement.

[55] Newman, *supra* note 5, at back cover.

[56] *See Justice Black Dies at 85*, *supra* note 14 (quoting Black, "I know what they're saying [about me]. . . . "Well I don't think I'm old yet. And I think I can state categorically that I have not changed my basic constitutional philosophy in at least 40 years.").

[57] *See Justice Black Dies at 85*, *supra* note 14 (describing Black as becoming more conservative, and using *Tinker* as evidence for the change in mentality).

[58] *See* Garrow, *supra* note 10.

[59] Newman, *supra* note 5, at 589.

court, Justice Hugo Black presented numerous notable and distinct arguments limiting speech and civil liberties.

1. *Korematsu v. United States*

"There is one time when Justice Black will support action by the Federal Government that normally he would rule out as unconstitutional. That is when the Nation is engaged in war for survival."[60] Irving Dilliard stumbled upon a new theory as he tried to explain Black's opinion in *Korematsu v. United States*. However, Dilliard's thoughts upon the *Korematsu* opinion stand in scholarly isolation. Not only did he not cite any authority to support his theory, Dilliard also failed to explain his reasoning. Despite the lack of support for the theory, Dilliard's views on Black and war provide a good starting point in examining cases in which Black supported a limitation on civil liberties and symbolic speech when the nation was at war. As Dilliard notes, Black falls outside his usual stance on civil liberties when he delivers the opinion in *Korematsu*.[61]

Before the Civil Rights Movement and the Vietnam War, Black, fairly early in his career on the bench (in 1944), delivered an extremely controversial opinion in *Korematsu v. United States*.[62] In a case concerning a racially based evacuation of Japanese-Americans during World War II following the Japanese attack on Pearl Harbor, Black delivered the opinion upholding the executive order requiring evacuation based on race.[63] Black found that the government's claim, which was based on military intelligence, that there was a serious risk having Japanese-Americans in military areas was constitutional.[64]

Deferring to the military's judgment was necessary in Black's mind.[65] This was made evident when he stated, "because Congress, reposing its confidence in this time of war in our military leaders—*as inevitably it must*—determined that they should have the power to do just this."[66] With this thought process, the military officials and those relying on the military's judgment were in the best position to make such a decision—even if it would result in a restriction of liberties. "Citizenship has its responsibilities as well as its privileges, and in time of war the burden is always heavier."[67]

Here, Black allowed the military to proceed with what the commanding officials felt was necessary for the safety of the nation—something Black had come to understand during his service in the military. Although he had

---

[60] *See* Irving Dilliard, ONE MAN'S STAND FOR FREEDOM: HUGO LAFAYETTE BLACK 113 (1963) (prefacing Black's opinion in *Korematsu*).

[61] *Id.*

[62] *Korematsu*, 323 U.S. at 215 n.43.

[63] *Id.* at 216.

[64] *Id.* at 219 (Black upholding constitutionality of the exclusion order).

[65] Tony Freyer, HUGO L. BLACK AND THE DILEMMA OF AMERICAN LIBERALISM 92 (1990).

[66] *Korematsu*, 323 U.S. at 223 n.43 (emphasis added).

[67] *Id.* at 219.

exchanged his army uniform for a judge's black robe, Black's opinion in *Korematsu*, which deferred to the military's judgment, is consistent with his primary duties as a Captain in World War I. Both in his *Korematsu* opinion and as a Captain, Black does not allow a third party to interfere with the military's judgment in protecting the nation.

Able to gain enough votes to deliver the opinion, Black was joined by fellow former members of the military. Of the nine members of the *Korematsu* Court, four of the Justices had served in the military.[68] However, the breakdown of which Justices served in the military, and which ones had not, seems to show no absolute pattern in the voting.[69] This does not support the idea that a military background affected all the Justices' opinions, but it should not affect the theory that Black was influenced by his military experiences. Additionally, this theory does have its limits as Black did not allow the military to have sweeping authority over any issue.[70]

Yet Black never backed down from his support in the military's judgment in *Korematsu*. In fact, years after the delivery of the opinion and the open criticisms of it, Black, after being questioned on his decision in the case, reiterated his opinion in *Korematsu*. "Yes, given the circumstances I would still write *Korematsu* the same way."[71]

2. Civil Rights Movement

Order is valued in the military. Whether in regard to marching, levels of hierarchy, or a uniform appearance, there is appreciation for order in the military. After undergoing training and other experiences in military service, a sense of order may remain with the soldier after his discharge.

Order was something Justice Hugo Black appreciated. Without even looking to his personal opinions on order, a quick look over his decisions covering disruption of the peace, trespass and symbolic speech in the form

[68] *See generally* Korematsu v. United States, THE OYEZ PROJECT AT IIT CHICAGO-KENT COLLEGE OF LAW, http://www.oyez.org/cases/1940-1949/1944/1944_22 (last visited May 1, 2013) (displaying the breakdown in votes by showing images of the Justices and how he or she voted, the site hyperlinks the Justice's images to include biographical information containing information on their early life—which includes information on military experience); ARLINGTON NATIONAL CEMETERY, www.arlingtoncemetary.net (last visited May 1, 2013) (listing individuals with military experience who were interred at the cemetery).

[69] *Id.* Three of the six Justices voting to uphold the evacuation order had served in the military—Justices Black, Douglas, and Reed. Justice Frank Murphy, who joined the dissent, had served in the military.

[70] *See, e.g.*, Trop v. Dulles, 356 U.S. 86, 87 (1958) (Black, J. concurring) (adding that citizenship could not be divested by a military tribunal on a finding of military desertion, Black wrote that such an issue should be determined by a civilian court, instead of a military tribunal); *see also* New York Times Co. v. U.S., 403 U.S. 713, 717 (1971) (Black, J. concurring) (arguing against abridging the freedom of the press in an issue of prior restraint concerning national security: "The greater the importance of safeguarding the community from incitements to the overthrow of our institutions by force and violence, the more imperative is the need to preserve inviolate the constitutional rights of free speech, free press and free assembly in order to maintain the opportunity for free political discussion. . . .").

[71] Black & Black, *supra* note 15, at 72.

of conduct reveal his desire for civil and social order.[72] He even extended his appreciation to those who maintained the order of law, stating, "I then considered and still consider policeman to be soldiers in the cause of the law."[73] Cases involving order coupled with an appreciation for law enforcement personnel who attempt to maintain order often resulted in Black believing those who disrupted order were unprotected by the First Amendment.[74] The transition from speech to acts resulted in a change in position on whether the First Amendment protected such behavior—and often Black responded in a dissent with a solid no.[75]

Consider Justice Black's opinion in *Adderley v. Florida*. A group of about 200 Florida A&M students marched from the school to a nearby jail to protest the arrests of other protesting students the day before.[76] However, this protest violated a Florida trespass statute. Because the students did not leave after the sheriff's warnings, some of the students were arrested for trespass with a malicious and mischievous intent.[77] The students were able to bring the case before the Supreme Court arguing that their freedom of speech was denied when the Florida District Court of Appeals affirmed their convictions of the violation of the Florida statute, which prohibited their demonstration at the jail.[78]

Black delivered the 5–4 majority opinion, affirming the convictions and discrediting the students' arguments for freedom of speech protection.[79] "Such an argument has as its major unarticulated premise the assumption that people who want to propagandize protests or views have a constitutional right to do so whenever and however and wherever they please. That concept of constitutional law was vigorously and forthrightly rejected. . . ."[80] Here, Black drew the line between speech and acts. "Leaving only the question of whether conviction of the state offense, thus defined, unconstitutionally deprives petitioners of their rights to freedom of speech, press, assembly or petition. We hold it does not."[81]

---

[72] *See, e.g.*, Cox v. Louisiana, 379 U.S 559, 575 (1965) (Black, J., dissenting) ("The streets are not now and never have been the proper place to administer justice."); *see also* Brown v. Louisiana, 383 U.S. 131, 151 (1966) (Black, J., dissenting) ("Though the First Amendment guarantees the right of assembly and the right of petition along with the rights of speech, press, and religion, it does not guarantee to any person the right to use someone else's property . . . as a stage to express dissident ideas); Adderley v. Florida, 385 U.S. 39 (1966) ("[T]here is no merit to the petitioner's argument that people who want to propagandize protests or views have a constitutional right to do so whenever and however and wherever they please.").

[73] Black & Black, *supra* note 15, at 38.

[74] *See Adderley*, 385 U.S. at 39 n.72.

[75] *See Cox*, 379 U.S. at 575 n.72.

[76] 385 U.S. at 39, 41 (1966).

[77] *Id.* at 40.

[78] *Id.*

[79] *Id.*

[80] *Id.* at 48.

[81] *Id.* at 46.

Also consider *Cox v. Louisiana*, which involved Southern University students led by the Reverend Elton Cox as they picketed stores that maintained segregated lunch counters.[82] The early part of the demonstration was considered "peaceful" by the Sheriff. However, when Cox urged the students to sit at the segregated lunch counters, the atmosphere changed.[83] The Sheriff found Cox's statements "inflammatory" and notified everyone that their demonstration was now in violation of disturbing the peace laws; in the end the crowd was disbursed by use of tear gas.[84] The next day, Cox was arrested for disturbing the peace.[85]

After reviewing the case, the Court overturned Cox's conviction because there was virtually no evidence that the students were violent or threatened violence.[86] Black disagreed with the majority. In his dissent, he wrote, "Minority groups in particular need always to bear in mind that the Constitution, while it requires States to treat all citizens equally and protect them in the exercise of rights granted by the Federal Constitution and laws, does not take away the State's power, indeed its duty to keep order. . . ."[87] Again and again, order finds priority over freedom of expression for Black.

These cases go against the norm of the man known to defend the First Amendment.[88] Why was Hugo Black consistently against the demonstrations and protests? Some critics had pointed to Black's past involvement with the Ku Klux Klan[89] as an answer to his unusual stance during the Civil Rights Movement.[90] One of those mentioning Black's involvement with the Ku Klux Klan sat beside him on the bench. Not only was Abe Fortas shocked by Black's dissent in *Tinker*, but also by Black's views in *Brown v. Louisiana*, which involved a library sit-in.[91] Fortas went so far as to accuse Black of racism, saying: "'Look, Hugo was in the Klan and now he's coming to the aid of southern white womanhood.'"[92] The reference to southern white womanhood was likely referring to the librarians in the case![93]

A closer look at Black's opinions and work in the past would have provided ample evidence to discredit accusations of racism.[94] For example,

---

[82] 379 U.S. 536, 538 (1965).

[83] *Id.* at 543.

[84] *Id.*

[85] *Id.* at 544.

[86] *Id.* at 550.

[87] *Id.* at 575.

[88] *See Justice Black Dies at 85, supra* note 14 (describing Black's admirers as "shocked and saddened" by his positions on civil rights protests).

[89] Newman, *supra* note 5, at 91 (explaining that Black joined the Klan on Sept. 13, 1923).

[90] *Id.* at 589.

[91] *Id.*

[92] *Id.* at 590.

[93] *Id.*

[94] *See, e.g.*, Loving v. Virginia, 388 U.S. 1 (1967) (holding unanimously that miscegenation statutes adopted to prevent the marriage of individuals from different races, as in this case a

early in Black's career when he ran for County Solicitor of Jefferson County, Black promised to clean up the backlogged docket.[95] The jail was overflowing with prisoners—some were professional gamblers and others were "honest-to-goodness working payday crapshooters."[96] These working payday crapshooters were still in jail because of their inability to make bond.[97] Because of the fee system in place, in which the state paid the fees and the prisoners paid the costs, sheriffs and jailers—all of them white people—were making money off the black crapshooters unable to get out of jail.[98] Black, in targeting the professional gamblers, sought dismissals for all the working payday crapshooters.[99] Because the dismissals were against "colored payday crapshooters," Black found himself with friends and supporters complaining.[100] Others even talked of his impeachment.[101] As an elected official, Black was likely aware of the consequences of dismissing the hundreds of cases against the black gambling workers, but he did it anyway. Unwilling to yield to the beliefs of the day, Black did what he thought was best for his county.[102]

Another example of Black standing against racial prejudices is evident in the case of *Chambers v. Florida*. In this case, young black men were accused of murdering a white man.[103] They were held without counsel for five days, subjected to a hostile environment and abusive treatment.[104] On the eighth day, the petitioners confessed to the murder.[105] In determining whether the tactics used to procure the confessions of the men failed to afford the protection of Due Process of law guaranteed by the Fourteenth Amendment, Black wrote that the Constitution proscribed such "lawless means."[106] Black argued that Due Process of law was preserved for all by the Constitution—"of whatever race, creed or persuasion."[107] Years later, Elizabeth Black, Black's second wife, recalled that Black felt so strongly about

white man and a black woman, were a violation of Equal Protection and Due Process of law).

95 Black & Black, *supra* note 15, at 44 (explaining why the county's docket was so bogged down).

96 *Id.*

97 *Id.*

98 *See* John P. Frank, MR. JUSTICE BLACK: THE MAN AND HIS OPINIONS 22 (1949).

99 Black & Black, *supra* note 15, at 44.

100 *Id.*

101 *Id.*

102 *Id.* at 48.

103 Chambers v. Florida, 309 U.S. 227, 229 (1940).

104 *Id.* at 231.

105 Black & Black, *supra* note 15, at 73.

106 *Chambers*, 309 U.S. at 241 n.102.

107 *Id.*

that case that "he would never read aloud from his opinion without tears streaming down his face."[108]

Concerning Black's prior membership in the Ku Klux Klan, Black had explained to Elizabeth why he had joined.[109] "The main reason he joined was so that he would have an equal chance in trying cases before jurors who were largely Klan members in Alabama. . . ."[110] Elizabeth acknowledged other reasons had been given for Black's reasoning in joining the Klan; however, she wanted his actual words to stand as evidence.[111]

3. Other Interesting Outcomes

During the Vietnam War, other issues arose involving symbolic speech. Episodes of young people burning draft cards or wearing clothes noticeably opposing the draft all occurred during Justice Black's latter years of service on the Supreme Court. While these cases were not widely recognized as notable cases during Black's tenure because he did not deliver the opinion, they do provide more evidence supporting the theory that his military background influenced Black.

In *United States v. O'Brien*, O'Brien and three of his companions burned their draft cards on the steps of the South Boston Courthouse in opposition to the Vietnam War.[112] This act of burning the draft cards violated a federal law, which made it a crime to "knowingly destroy" draft registration certificates.[113] O'Brien testified in District Court that he had burned his draft card publicly to "influence others to adopt his antiwar beliefs, as he put it, 'so that other people would reevaluate their positions with Selective Service, with the armed forces, and reevaluate their place in the culture of today, to hopefully consider my position.'"[114] Despite his argument that his speech was abridged because of the statute criminalizing the act, O'Brien was convicted of violating the statute by the District Court.[115]

Upon review, the Court, with Black a party to the majority opinion, found that the statute was constitutional because the government's interest was greater than the message O'Brien was attempting to make by burning his draft card.[116] The Court reasoned: "This Court has held that when 'speech' and 'nonspeech' elements are combined in the same course of conduct, a sufficiently important governmental interest in regulating the

[108] Black & Black, *supra* note 15, at 73.

[109] *Id.* at 70.

[110] *Id.*

[111] *Id.* at 71.

[112] United States v. O'Brien, 391 U.S. 367, 369 (1968).

[113] *Id.* at 370.

[114] *Id.*

[115] *Id.* at 369.

[116] *Id.* at 367.

nonspeech element can justify incidental limitations on First Amendment freedoms."[117]

In *Cohen v. California*, Cohen was convicted of disturbing the peace because he wore a jacket into the courtroom containing a profanity directed against the draft during the Vietnam War.[118] Cohen later testified that "he wore the jacket knowing that the words were on the jacket as a means of informing the public of the depth of his feelings against the Vietnam War and the draft."[119]

The Court believed that the State could not punish Cohen for the content of his speech.[120] As a result, the Court found that the state had no right to prohibit speech simply because others might find it offensive.[121] Yet Black, who had argued against obscenity laws because of the restriction on speech,[122] joined the dissent with the belief that Cohen's "absurd and immature antic . . . was mainly conduct and little speech."[123] Here conduct, disorder, and speech against the military draft—all things that, as previous cases demonstrate, Black was not particularly fond of—are all present in one case. There were no surprises in the outcome here: Black joins the dissent in Cohen arguing against the majority overturning Cohen's conviction.

Cases not involving symbolic speech but occurring during war, much like *Korematsu*, display Black's willingness to limit individuals' civil liberties in a time of war.[124] In *Cramer v. United States*, Cramer, a naturalized American citizen of German background, was convicted of treason.[125] The Court reversed Cramer's conviction based on the lack of evidence of Cramer "levying War," which was required as part of the definition of treason.[126] The facts revealed that Cramer was affiliated with two German saboteurs in 1942.[127] Despite this association, the Court found this association with the saboteurs did not meet all the elements of treason.[128]

An interesting fact to note, though, is that before the treason conviction, Cramer had previously served in the German Army against the United States in 1918.[129] Cramer's service in the German Army happened to co-

---

[117] *Id.* at 377.

[118] Cohen v. California, 403 U.S. 15, 27 (1971) (Black, J. dissenting).

[119] *Id.* at 16.

[120] *Id.* at 18.

[121] *See* Erwin Chemerinsky, CONSTITUTIONAL LAW PRINCIPLES AND POLICIES 1068 (4th ed. 2011) (noting one major principle of the *Cohen* case).

[122] *See* Roth v. United States, 354 U.S. 476, 508 (1957) (Black, J., dissenting, arguing the First Amendment protects obscene material).

[123] *Cohen*, 403 U.S. at 27 n.118.

[124] Freyer, *supra* note 65, at 95.

[125] Cramer v. United States, 325 U.S. 1, 3 (1945) (Black, J. dissenting).

[126] *Id.* at 6.

[127] *Id.* at 3.

[128] *Id.*

[129] *Id.*

incide with Black's service in the U.S. Army in World War I. Considering the opinion was delivered in April of 1945,[130] which was during World War II, and that Cramer had fought against the army that Black had been a part of, it follows that Black would join the dissent in favor of upholding Cramer's conviction. Black's legal reasoning here was thought to be the result of his belief that anyone affiliated with the enemy deserved "only the most elemental due process rights."[131] With Cramer's past involvement in World War I and his affiliation with German saboteurs in World War II, Black was against having to require enough evidence to uphold a treason conviction. This case exemplified his unwillingness to broaden civil liberties, which five of his fellow Court members did, to anyone classified as an enemy to the nation.[132]

4. Overview

Again and again, Black found that the First Amendment or other civil liberties are trumped by an alternate interest—the government's—when a war is involved. This is not to suggest that Black did not wish to afford protection to most speakers in most First Amendment cases. Rather, this essay demonstrates that war and civil unrest affected Black's opinions concerning symbolic speech. In the cases listed above, civil and social order seems to be a quality Black promoted—a preference or trait he may have learned to appreciate (or that may have been reinforced) during his military service. While there is nothing but his cases and thoughts to further this theory, Black unquestionably saw a distinction between pure speech and conduct. Interestingly, though, Black's fight against protection of speech that fell under the subcategory of conduct was typically called forth by a direct or indirect act against government rules or policies during a time of war. Considering his background and opinions throughout his tenure on the Supreme Court bench, a common line of thinking is noticeable.

IV. The Man Against the Majority: Hugo Black, the Great Dissenter

A. In a Landmark Case, Hugo Black Finds Himself on the Other Side of the Mark

The great dissenter, Hugo Black, had rightfully earned his title. During his 1968–1969 term, Black dissented 18 times, which is the highest number of dissents of any Court member during that term.[133] Black did not ease up on his dissents when the issue of children's right to symbolic speech in the classroom came before the court. In fact, Black delivered one of his most

---

[130] *Id.* at 1.

[131] Freyer, *supra* note 65, at 95.

[132] *Id.*

[133] Johnson, *supra* note 2, at 176.

powerful opinions against symbolic speech in his dissent in *Tinker v. Des Moines*.[134]

The Supreme Court had granted certiorari to hear a case involving students wearing black armbands to school in protest against the Vietnam War.[135] In December of 1965, a group of parents and students met to determine a way to publicize their objections to the hostilities in Vietnam.[136] A decision was made to wear black armbands during the holiday season to show their support for a truce.[137] The problem was the school administration had learned of the plan for students to wear black armbands, so they passed a policy prohibiting the wearing of a black armband.[138] On December 16, the petitioners—junior high and high school students—wore their black armbands to school.[139] As a result, the students were sent home from school and suspended.[140]

In finding that the regulation prohibited student speech, the Court found that the First Amendment applied to students as well as to adults.[141] "First Amendment rights, applied in light of the special characteristics of the school environment, are available to teachers and students," Fortas wrote.[142] He added, "It can hardly be argued that either students or teachers shed their constitutional rights to freedom of speech or expression at the schoolhouse gate."[143] Examining the evidence that there was little disturbance as a result of the wearing of the black armbands, the Court found that the regulation violated student speech.

This is not the case for Black. Instead, Justice Black, now the most senior member of the Court, came out fighting.[144] ". . . [T]he record amply shows that public protest in the school classes against the Vietnam War 'distracted' [from the purpose of the school as an institution]."[145] Black supported this argument by pointing to evidence demonstrating that comments were made to the students that day, that other students had warned the petitioners and that the petitioners were poked fun at.[146] The minor distractions were not the only problem Black had with this case. In addition to pointing out the distractions in the school, Black goes further to point out

---

[134] *Id.*

[135] *Tinker*, 393 U.S. at 503 n.1.

[136] *Id.* at 504.

[137] *Id.*

[138] *Id.*

[139] *Id.*

[140] *Id.*

[141] *Id.* at 506.

[142] *Id.*

[143] *Id.*

[144] Johnson, *supra* note 2, at 166.

[145] *Tinker*, 393 U.S. at 524.

[146] *Id.*

the subject about which the students were protesting. In the midst of a highly sensitive war, he wrote, the students had decided to protest on this divisive and disruptive issue: "Members of this Court, like all other citizens, know, without being told, that the disputes over the wisdom of the Vietnam War have disrupted and divided this country as few other issues have."[147]

The nation was at war, and these students had supposedly caused disorder by protesting the war at school. Black did not hide the fact that he was very aware of the underlying issue at hand, an issue that had caused a great deal of disruption to the country, not just a school in Iowa—the Vietnam War. Following with his previous opinions, Black distinguished the petitioners' act of wearing black armbands as conduct, which can be limited. "While I have always believed that under the First and Fourteenth Amendments neither the State nor the Federal Government has any authority to regulate or censor the content of speech, I have never believed that any person has a right to give speeches or engage in demonstrations where he pleased and when he pleases."[148] Because the students' speech took place in a classroom, which he found to cause disorder, Black finds no Constitutional protection able to protect the students' deliberate disregard of the school policy. If schools followed the Court's opinion, Black worried that educators would be left without the ability properly to instill order in their pupils.[149] As a result of the Court's decision on *Tinker*, Black believed the Court had now subjected the "public schools in the country to the whims and caprices of their loudest-mouthed, but maybe not their brightest, students."[150]

B. Theories on Black's Dissent in Tinker

While the media was abuzz with headlines reporting the results in *Tinker*,[151] other rumors spread on why Black spoke so harshly against the students.[152]

One theory was that Black's harsh dissent was in response to trouble his grandson had recently gotten into at his high school. Roger Newman, in his biography on Black, points out that Black had learned that his grandson, Sterling, Jr., had been suspended from high school shortly before the Court heard oral arguments for *Tinker*.[153] The suspension was a result of Sterling, Jr.'s helping to write an underground newspaper.[154] In this newspaper, Sterling, Jr. described his school's administration as "brutal" and "vicious"

---

147 *Id.*

148 *Id.*

149 *Id.*

150 *Id.* at 525.

151 *See Armbands Yes*, *supra* note 6 (editorializing the newspaper staff's opinion on the outcome of *Tinker*).

152 Newman, *supra* note 5, at 592.

153 *Id.*

154 *Id.*

"Hugo Lafayette Black in Uniform"

From the Bounds Law Library of the University of Alabama.

Courtesy W.S. Hoole Special Collections Library, University of Alabama, used by permission

and even called them "finkos."[155] Black felt no remorse for his grandson concerning the suspension; instead he wrote in a letter to Sterling, Jr.'s mother that he thought "'the school has done exactly right'. . . ."[156] Taking into account the timing of the suspension and the Court's hearing of the oral argument, it is quite possible that his grandson's actions were on Black's mind as he wrote his dissent in *Tinker*. Arguably, this may be a reason for Black's particularly harsh words against the students. Yet, however upsetting it may have been to learn of his grandson's behavioral issues at school, Black—or any Justice, for that matter—would not do well to use family problems as a basis for determining the constitutionality of an issue. To believe a grandson's actions had such power in determining Supreme Court cases would be both hard to prove and disturbing.

In addition, *Tinker* was not the first case in which Black sided against the speaker when the issue was dealing with students and symbolic speech. After all, *Adderley* involved students demonstrating at a jail a few years prior to the hearing of the *Tinker* case.[157] Although the students were college students instead of junior high school or senior high school students,[158] the students violated a policy that was set in place to contain order. Though not as harsh, Black had already dealt with students protesting three years earlier in *Adderley*. Also, it is important to note that during the time *Adderley* was being decided, there were no recorded family crises occurring. What was present in that case were the same elements, which have time and again steered Black into considering that conduct fell outside the protections of the First Amendment. While the harsher words in *Tinker* may be attributed to his anger with his grandson, the idea that Black's dissent was largely the result of Sterling, Jr.'s actions overlooks his opinion in *Adderley* made only three years earlier.

Another theory noted by Newman was that Black's age was affecting his mind. It was noted that Black told a former clerk in 1967, "My mind isn't as quick."[159] A couple of years later, Black began having strokes.[160] Afterward, fellow Justices began to notice Black making remarks that did not make any sense.[161] As a man in his eighties at the time the *Tinker* opinion was delivered, Black's age had begun to affect his body and his mind. The argument that Black's weakening mental capacity affected his later decisions is a strong one. Yet, it is important to reflect over Black's entire time on the Court. Although his mind may not have been as quick later in life, Black had written some controversial opinions throughout his

155 *Id.*

156 *Id.*

157 The opinion in *Adderley* was delivered in 1966, and the opinion in *Tinker* was delivered in 1969.

158 *Tinker*, 393 U.S. at 504 n. 1.

159 Newman, *supra* note 5, at 589.

160 *Id.*

161 *Id.* (noting that Justice Douglas had recalled Black making unexpected remarks).

career. *Tinker*—which was decided prior to Black's strokes[162]—was certainly not the first case in which Supreme Court observers were surprised by Black's position, especially considering that Black delivered the opinion in *Korematsu* in 1944.

V. Conclusion

No one will ever truly know the reasons for Black's decisions in cases such as *Tinker* and *Korematsu*. His death in 1971 left academics with cases, interviews, biographies and memoirs to piece together answers about one of the most notable Supreme Court justices in the history of the United States. Black did take it upon himself to begin recording his life story. He was able to chronicle his early childhood through his mid-thirties in his memoir before he died.[163] Leaving a significant portion of his life untouched, his memoir sheds light only on his early years.[164] Although a full story would better explain Black's thoughts on the various cases throughout the years, the early years provided a valuable insight into his young mind that was shaped by early influences, a mind that in many respects endured throughout his life.

One of those influences happened to be Black's military experience, as evident in the detail with which Black described his time in the service. Yet, in spite of the importance Black placed on his service in the military, little mention is made of the fact that he served in World War I. Not only do most scholars fail to mention or acknowledge Black's service in the military, others (typically, outside the legal world) fail to include this era of Black's life. In the more than 5,500-word obituary recounting the life of Hugo Black, the *New York Times* failed to mention that Black ever served in the military, much less that he was a commissioned officer in World War I.[165] Perhaps the lack of acknowledgment of Black's military background leaves academics and critics turning to other theories for Black's decisions.

Knowing Black served his country when he was not required to do so, knowing his thoughts on earning his commission, and knowing the importance he placed on that time of his life changes many things. The military background provides a lens one can look through to see things as Black quite possibly viewed them. Someone so steady in his beliefs did not waver over time. No, he stood strong in his views supporting order and giving preference to military judgment over those who took part, as he saw it, in disruptive symbolic speech. In a battle between symbolic speech and order,

---

162 *Id.*

163 Black & Black, *supra* note 15, at 68. Hugo Black's own detailed memories end in 1921. His wife, Elizabeth, picks up his story from that point forward.

164 Newman, *supra* note 5, at 589.

165 *See Justice Black Dies at 85, supra* note 14. Featured on the front page, the obituary continues to page 3 with multiple pictures and multiple subsections detailing Black's life and years on the Court. No mention is made of his service in the military during World War I.

the former Captain Black sought to maintain order in his service to his country during the multiple wars he witnessed from the high bench.

THE "BREAKTHROUGH VERDICT": *STRANGE V. STATE*

Ellie Campbell

"If the Klan don't get you, the police will; if the police don't get you, the courts will."
— Rev. Fred Shuttlesworth[1]

On December 2, 1965, in Anniston, Alabama, for the first time in Alabama history, a state court jury convicted a white man for the racially motivated murder of a black man. On a hot July evening a little over four months earlier, Hubert Damon Strange leaned out of the passenger side window of a friend's car and fired a rifle three times into a passing car containing four black men. One shot hit the driver, Willie Brewster, in the back of the neck. Brewster died in Anniston Memorial Hospital three days later. In an extraordinary move, a group of local citizens took out a full-page ad in the Anniston Star to announce a $20,000 reward for information on the killing. A witness stepped forward, and his information led to the arrest and eventual conviction of Damon Strange for the murder of Willie Brewster.[2]

Why Anniston? Why 1965? Why, through these people and in this place, was justice finally done in Alabama? Part of the answer lies in the long road travelled by the civil rights movement; by 1965, many Alabamians were tired of violence, tired of bombs, tired of marches met with police dogs and fire hoses and bad press. They were tired of being held hostage by society's worst elements, and wished to enforce peace and order. Another part of the answer lies in the laudable efforts of Anniston's Judge Robert Parker, who oversaw every step of the trial process to ensure a just resolution. The Strange case also illuminates the continued struggle in Southern race relations even after the passage of the Civil Rights Act of 1965 and the desegregation of local schools. Although the Civil Rights Movement achieved great local and national victories during the 1960s, it was only the beginning of a struggle for equality played out in thousands of towns like Anniston. This paper will explore the historical, social, economic, political, and legal circumstances that led to the conviction of Damon Strange for the murder of Willie Brewster.

---

[1] Diane McWhorter, CARRY ME HOME 136 (Simon and Schuster 2001).

[2] Gary Sprayberry, "'Can We Say We Are All Innocent?': The 1965 Murder of Willie Brewster and the Limits of Political Violence" (January 1, 2006) (unpublished article, on file at the Calhoun County Public Library). Note that there are no page numbers, so I cite to the article generally.

Anniston is a small city located in Appalachian foothills in northeast Alabama, about halfway between Birmingham and Atlanta. In an area of the state mostly made up of small farms, Anniston was founded as a company town shortly after the end of the Civil War in order to take advantage of the coal and iron ore deposits in the surrounding hills.[3] Later, in the early decades of the twentieth century, Anniston expanded with the addition of Fort McClellan to the north and the Monsanto chemical plant and Anniston Army Depot along Highway 202 to the west.[4] At the time, Highway 78 ran through the middle of town, bisecting Noble Street and providing the direct route from Birmingham to Atlanta. Anniston's easy access to bigger cities, as well as its rotating population of servicemen and women and influx of federal military spending, gave the small city a cosmopolitan air that belied its size.

Like the rest of Alabama, Anniston did not escape the violence that accompanied the Civil Rights Movement. The modern Civil Rights Movement began in Alabama with the Montgomery bus boycott in 1955–1956. The boycott not only pioneered many of the larger movement's strategies and introduced Dr. Martin Luther King, Jr. to the world, but also prompted the state's die-hard segregationists to start organizing as well.[5] Klan membership grew rapidly after *Brown v. Board of Education* and during the bus boycott, and an Alabama chapter of the White Citizens' Council started up in 1956.[6] The segregationists also had the full support of many in the legal profession, including Montgomery judge Walter B. Jones, who founded and edited the Alabama Bar Association's official journal, the *Alabama Lawyer*.[7] The journal became "a forum for segregationists."[8]

Although the White Citizens' Council publicly disavowed lawlessness and vigilantism, violent attacks and bombings directed at Alabama's African-American community increased after the bus boycott. Those attacks met with little public reproach and tacit approval from the middle and upper class whites throughout the state. In late January 1956, bombs were set off outside the homes of Dr. King and other Montgomery leaders.[9] Snipers fired on newly desegregated buses in 1957.[10] The violence spread beyond Montgomery; in Birmingham, the black Fountain Heights neighborhood was bombed seven times in 1957, earning it the nickname "Dynamite Hill."[11]

---

[3] Dennis Love, MY CITY WAS GONE 52-53 (Harper Perennial 2006).

[4] *Id.* at 61-64.

[5] William Warren Rogers, *et al.*, ALABAMA: HISTORY OF A DEEP SOUTH STATE 548-49 (University of Alabama Press 2004).

[6] *Id.* at 548.

[7] *Id.*

[8] *Id.*

[9] *Id.* at 554.

[10] *Id.*

[11] *Id.*

Some of the violence came at the hands of men who would become key figures in various white supremacist groups around the state. Asa Carter first became associated with segregationist forces in Alabama when he was hired as the American States Rights Association's radio personality. He later founded a Birmingham chapter of the Klan that was responsible for a number of violent attacks during 1956–1957.[12] Carter and his followers participated in attacking Autherine Lucy on the University of Alabama's campus, beat Birmingham minister Fred Shuttlesworth, and kidnapped and castrated "Judge" Edward Aaron, an African-American veteran from Tarrant City.[13] Carter then became George Wallace's speechwriter, gaining him access to the most powerful man in Alabama. He is most famous for authoring the "segregation today, segregation tomorrow, segregation forever" line from Wallace's 1962 inaugural address.[14] Carter was at one time or another connected to the most infamous terrorists the white supremacy movement had to offer, including several that played a part in the Strange trial.

For example, Carter and J. B. Stoner both ran various white supremacist organizations in Birmingham in the 1960s. Stoner was Damon Strange's attorney in 1965. Stoner first appeared at the Dixiecrat convention in 1948, in an attempt to enlist support for a Congressional campaign on his own Anti-Jewish Party ticket.[15] He later worked as an insurance claims adjuster out of Georgia after getting a law degree from a night school in Atlanta, and was believed to be responsible for a series of bombings directed at synagogues and black schools across the South.[16] After being arrested, though not convicted, for supplying the dynamite for a temple bombing in Atlanta, Stoner was fired from his insurance job.[17] He then founded the National States' Rights Party, which moved its headquarters to Birmingham in 1960.[18] Stoner soon found an opportunity to return to the center of Birmingham's segregationist forces when the Freedom Ride buses rolled into Alabama in the spring of 1961, bringing national attention back with them. While Stoner's National States' Rights Party clashed with Asa Carter's Klan over who got to meet the Freedom Riders in Birmingham, local segregationists in Anniston got there first, catapulting the city into national attention in its first brush with outright resistance to the Civil Rights Movement.[19]

At the time, Anniston was the home of notorious local segregationist Kenneth Adams. Adams had been part of a group of Asa Carter followers

---

[12] *Id.*

[13] *Id.* at 555; *see also* McWhorter, *supra* note 1, at 124-26; Dan Carter, THE POLITICS OF RAGE: GEORGE WALLACE, THE ORIGINS OF NEW CONSERVATISM, AND THE TRANSFORMATION OF AMERICAN POLITICS 107 (Louisiana State University Press 1995).

[14] Carter, *supra* note 13, at 109.

[15] McWhorter, *supra* note 1, at 71.

[16] *Id.* at 133.

[17] *Id.* at 200-01.

[18] *Id.* at 201.

[19] *Id.*

who assaulted Nat King Cole when the singer broke the color line to perform for a white audience at Birmingham's municipal auditorium in 1956.[20] Adams ran a gas station in north Anniston that was known for displaying a "NO NIGGERS" sign out front. When people complained, Adams would occasionally change it to "WHITES ONLY."[21] Adams heard about the Freedom Rides from leaders in the Birmingham Klan, who had gotten the information from a series of FBI memos sent to the Birmingham Police Department.[22] Adams's orders were to gather a group of men to go down to the Anniston Bus Station and "bring ball bats and clubs ... to greet the Freedom Riders."[23]

The Freedom Riders' bus left Atlanta around 11:00 A.M. on Mother's Day, Sunday, May 14, headed for Birmingham with an Anniston stop on the way.[24] Two undercover plainclothes agents from the Alabama Bureau of Investigation, Ell Cowling and Harry Sims, accompanied the seven Riders on board. They had instructions from Alabama Governor John Patterson to gather information on the Riders.[25] When the bus reached Anniston, a mob of about fifty men, led by Kenneth Adams, attacked the bus with crowbars, pipes, and chains for about twenty minutes before the police arrived.[26] The police cleared a path for the bus to leave but did not bother to arrest any of the attackers.[27] The mob had also slashed the bus's tires, and about five miles out of town on Highway 202, the bus was forced to pull off onto the side of the road.[28]

The mob had followed from the bus station, and proceeded to smash in several windows.[29] One attacker threw a bomb inside, which exploded and quickly enveloped the bus in smoke and flames.[30] Several of the Riders made it out the windows and across the road, while others were trapped in the bus until the mob, afraid the flames might reach the gas tank, retreated.[31] The mob quickly surged forward again and beat several of the Riders until the police arrived and scared them off.[32] The bruised and bleeding Riders were taken to the Anniston hospital, where the staff, frightened by

---

[20] *Id.* at 203; *see also* Rogers, *supra* note 5, at 549.

[21] Love, *supra* note 3, at 22-23, *see also* Rogers, *supra* note 5, at 535.

[22] Raymond Arsenault, FREEDOM RIDERS: 1961 AND THE STRUGGLE FOR RACIAL JUSTICE 136 (Oxford University Press 2006).

[23] *Id.* at 138.

[24] *Id.* at 141.

[25] *Id.*

[26] *Id.* at 143.

[27] *Id.*

[28] *Id.*

[29] *Id.*

[30] *Id.*

[31] *Id.* at 144.

[32] *Id.*

the following mob, refused the Riders treatment and did not allow them to stay overnight.[33] One of the Riders finally communicated with Rev. Shuttlesworth in Birmingham, who sent a group over to pick them up.[34]

Later that month, the U.S. Justice Department sought a "novel injunction" against the Klan for "interfering with the safe travel of persons in the state."[35] Federal District Judge Frank M. Johnson, Jr. held a hearing featuring one of the men accused of throwing the firebomb at the bus in Anniston.[36] J. B. Stoner was the lawyer for the defense that day, and he and his clients endured Judge Johnson's wrath.[37] Unfortunately, Governor George Wallace turned the issue into a "protest against the aggression of Big Government" and condemned Johnson's efforts.[38] Eventually the U.S. Justice Department saw all four of its "seemingly open-and-shut" cases against those who attacked the Freedom Riders, including Kenneth Adams, end in hung juries or outright acquittals.[39] None of the assailants were ever convicted for their involvement.[40]

After the Freedom Ride debacle, Anniston had its own activists in the African-American community who were looking to challenge the city's racial barriers. William B. McClain, the pastor of the African-American Haven Chapel Methodist Church, and Nimrod Q. Reynolds, the pastor of the African-American Seventeenth Street Baptist Church, eventually found a willing ear in Phil Noble, the pastor of the white First Presbyterian Church.[41] McClain was twenty-four upon his arrival in Anniston in 1962, and his experiences in college, divinity school, and missionary work had convinced him that the South's old racial order did not have to stand.[42] Reynolds was a veteran of the Civil Rights Movement, having participated in the Montgomery bus boycott and the Southern Christian Leadership Conference (SCLC). Reynolds formed the Calhoun Community Improvement Association in 1960, a local version of the NAACP, which greatly increased its membership after the bus burnings.[43] Phil Noble was one of the few white men in Anniston willing to meet with Reynolds and McClain; Noble's experience working with African-Americans after being appointed to the board of Stillman College, a small black college in Tuscaloosa,

---

33 *Id.*

34 *Id.* at 143-48.

35 McWhorter, *supra* note 1, at 240.

36 *Id.*

37 *Id.*

38 *Id.* at 241.

39 *Id.* at 246-47.

40 *Id.*

41 Gary Sprayberry, *"One Doesn't Integrate on Sunday": The Creation of the Human Relations Council and the Origins of Desegregation in Anniston, Alabama, 1961–1963*, 61 THE ALABAMA REVIEW 105, 113 (Apr. 2008).

42 *Id.* at 114.

43 *Id.* at 115.

challenged his previous acceptance of the South's segregationist culture.[44] Sometime in early 1962, Reynolds and McClain finally got Noble to meet with them.[45]

The three ministers continued meeting monthly during the summer of 1962, adding more pastors from both black and white churches.[46] The group went public as the Anniston Ministerial Association and met with some resistance from the community, but few seemed to care until the next summer when Kenneth Adams struck again.[47] He and several fellow Klan members fired shotgun blasts over cars driven by blacks in north and west Anniston, and then into St. John's Methodist Church.[48] In response to the Freedom Ride violence and increasing attacks on civil rights protesters all over the state, the candidates in Anniston's 1962 mayoral race promised better race relations in the city's future.[49] Adams's latest attacks put those promises to the test. Building on McClain, Reynolds, and Noble's group of ministers, Anniston mayor Claude Dear commissioned the Human Relations Council, a biracial group of leaders from both communities.[50]

At one of the first meetings, the African-American ministers presented their white counterparts on the Council with a list of grievances they wanted the council to address.[51] The list included opening city jobs like policeman and fireman to blacks; desegregating public facilities like the library, the city parks, swimming pools, and golf courses; desegregating public transportation and theaters; opening restaurants, soda fountains, and lunch counters to blacks; letting whites and blacks use the same bathrooms and water fountains; and desegregating the unions that operated in the pipe shops and foundries on Anniston's West Side.[52]

The Human Relations Council was slow to address the concerns of the African-American community; Phil Noble later characterized his fellow members' attitude as "how little we can give and still keep demonstrations and boycotts from happening."[53] The whites on the Council were often more interested in keeping the peace than in addressing the black communities' concerns. Nevertheless, the Council began first by meeting with local businessmen and slowly desegregating Anniston's public spaces: parks, stores,

---

44 *Id.* at 113.

45 *Id.*

46 *Id.* at 116.

47 *Id.* at 117.

48 *Id.* at 118.

49 *Id.* at 117.

50 *Id.*

51 *Id.* at 124.

52 Phil Noble, BEYOND THE BURNING BUS: THE CIVIL RIGHTS REVOLUTION IN A SOUTHERN TOWN 102-03 (NewSouth Books 2003).

53 *Id.* at 103.

restaurants, and lunch counters.[54] Little did Anniston's leaders know in 1962 what waited in the years ahead.

Although Anniston did not garner the international attention of events like Wallace's stand in the schoolhouse door at the University of Alabama or the bombing of the 16th Street Baptist Church in Birmingham, the city did not escape further violence. On the same day as the church bombing in Birmingham, Anniston's Human Relations Council, including Reverends Reynolds and McClain, attempted to desegregate the Calhoun County Public Library.[55] With the approval of most of the city commission and the library board, the men stepped onto the sidewalk in front of the library.[56] A crowd of fifty to a hundred white men, including several of Adams's friends, met them at the library armed with sticks, bats, chains, and broken beer bottles. Reynolds was slashed across the face with a chain and stabbed twice.[57] McClain dragged his companion away, and the two men managed to fight their way to safety.[58]

Anniston's leadership would face another challenge over the course of 1964 and 1965 when Anniston High School was desegregated. The Civil Rights Act of 1964 had recently been passed when a group of community members met that fall to discuss its potential effect on the city. The white community felt that it would be better to wait for a time when emotions were not running quite so high. Many in the black community were unhappy with this plan. A group of citizens from the Calhoun County Improvement Association took out a full-page ad in the Sunday *Anniston Star*. The title read, "Anniston Manifesto," and the ad listed grievances, demands, and areas for improvement within Anniston and Calhoun County.[59] The ad derided the stopgap measures employed by the city so far and declared: "We want equal representation in jobs and accommodations, and we want it now. We want the veil of segregation and discrimination lifted and we want it lifted now. We want our freedom and we want it now."[60] The *Star* ran an opinion article chastising the CCIA for asking for too much too soon and calling for more patience.[61] Meanwhile the HRC continued its efforts to slowly desegregate places around Anniston.[62]

Kenneth Adams and his followers fought back. J. B. Stoner's National States' Rights Party sponsored a series of rallies around town in October of 1964 and presented the police department with a "Petition for the Redress

---

[54] *Id.*

[55] *Id.* at 128.

[56] *Id.* at 129.

[57] *Id.*

[58] *Id.*

[59] Sprayberry, *supra* note 2.

[60] *Id.*

[61] *Id.*

[62] *Id.*

of Grievances" that called for the dissolution of the HRC.[63] A bomb was set off outside a City Commissioner's hardware store.[64] A tear gas canister was set off inside Kitchens, a local department store.[65] In response, a group of community leaders took out yet another full-page ad in the *Anniston Star* entitled "Where We Stand."[66] It demanded: "Order and respect for the law must be maintained."[67] Tolerance for terroristic acts was growing thin.

Meanwhile, the superintendent announced plans in April to desegregate Anniston City Schools the next fall.[68] A week later, thousands attended a Klan rally at the city auditorium.[69] Later that week a small African-American church was bombed, and the *Anniston Star* led fundraising efforts to rebuild it.[70] The *Star* wrote, "We know what to expect if this community fails to rise up in protest. We will open the door to further incidents that may come ... unless the floods of violence are turned off, we can expect to draw unto us another incident tomorrow, another next week and the next until all the bitter poison of racial hatred is brought down on our heads."[71]

On the night of Thursday, July 14, 1965, there was yet another white supremacist rally in downtown Anniston, this one on the steps of the Calhoun County courthouse. Speakers included Kenneth Adams and J. B. Stoner. Over on the west side of town, Willie Brewster and his friends, Jeremiah Adams, Henry Lewis Beavers, and Elgin Parker, were just getting off the late shift from the pipe shop and the foundry.[72] As they headed home to Talladega and Munford on Highway 202, three shotgun blasts were fired from a passing car. The first shattered the back windshield, and the second hit Willie Brewster in the back of the neck. Brewster managed to pull the car off to the side of the road, close to the site of the bus burning four years earlier, and his friends ran to the nearest house to call the police, and for an ambulance. The *Anniston Star* published an article the next day titled "Bullet Hits Negro Driving in County." The article linked the shooting to the rally, quoting speaker Rev. Connie Lynch's ultimatum, "If it takes killing to get the Negroes out of the white man's streets and to protect our constitutional rights, I say, yes, kill them."[73]

Over the weekend, a group of Anniston citizens, headed by Harry M. Ayers, the publisher of the *Anniston Star*, and Thomas S. Potts, owner of a

---

63 *Id.*

64 *Id.*

65 *Id.*

66 *Id.*

67 *Id.*

68 *Id.*

69 *Id.*

70 *Id.*

71 *Id.*

72 John McCaa, *Bullet Hits Negro Driving in County*, ANNISTON STAR, July 16, 1965.

73 *Id.*

local radio station, set up a phone tree to gather money for a reward for information in the shooting. They ran a full-page ad in the *Anniston Star*, on Sunday, July 18, declaring:

> We, as a community, are determined that those who advocate and commit secret acts of violence will not control this county. We are determined to fight with the weapons of law to retain the dignity of this community and to punish those who struck down a respectable and industrious citizen. Therefore, we, the undersigned, pledge the sum of $20,000 to the person who supplies information leading to the arrest and conviction of those responsible for the shooting Thursday night of Willie Brewster.[74]

The list of names included over 250 citizens of Anniston, Oxford, Jacksonville, and the surrounding communities.[75] A further article gave instructions on how to contact the paper anonymously.

Meanwhile, the FBI and the Alabama Attorney General's office joined the search, in what the *Anniston Star* called "one of the area's largest manhunts."[76] Brewster passed away during the night on July 17, leaving his wife and two children behind. The sheriff immediately ordered an autopsy, hoping the bullet would provide a clue. Little else was heard about the case until a month later, when three men were arrested in conjunction with the murder: Damon Strange, Johnny Ira DeFries, and Lewis Blevins. The case landed on the bench of Judge Robert Parker. Local leaders in the community were initially worried because Parker had previously represented Kenneth Adams a couple of times on small criminal charges.[77]

Alabama's courts offered little help to seekers of racial justice. Not only was the opinion of the white community solidly against equal rights and justice for African-Americans, the state's legal system operated on an "outmoded procedural system" that had not changed substantively since the 1852 Code.[78] The state's legal system was tied "to a system so formal that substantial justice was frequently sacrificed to precision of wording."[79] Cases and their appeals could, and did, turn on the proper use of grammar.[80] "Where blacks were accused of crimes against whites, court officials, though there were honorable exceptions, often took only the most perfunctory steps to achieve impartial verdicts."[81] Likewise, the courts often did

74 *$20,000 Reward*, ANNISTON STAR, July 18, 1965, at 5A.

75 Those names included my grandfather, J. J. Campbell.

76 Jean Quillen, *Bullet From Body May Provide Clue in Ambush Killing*, ANNISTON STAR, July 14, 1965.

77 *Id.*

78 Tony A. Freyer and Paul M. Pruitt, Jr., *Reaction and Reform: Transforming the Judiciary Under Alabama's Constitution 1901–1975*, 53 ALABAMA LAW REVIEW 77, 96 (2001).

79 *Id.*

80 *Id.* at 109.

81 *Id.* at 104.

little to ensure impartial verdicts when whites were accused of crimes against blacks. However, Judge Parker defied judicial trends and refused to tolerate frivolous pleas. Backed by community support, he insisted upon due process and justice for Willie Brewster's murder.

Judge Parker quickly called a grand jury. The witnesses included Harry Sims, the ABI investigator who had ridden on the first Freedom Ride bus, and was now investigating the Brewster case.[82] The grand jury quickly indicted Strange, DeFries, and Blevins.[83] Clarence Williams, the District Attorney for Calhoun County, would be the prosecutor, and two local lawyers, Hugh Merrill and Douglas Stewart, were assigned to the defense.[84] The trial date was set for late November.[85]

In the meantime, Judge Parker and other members of Anniston's legal community paid close attention to every aspect leading up to the trial. At the time in Calhoun County, a jury commission pulled jury pools from registered voters in Calhoun County. The initial jury pool for the Strange case was a striking "blue ribbon" panel, made up of community and business leaders from all over Calhoun County.[86] Potential jurors included upper management and owners of local banks and businesses like Farmers and Merchants, Monsanto, Southern Bell, First National Bank, Sawyer Office Supply, Sunset Land Company, and the First State Bank of Oxford.[87] They also included management at the local Social Security Administration and Fort McClellan, and the mayor of Jacksonville.[88] Highly unusually for the time, the potential jurors also included eleven black men.[89] Leadership within the legal community clearly hoped to send a message to the community that overtly racist and violent behavior would no longer be tolerated in Anniston.

Judge Parker also had to address another concern. On November 5, Strange filed for a new lawyer: J. B. Stoner. Kenneth Adams called Stoner in on a favor, but Stoner was only licensed to practice in Georgia. Judge Parker worried about letting an out-of-state attorney in on the case, but a fellow judge from Sylacauga who had presided over another case Stoner had worked on advised him to let Stoner take the case.[90] Stoner was not known to be a particularly good lawyer.

---

[82] Jean Quillen, *County Grand Jury Recalled, May Indict in Brewster Case*, ANNISTON STAR, August 27, 1965.

[83] *Id.*

[84] Transcript of Record, *Strange v. State*, 197 So.2d 437 (Ala. Ct. App. 1966).

[85] *Id.*

[86] James M. Campbell, Memo on the *Strange v. State* Venire Roll (October 26, 2011) (in the possession of the author).

[87] *Id.*; see also venire roll.

[88] *Id.*

[89] *Id.*

[90] Interview with Judge Robert Parker (Oct. 16, 2011). [Transcript in possession of the author.]

Parker sat down with Strange and explained the pros and cons of hiring an out-of-state attorney, but Strange wanted Stoner.[91] Stoner's first act as Strange's attorney was to file three charges, that the court could not return a guilty verdict for manslaughter, first, or second-degree murder.[92] Parker turned down every one. Judge Parker also had to allay the fears of District Attorney Clarence Williams. Williams was "scared to death" of retaliation from Kenneth Adams and his followers, so Parker called the highway patrol and had them send over eight or ten troopers to protect the courtroom.[93]

The trial started on November 29, 1965, and took four days. There was never any doubt that this case was much more than a simple murder trial. In a show of solidarity, Kenneth Adams sat at the table for the defense with Stoner. Williams immediately asked the jury pool if any were familiar with Adams, which Stoner objected to and Parker overruled.[94] Adams moved outside the rail with the rest of the audience.[95] Stoner also objected and was overruled when Williams asked if any of the jury pool were members of the National States' Rights Party.[96] In turn, Stoner brought up the specter of the movement, saying, "I think that most of you jurors have heard threats by Martin Luther King that if a jury failed to convict white persons charged with an offense against members of his race, he would march on the courthouses here in Alabama."[97] Williams objected to this and Parker sustained it. Stoner also asked if any of the potential jurors were members of the NAACP and whether they "consider[ed] this a civil rights case?"[98] Williams objected, claiming, "Nobody has interjected civil rights in here except Mr. Stoner."[99]

Two of the black jurors did claim to be members of the NAACP and the Calhoun County Improvement Association. Stoner struck all the black members of the pool, and after the lunch break the case had its jury. It included Floyd Marbut, the mayor of Jacksonville, Olin Deason, a member of Jacksonville's city council, and Roy Rigney, owner of Rigney Typewriter Co. and the jury foreman.[100] Issues with the jury members did not end there. They were sequestered during the trial, which meant staying overnight at the courthouse on the fourth floor.[101] This was an unpleasant prospect in the best of

---

91 *Id.*

92 Transcript, *supra* note 84.

93 Interview with Judge Parker, *supra* note 90.

94 Transcript, *supra* note 84.

95 *Id.*

96 *Id.*

97 *Id.*

98 *Id.*

99 *Id.*

100 John McCaa and Jean Quillen, *Juror's Sickness Raises Possibility of Mistrial in Damon Strange's Trial*, ANNISTON STAR, November 30, 1965.

101 Interview with Judge Parker, *supra* note 90.

times, as the top floor had neither air conditioning nor heating.[102] Deason nearly caused the case to go to mistrial on the second day when he became ill, but Judge Parker let everyone go to lunch early and talked him into staying on the jury.[103] Parker called a doctor to attend to Deason during jury deliberations.[104] Another shock came two days into the trial when a man was escorted from the courtroom; the police had found a gun in his pocket.[105]

Williams called his first witness: Lestine Brewster, Willie Brewster's widow. She testified that he had been her husband and that he was now deceased.[106] Williams's second witness, Dr. William H. Sellers, was the physician who treated Brewster at Anniston Memorial Hospital.[107] Dr. Sellers testified that Brewster had been admitted to the hospital on the night of July 15 with "a bullet wound in the upper chest," and that bullet caused his death a little over two days later.[108]

After Williams established the fact and timing of Brewster's death, he called the three men who were in the car with Brewster that night: Jeremiah Adams, Henry Lewis Beavers, and Elgin Parker.[109] The men all told the same basic story. All of them worked at Alabama Pipe or Union Foundry, and had just gotten off the late shift that night.[110] The first three went to Dear's Curb Market to get their checks cashed, then picked up Elgin Parker and ran by Tenneco Service Station on West 10th Street to get some gas and transmission fluid.[111] Jeremiah Adams and Henry Beavers remembered seeing a "dull color yellow '55 Chevrolet" with a missing front bumper at the gas station.[112] One remembered seeing a red Volkswagen as well, whose driver spoke to the men in the yellow Chevy.[113] Elgin Parker remembered another car, but had no description.[114]

Jeremiah Adams had been driving, but switched with Brewster at the station because his feet hurt after a long day at work.[115] They got back in the car and pulled onto Highway 202 going west, followed by the yellow Chevy.[116] A few miles past the city limits, they heard three shots.[117] The first

---

102 *Id.*

103 *Id.*; McCaa, *supra* note 100.

104 Interview with Judge Parker, *supra* note 90; McCaa, *supra* note 100.

105 *Id.*

106 Transcript, *supra* note 84.

107 *Id.*

108 *Id.*

109 *Id.*

110 *Id.*

111 *Id.*

112 *Id.*

113 *Id.*

114 *Id.*

115 *Id.*

116 *Id.*

shattered the back windshield; the second followed immediately after and hit Brewster in the neck. Brewster cried, "I'm hit! Take the wheel!" and Adams, who was in the passenger seat, struggled to pull the car off the road. They heard the third shot as they pulled onto the gravel near Forsythe Grocery, close to the site of the bus burning four years earlier.[118] On cross-examination, Stoner focused on Adams and Beavers' later interaction with the police; the two were picked up and driven around until they identified the yellow Chevy.[119] Adams pointed the car out to the officers without prompting, but Beavers only said it looked like the same one after the police pointed it out to him.[120]

After establishing the events inside the car, Williams called several more witnesses who lived near Forsythe Grocery and who testified to hearing the shots that night.[121] He also called the state troopers who had been called to the scene, and Anniston's police sergeant, who testified to seeing Damon Strange, Johnny DeFries, Kenneth Adams, Bill Dozier, and Jimmy Glen Knight leaving the rally that night around 10:30 P.M.[122] The sergeant also testified to having seen Knight in an off-white colored car, possibly yellow.[123] Williams then called Dr. Robert D. Johnson, the state toxicologist who performed Brewster's autopsy. Johnson described pulling the bullet slug from Brewster's neck, and claimed that the bullet most likely came from a 12-gauge shotgun.[124]

After lunch on the second day, Williams called his final witness: Jimmy Glen Knight. Knight testified to having been at the rally that evening with his wife and Damon Strange.[125] The three of them left the rally and went back to Bill Dozier's house on Eulaton Road, where Johnny DeFries and Lewis Blevins joined them.[126] Strange left the house with DeFries and Blevins and came back around 11:30 P.M.[127] Knight and Dozier were in the front yard, on their way to pick up some more beer. Knight said Strange and the others pulled up in a light-colored 1955 Chevy with a missing front bumper. DeFries jumped out of the car and said, "we got us a nigger."[128] DeFries made everyone help get rid of the shell casings.[129] Knight, Strange,

---

117 *Id.*

118 *Id.*

119 *Id.*

120 *Id.*

121 *Id.*

122 *Id.*

123 *Id.*

124 *Id.*

125 *Id.*

126 *Id.*

127 *Id.*

128 *Id.*

129 *Id.*

Blevins, and Dozier piled into Knight's car to go to the store and drove by the spot, where the policemen on the scene waved them past.[130] Blevins said, "Damon got a pumpkin ball in him."[131] Knight asked Strange how many he got, and Strange replied, "I got one, I am pretty sure, because the car was swerving off the road."[132]

Knight also told the jury that he testified during the grand jury hearing, and that shortly after, Strange and his brother, Robert, found him and threatened to kill him.[133] Damon Strange hit Knight over the head, and Robert asked his brother for his gun.[134] Knight had been knocked to the floor, and he came up with his own gun, wrestled Damon's gun away from Robert, and shot Damon in the chest.[135] Robert wrestled Knight's gun away from him, and Knight jumped the counter and escaped out the back door.[136]

On cross-examination, Stoner prompted Knight to reveal that he was being held in the county jail on two counts each of burglary and grand larceny when he heard about the reward for information in the Brewster case and asked to speak to the officers concerned.[137] He already had a DWI and a charge for carrying a concealed weapon.[138] Knight talked to Harry Sims from the ABI and Joe Landers from the FBI. Stoner tried to get the court to produce his statements, but couldn't cite any cases in which the court allowed this. After calling one final witness from the bar Knight and Strange visited later that night, the prosecution rested.

Stoner's main tactic on the defense was to make Knight look as bad as possible, and then give the jurors an out by providing Strange with an alibi. He called a series of people, including Kenneth Adams's son, who testified that Knight's "general reputation for truth and veracity is bad."[139] Stoner then called a series of witnesses, including Harry Ayers, the publisher of the *Anniston Star*, to testify about the reward offered in the paper.[140] Stoner also called the manager of the gas station, who testified that he saw the four black men that night but no one else.[141] Finally, Stoner called Bill Dozier and his wife, who both testified that Strange was at their house all night, but that Jimmy Knight had come and gone with a shotgun.[142] After making an

---

130 *Id.*

131 *Id.*

132 *Id.*

133 *Id.*

134 *Id.*

135 *Id.*

136 *Id.*

137 *Id.*

138 *Id.*

139 *Id.*

140 *Id.*

141 *Id.*

142 *Id.*

overruled motion to direct a verdict of acquittal on the grounds that the State failed to produce enough evidence, the defense rested.[143]

Williams called two rebuttal witnesses to briefly address portions of the gas station manager's testimony and Bill Dozier's testimony, and then he rested his case.[144] Both sides gave closing arguments on the morning of Wednesday, December 1.[145] Williams reinforced the community's hopes that racial violence would no longer be tolerated; he told the jury, "we must see that law violators are punished for what they are doing," and defended the reward, claiming that "we should be thankful we have men who believe in law enforcement enough in this county to back it up with their money."[146] On his turn, Stoner hammered Knight's character, arguing that the case "boils down to whether you're going to believe a liar and a thief against an innocent man when there is no other evidence pointing toward the defendant."[147] Stoner also accused the community of using the reward to create an atmosphere of "convict, convict, convict."[148] Judge Parker read a series of instructions on manslaughter, first, and second degree murder to the jury and then released them.[149]

The jury reported back to Judge Parker several times over the next day, asking for a mistrial.[150] Parker "went back a couple of times and give 'em pep talks ... [like] whatever your decision is we'll back it."[151] Parker urged the jurors, "this case is tried as good as it will ever be tried and twelve people have got to decide it. Y'all are good citizens. Compromise, don't forget a conviction you have about something, but rethink your case."[152] When Olin Deason got sick and scared, Parker called a doctor in for him and persuaded him to stay on the jury.[153] The jury stayed overnight and returned a verdict the next morning: Strange was found guilty of murder in the second degree, with a twenty-year sentence.

The *Anniston Star* reported "Verdict Shocks Parties," and called it "the first Alabama conviction in recent history of civil rights strife of a white man charged with killing a Negro."[154] Civil Rights demonstrators tore up pre-

---

143 *Id.*

144 *Id.*

145 *Id.*

146 John McCaa, *Jurors Get Instruction*, ANNISTON STAR, December 1, 1965.

147 Jean Quillen, *Jury Decision Expected in Damon Strange Case*, ANNISTON STAR, December 2, 1965.

148 *Id.*

149 Transcript, *supra* note 84.

150 Interview with Judge Parker, *supra* note 90.

151 *Id.*

152 *Id.*

153 *Id.*

154 Jean Quillen, *Strange, Convicted of Slaying Negro, Sentenced, Placed on $10,000 Bond*, ANNISTON STAR, December 3, 1965.

printed leaflets protesting Strange's acquittal in the courtroom.[155] The story spread all over the nation; the *New York Times* reported "a white man can be convicted in the South," though the paper expressed concern that convictions might still be rare.[156] *Time Magazine* claimed that "it had become axiomatic that Southern white men do not convict other Southern white men for racist murders," and that the Strange case, along with a conviction several days later in the killing of Viola Liuzzo issued in Judge Frank Johnson's federal district court, gave hope "for the survival of the local jury system."[157]

Back in Anniston, Kenneth Adams, J. B. Stoner, and other friends raised Strange's bond, and he was let out in early January. Stoner continued to pursue an appeal, which was argued on May 26, 1966, and decided by the Alabama Court of Appeals on August 23, 1966.[158] The court handed down its opinion affirming the conviction, and then later denied rehearing on September 19.[159] Strange never served a day of his time. He was shot to death in November during a bar brawl.[160]

In his mammoth work on the history of the Civil Rights Movement, Taylor Branch called the Strange case "a breakthrough verdict."[161] No one expected a state court jury to find Strange guilty. No one expected that this kind of justice could be done in the South. Even in this case, only the greatest effort of a community, sick of racist violence and terrified of a Civil Rights media storm, allowed twelve men cherry-picked from local leadership to render their verdict. The facts were not stellar; the prosecution had no eyewitness to the attack who could directly identify Damon Strange. Their star witness had pending felony charges. Stoner, though no great lawyer, offered the jury an easy out when Dozier and his wife offered Strange an alibi. Twelve men, guided by Judge Robert Parker, with the eyes of the world upon them, finally managed to do the right thing.

Judge Parker's adherence to justice under the law, regardless of race, foreshadowed later legal reform by Alabama Supreme Court Chief Justice Howell Heflin in the early 1970s. Heflin's campaign to reform legal procedure and the judicial article of the state constitution depended, in part, on "undercut[ting] the racially coded, anti-federal government demagoguery which had defeated constitutional reform during the mid-1950s."[162] By taking race out of politics and casting justice under the law as something

---

155 *Id.*

156 Fred Graham, *A White Man Can Be Convicted in the South But*, N.Y. TIMES, December 5, 1965.

157 *Turn in a Dark Road*, TIME, December 10, 1965, at 27-28.

158 Strange v. State, 197 So.2d 437 (Ala. Ct. App. 1965).

159 *Id.*

160 *Obituaries, Hubert D. Strange*, ANNISTON STAR, November 7, 1966; *see also* Interview with Judge Parker, *supra* note 90.

161 Taylor Branch, AT CANAAN'S: AMERICA IN THE KING YEARS, 1965–1966 391 (2007).

162 Freyer and Pruitt, *supra* note 78, at 132.

desirable across racial and class lines, Heflin managed to push through reform of Alabama's outdated legal procedure. Likewise, Judge Parker guided a case to a just conclusion against great odds.

However, a dedication to due process and law and order in the narrow issues of procedure did little to address larger inequities that still existed between the black and white communities in Alabama. Though the Strange case set a precedent in Anniston that vigilante violence on behalf of white supremacy would no longer be tolerated, the resolution of one trial did little to address the concerns of the African-American community. Fed up with limited response to their demands for a full desegregation of Anniston High School, black and white students rioted at the annual Homecoming Parade in the fall of 1970.[163] Shortly thereafter, whites began fleeing Anniston City Schools for private or county schools. Many moved to Oxford, the town directly south of Anniston, which had a much smaller black population.

At present date, Anniston's schools systems have been under a thirty-year-old desegregation suit, this time for being over 90% black. Anniston still has not managed to bridge the gap between its white and black communities. But the verdict in the Strange case was a step forward. Not an end in and of itself, but a moment when the community stepped up. Racist violence had long been openly encouraged by Alabama's leadership, then tolerated, and finally, starting with Damon Strange, condemned.

[163] Sprayberry, *supra* note 2.

INDEX

www.ingramcontent.com/pod-product-compliance
Lightning Source LLC
LaVergne TN
LVHW011818200926
848484LV00005B/1232